EYEWITNESS TRAVEL

MADRID

EYEWITNESS TRAVEL

MADRID

MAIN CONTRIBUTOR: MICHAEL LEAPMAN

DK

LONDON, NEW YORK,
MELBOURNE, MUNICH AND DELHI
www.dk.com

PROJECT EDITOR Helen Townsend
ART EDITOR Gillian Andrews
EDITORS Elizabeth Atherton, Sophie Warne
DESIGNERS Carolyn Hewitson, Nicola Rodway
MAP CO-ORDINATOR David Pugh
DTP DESIGNER Pamela Shiels
PICTURE RESEARCHER Monica Allende

MAIN CONTRIBUTORS
Adam Hopkins, Mark Little,
Edward Owen

PHOTOGRAPHERS
Peter Wilson and Kim Sayer

ILLUSTRATORS
Richard Bonson, Stephen Gyapay, Claire Littlejohn, Isidoro González-
Adalid Cabezas (Acanto, Arquitectura y Urbanismo S.L.), Maltings
Partnership, Chris Orr & Associates

Reproduced by Colourscan (Singapore) Printed and bound by South
China Printing Co. Limited (China)

First published in Great Britain in 1999
by Dorling Kindersley Limited
80 Strand, London WC2R 0RL

Copyright 1999, 2009 © Dorling Kindersley Limited,
London A Penguin Company

**Reprinted with revisions 2000, 2001, 2002, 2003, 2004, 2005, 2006,
2007, 2009**

Front cover main image: Statue of Felipe III in Plaza Mayor

**The information in this
DK Eyewitness Travel Guide is checked regularly.**
Every effort has been made to ensure that this book is as up-to-date
as possible at the time of going to press. Some details, however,
such as telephone numbers, opening hours prices, gallery hanging
arrangements and travel information are liable to change. The
publishers cannot accept responsibility for any consequences arising
from the use of this book, nor for any material on third party
websites, and cannot guarantee that any website address in this
book will be a suitable source of travel information. We value the
views and suggestions of our readers very highly. Please write to:
Publisher, DK Eyewitness Travel Guides,

CONTENTS

Winged Victory on the dome of
the Edificio Metrópolis *(see p74)*

INTRODUCING
MADRID

Madrileños enjoying the May-time
Fiesta de San Isidro *(see p34)*

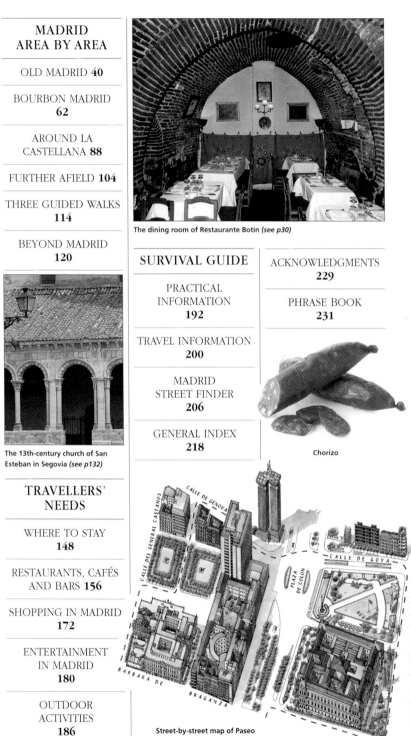

The dining room of Restaurante Botín *(see p30)*

Chorizo

The 13th-century church of San Esteban in Segovia *(see p132)*

CALLE DE GENOVA

CALLE DEL GENERAL CASTAÑOS

CALLE DE GOYA

PLAZA DE COLON

BARBARA DE

BRAGANZA

Street-by-street map of Paseo de Recoletos *(see pp90–91)*

INTRODUCING MADRID

FOUR GREAT DAYS IN MADRID

Brooch from a Madrid boutique

Although Madrid has quadrupled in size in the last 50 years, the places of real interest are still in the centre. The first three suggestions for a day out can all be undertaken on foot. For the family day you will need transport, but taxis are plentiful and cheap. Almost all the places are cross-referenced so you can check out more details of each place in this guide before you set out. The prices include cost of travel, food and admission fees.

Palm trees in the Real Jardín Botánico

HISTORY AND ART

- Fabulous art at the Prado
- Relaxing Real Jardín Botánico
- Picasso at the Reina Sofía
- Cocktails at the Westin Palace hotel

TWO ADULTS allow at least 60 euros

Morning
Start at the **Museo Thyssen-Bornemisza** *(see pp70–73)* and enjoy the world's greatest private art collection, acquired by Spain thanks in part to the late Baron Thyssen-Bornemisza's Spanish wife. There is also a good bookshop on the premises. Then head to the **Museo del Prado** *(see pp78–81)*, whose small size belies the treasures within. Make sure you get a plan at the entrance to find your way around and to be able to enjoy fully the best that Spanish art has to offer. Among the highlights are works by Goya and El Greco. There is also a café near the far exit, making an ideal lunch stop, and it is opposite the entrance to the **Real Jardín Botánico** *(see p82)*, a lovely oasis in central Madrid.

Afternoon
Next walk across to the **Centro de Arte Reina Sofía** modern art museum *(see pp84–7)*, whose highlight is Picasso's *Guernica*. Walk back towards the Thyssen for a cocktail in the lovely **Westin Palace** hotel *(see p69)*.

Centro de Arte Reina Sofía

OLD MADRID

- Art treasures and monasteries
- *Tapas* on Plaza de Oriente
- The majestic Palacio Real
- Explore Cava Baja

TWO ADULTS allow at least 60 euros

Morning
Start at the **Monasterio de las Descalzas Reales** *(see p52)* to see the fabulous art treasures collected by Felipe II's wife, Juana, and her royal nuns, then continue to see more at the **Monasterio de la Encarnación** *(see p53)*, opened by Felipe III's spouse, Margaret of Austria. Walk to **Plaza de Oriente** *(see p58)* and have a *tapas* lunch at either the Taberna de Alabardero (Felipe V 4) or the **Café de Oriente** *(see p166)*.

Afternoon
Cross the Plaza de Oriente to visit the **Palacio Real** *(see pp54–7)*. A visit to the amazing armoury is essential. After the palace head for the vast and majestic **Plaza Mayor** *(see p44)*. This was once the

Allegorical paintings on the Casa de la Panadería, Plaza Mayor

Smart boutiques along Calle Serrano

scene of Spanish Inquisition trials, as well as bullfights, and you can see gory bullfighting photos in the Torre de Oro bar while you enjoy a drink. Today it is an altogether calmer place. Also don't miss the murals on the Casa de la Panadería. Continue straight on and pass Casa Botin (Cuchilleros 17), purportedly the world's oldest restaurant, cross to Cava Baja and explore the streets of the city's Old Quarter off to the right.

FASHION AND SHOPPING

- Nineteenth-century mansions
- Exclusive boutiques
- Stop for a wine bar lunch
- Enjoy archaeological finds

TWO ADULTS allow at least 70 euros

Morning
Before you begin your day's shopping, step back in time and see what stylish people wore and how they lived at two private houses, now museums, dedicated to their 19th-century owners: **Joaquín Sorolla**, the painter *(see p100)* and **Lázaro Galdiano**, the collector *(see pp98–9)*. For a quick snack, opposite the second museum in Calle Serrano is José Luis, a popular *tapas* bar for the well heeled. Walk a short way down Calle Serrano to the ABC shopping centre on the

right and the smaller Multi-centro on the left for one-stop retail opportunities. Then, for a relaxed lunch in a fashionable wine bar walk a few blocks to Lagasca 74 and O'Caldino, a traditional Galician *tapas* bar.

Afternoon
The area bordered by the Lagasca, Serrano and Goya streets is packed with fashion boutiques, including designer names, as well as two branches of the **El Corte Inglés** department store *(see p173)*. Expensive Serrano shops continue alongside the **Plaza de Colón** *(see p96)* and opposite the excellent **Museo Arqueológico Nacional** *(see pp94–5)*, which displays a treasure trove of archaeological finds. Finally, enjoy gourmet treats for dinner at the Mallorca restaurant (Calle Serrano 6).

A FAMILY DAY

- Real Madrid stadium
- Dinosaurs at the Natural History Museum
- Lunch in the park
- Interactive science & technology

FAMILY OF 4 allow at least 200 euros

Morning
Start at Calle de Alfonso XII 3, where you can visit the old **Observatorio Astronómico** *(see p82)*. Join a guided tour (11am Fridays only) to see the large Foucault pendulum and the collection of telescopes. Then take a short taxi ride to Real Madrid's **Estadio Santiago Bernabéu** (open 10:30am–6:30pm daily) just off the Paseo de la Castellana *(see p107)*. The impressive trophy room and soccer club's shop are both worth a look. Next, visit the **Museo de Ciencias Naturales** *(see p107)* with impressive displays including the skeleton of a dinosaur.

Afternoon
For lunch you can visit the **Parque del Retiro** *(see p77)* with lovely cafés near the lake, and afterwards take a turn in one of the rowing boats which can be hired here. Alternatively, eat in a 1930s dining car in the café at the **Museo del Ferrocarril** *(see p110)*. Here engines and trains are on display at the old Delicias station plus detailed model train layouts.

Dinosaur skeleton, Museo de Ciencias Naturales

Putting Spain on the Map

Spain, in southwestern Europe, covers the greater part of the Iberian Peninsula. The third largest country in Europe, it includes the Canary Islands in the Atlantic and the Balearics in the Mediterranean, and two small territories in North Africa. Its capital, Madrid, lies geographically in the centre of the country, some 650 m (2,130 ft) above sea level.

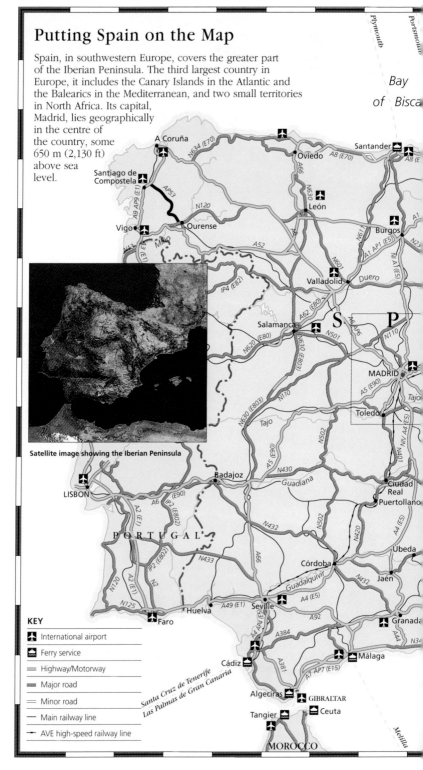

Satellite image showing the Iberian Peninsula

KEY

✈	International airport
⛴	Ferry service
═	Highway/Motorway
▬	Major road
═	Minor road
─	Main railway line
⊷	AVE high-speed railway line

THE CANARY ISLAND

Santa Cruz de la Palma

Puerto de la Cruz
Santa Cruz de Tenerife

San Sebastián de la Gomera

Valverde

Las Palmas de Gran Canaria

Maspalomas

Arrecife

Puerto del Rosario

Cádiz *Cádiz*

Biarritz

Bilbo (Bilbao)

Donostia (San Sebastián)

Iruña (Pamplona)

F R A N C E

ANDORRA

Perpignan

Huesca

Soria

Zaragoza

Girona

Lleida

Barcelona

Calatayud

Tarragona

S P A I N

adalajara

Cuenca

Valencia

Albacete

Maó

Palma de Mallorca

Eivissa (Ibiza)

Alacant (Alicante)

Murcia

Almería

Ebro

Júcar

Segura

Genoa

M e d i t e r r a n e a n   S e a

Oran

Melilla

0 kilometres 75

0 miles 75

Spain's Frontiers
Spain has borders with France, Portugal, Andorra and Gibraltar. The Strait of Gibraltar is only 13 km (8 miles) wide between Tarifa, the peninsula's southernmost point, and northern Morocco.

EUROPE AND NORTH AFRICA

NORWAY
SWEDEN
FINLAND
ESTONIA
RUSSIAN FED.
LATVIA
LITHUANIA
RUSSIAN FED.
BELARUS
DENMARK
IRELAND
UNITED KINGDOM
NETHERLANDS
POLAND
GERMANY
BELGIUM
LUXEMBOURG
CZECH REPUBLIC
SLOVAKIA
UKRAINE
FRANCE
SWITZERLAND
AUSTRIA
HUNGARY
SLOVENIA
CROATIA
ROMANIA
ITALY
BOSNIA AND HERZEGOVINA
SERBIA
MONTENEGRO
BULGARIA
GREECE

PORTUGAL
Madrid
SPAIN

MOROCCO
ALGERIA
TUNISIA
LIBYA

Putting Madrid on the Map

With a population of over 3 million, Madrid is the largest city in Spain. It lies in the centre of the Spanish *meseta* (high plain). The surrounding area is known as the Comunidad de Madrid, while further afield are the provinces of Guadalajara, Cuenca, Toledo, Avila and Segovia.

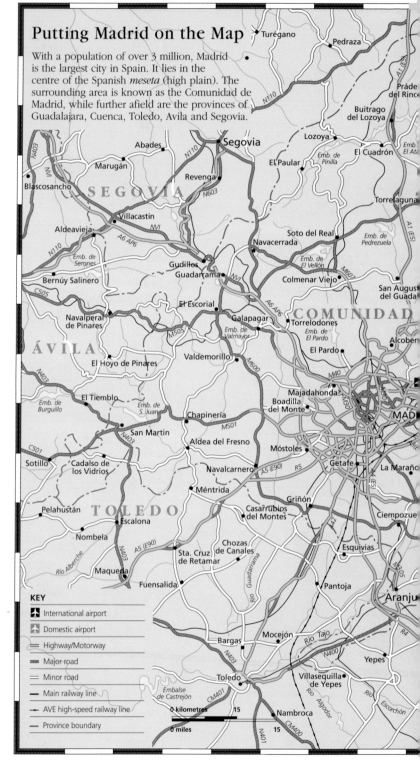

Turégano
Pedraza
Práde del Rinc
Buitrago del Lozoya
Abades
Segovia
Lozoya
El Cuadrón
Emb. El Ata
Marugán
Revenga
El Paular
Emb. de Pinilla
N110
Blascosancho
SEGOVIA
N603
Torrelaguna
Villacastín
NVI
A1 (E5)
Aldeavieja
A6 AP6
Soto del Real
Emb. de Pedrezuela
N110
Emb. de Serones
Gudillos
Navacerrada
M607
Bernúy Salinero
Guadarrama
NVI
Emb. de El Vellón
Colmenar Viejo
San Augus del Guada
C505
El Escorial
A6 AP6
COMUNIDAD
Navalperal de Pinares
Galapagar
Torrelodones
Emb. de El Pardo
Alcoben
ÁVILA
M505
Emb. de Valmayor
El Pardo
El Hoyo de Pinares
Valdemorillo
M40
Emb. de Burguillo
El Tiemblo
Emb. de S. Juan
Chapinería
M600
Majadahonda
M30
MAD
Boadilla del Monte
San Martín
MS01
N403
Aldea del Fresno
Móstoles
C501
Sotillo
Cadalso de los Vidrios
Navalcarnero
A5 (E90)
R5
Getafe
La Maraño
Méntrida
Griñón
Pelahustán
TOLEDO
Casarrubios del Montes
Ciempozue
Escalona
Nombela
Chozas de Canales
Esquivias
M305
N403
A5 (E90)
Sta. Cruz de Retamar
Aranju
Maqueda
Fuensalida
Río Alberche
Río Guadarrama
Pantoja
R4

KEY

✈ International airport

✈ Domestic airport

═══ Highway/Motorway

━━ Major road

═══ Minor road

━━━ Main railway line

━━━ AVE high-speed railway line

━━ Province boundary

Mocejón
Bargas
N400
Yepes
N403
Toledo
Villasequilla de Yepes
Embalse de Castrejón
CM401
Nambroca
CM400
N401

0 kilometres   15

0 miles   15

THE HISTORY OF MADRID

*A*lthough archeological evidence suggests that humans were attracted to the area in prehistoric times, the story of Madrid doesn't begin until AD852, when the Moors built a fortress near the Manzanares river. By Spanish standards, the city is a mere adolescent – it was born 21 centuries after the Phoenicians founded Cádiz and six centuries after the Romans constructed Itálica near Seville.

In the early 8th century, a Moorish army from North Africa landed at Gibraltar and, within a few years, conquered most of the Iberian peninsula. The Moors established an independent emirate based in Córdoba, southern Spain and, in 852, under Emir Mohamed I, they built a fortress (alcázar) to protect the northern approach to Toledo; it stood on the site of Madrid's present-day royal palace. Named Mayrit (later corrupted to Magerit, then Madrid), a small community arose around the alcázar.

Ornate Moorish warrior helmet

CHRISTIAN CONQUEST

Timidly at first, then with gathering strength, the Christians to the north rallied against the Moorish invaders, pushing southward in the so-called Reconquest. By the middle of the 11th century, the kingdom of Castile had arisen as the major Christian power, its territory extending as far south as the Cordillera central mountain range, within sight of Mayrit. In 1085, the Castilians under Alfonso VI mustered for the decisive thrust against Toledo. Mayrit stood in the path of the advancing army. According to one story, the troops mistook it for the much larger Toledo, which is why they bothered laying siege to it. Another legend has it that the Christian attackers subdued the town after some of the more intrepid soldiers clambered up the defence walls.

Once all the excitement was over, the town of Madrid settled back into its sleepy rural existence. Many of its earliest inhabitants were monks, encouraged by the Spanish rulers to establish monasteries there and thus breathe new life into the community. Before long, Madrid had 13 churches, more than enough to serve the spiritual needs of its small population.

Among the first *Madrileños* was San Isidro Labrador, a local farmer who founded a *cofradía* (religious brotherhood). It is also said he performed miracles, but little else is known about Madrid's rustic patron saint.

In the 13th century a dispute arose over hunting rights on land owned by the Church. It was agreed that, while the Church owned the soil, *Madrileños* had rights to all that was above it, namely, game. Thus Madrid acquired its symbol – a bear (the Church's emblem) sniffing a tree.

TIMELINE

711 Moors invade Iberian peninsula

932 Christian king Ramiro II temporarily occupies Madrid

1109 Moors unsuccessfully lay siege to Madrid

| AD700 | 800 | 900 | 1000 | 1100 | 1200 |

756 Emir Mohamed I founds emirate of Córdoba

852 Moors found Mayrit

Bronze stag from a Moorish palace

1085 Madrid captured by Castile

1202 Madrid granted the status of town

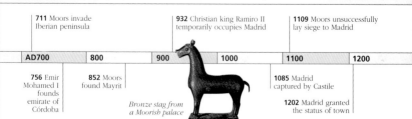

◁ **Tiled mural showing San Isidro Labrador, Madrid's patron saint, and another farmer tilling the soil**

Columbus setting foot in the Americas in the late 15th century

Isabel and Fernando visited often, most of the momentous events of the age, such as the final war against the Moors and Columbus' encounter with the queen, took place elsewhere. When Isabel died in 1504, her daughter Juana *"la Loca"* ("the Mad") was deemed unfit to rule. She and her husband, the Archduke of Austria, who were living in Burgundy, returned to Spain to reassert their rights. But the archduke soon died,

ROYAL HUNTING GROUND

Madrid's reputation as a hunting paradise attracted the attention of Castilian royals, whose visits became increasingly frequent. The city was especially favoured by Enrique IV de Trastamara who was, by all accounts, physically repellent, politically inept and morally perverted. Enrique was married to Juana of Portugal, but most people doubted that their daughter, Juana, was actually the king's; it was assumed her real father was the queen's lover, Beltrán de la Cueva, thus earning her the sobriquet, La Beltraneja (Beltrán's little one). On Enrique's death in 1474, a dynastic struggle ensued between supporters of La Beltraneja and those of Enrique's half-sister, Isabel, who went down in history as Isabel la Católica.

Madrid's nobility threw its support behind La Beltraneja, and the forces of Isabel and her husband Fernando of Aragón laid siege, conquering Madrid with the help of supporters within the town. Although

Fernando of Aragón, the Catholic Monarch

leaving Juana to slip further into dementia. Fernando of Aragón acted as regent until the couple's son, Charles of Ghent, acceded to the throne in 1517 as Carlos I, the first of the Spanish Habsburgs (later Holy Roman Emperor Charles V).

Carlos I (1516–56)

Carlos I ruled over a European empire that included the Low Countries, parts of Italy and Germany, and Spain's newly conquered possessions in the Americas. But he had been brought up in France, spoke no Spanish when he arrived to claim the throne and, although his reign lasted 40 years, he spent only 16 of them in Spain. The European wars and the Counter-Reformation kept him busy elsewhere. Finally, spiritually exhausted and plagued with gout, Carlos I retired to the monastery of Yuste in western Spain, where he died at the age of 58.

TIMELINE

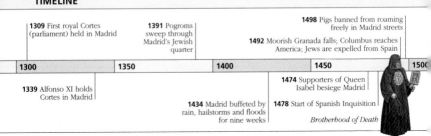

1309 First royal Cortes (parliament) held in Madrid

1339 Alfonso XI holds Cortes in Madrid

1391 Pogroms sweep through Madrid's Jewish quarter

1434 Madrid buffeted by rain, hailstorms and floods for nine weeks

1492 Moorish Granada falls; Columbus reaches America; Jews are expelled from Spain

1498 Pigs banned from roaming freely in Madrid streets

1474 Supporters of Queen Isabel besiege Madrid

1478 Start of Spanish Inquisition

Brotherhood of Death

1300   1350   1400   1450   1500

A CITY IS BORN

Since the beginnings of the kingdom of Castile, its rulers travelled ceaselessly from one part of the realm to another, with the entire court tagging along. Fed up with this migrant existence, Carlos I's successor, Felipe II, established a permanent capital in Madrid in 1561. It was centrally located in the Iberian Peninsula and small enough to lack the complex web of loyalties and intrigues of larger cities, such as Toledo.

Felipe V, the first Bourbon king

Artisans, cooks, poets, soldiers, thieves and hangers-on from around the peninsula flocked to the new capital. Within four decades, the population swelled from some 20,000 to 85,000.

Unlike his father, Felipe II spent most of his reign in Spain. Under him, the Inquisition became a major force, and the unsuccessful Spanish Armada was launched against England. The "Black Legend" has painted a dark picture of Felipe II, yet whatever his shortcomings, laziness and dishonesty were not among them and, during his reign, Spain's world power was virtually unchallenged.

Due to its sudden rise to prominence, Madrid's growth was haphazard. Yet under the Habsburgs the city acquired some of its most notable constructions. The best examples were built in the reigns of Felipe's successors, a period when the country enjoyed an age of cultural brilliance (the Siglo de Oro) just as Spain's military and political strength was declining. The Plaza Mayor *(see p44)*, the epitome of Habsburg Madrid, was built during the reign of Felipe III. His successor, Felipe IV, built a stylish new palace at El Retiro. At the same time, Cervantes, Lope de Vega, Velázquez, Zurbarán and Murillo *(see pp28–9)* were active in Madrid. Money poured in from the New World and, although most of it financed Spain's foreign wars and increasing debt, enough was left to fuel an artistic boom.

THE BOURBON ZENITH

It was too good to last. The inbred Habsburg dynasty produced the gentle but dim-witted Carlos II who died without an heir in 1700, leaving the Spanish throne in dispute. France favoured Philippe of Anjou, the grandson of Louis XIV. Alarmed at the implications of a French-Spanish alliance, England, Austria and Holland supported the Archduke Charles of Austria. This dispute led to the 14-year-long War of Spanish Succession. At the end of the conflict Philippe was crowned as Felipe V – the first Bourbon king – and Spain was securely in the French orbit.

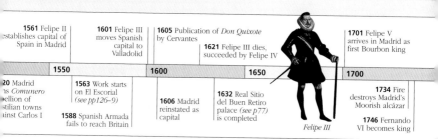

Bullfighting in Madrid's Plaza Mayor in the 17th century

The Bourbons were able administrators, availing themselves of French and Italian advisers who introduced modern improvements to Spain. Felipe V spoke little Spanish and his main concern was making Madrid look as French as possible. When the alcázar burned down in 1734, he ordered the construction of a royal palace *(see pp54–7)* modelled on Versailles, but died before it was completed. The first occupant was Carlos III, under whose rule the Bourbon dynasty, and Madrid, reached their greatest splendour. At this time the centre of the city shifted from the old Plaza Mayor to the new Paseo del Prado, and many new buildings were constructed. Such was Carlos's urbanistic zeal that he is still cited as the best "mayor" Madrid ever had.

Carlos III

The presence of foreign advisers did not sit well with *Madrileños*, however, and the Church encouraged sentiment against interloping outsiders. The most famous incident was the 1766 Esquilache affair in which the Marqués de Esquilache, adviser to the king, banned the traditional broad-brimmed hat and long cape, as they enabled weapons to be concealed. His men roamed the streets armed with scissors to trim the offending garb. The people took this as an attempt to make them conform to foreign fashions, and fierce riots ensued. The Jesuits were thought to be behind the disturbances, and the order was expelled from Spain.

On his death in 1788, Carlos was succeeded by his vacillating son, Carlos IV, who ushered in the decline of the monarchy. The real power sat with his domineering wife, María Luisa of Parma, and chief minister, Manuel Godoy.

A CITY IN ARMS

Godoy struck a deal with the France of Napoleon (who had declared himself emperor in 1804) to allow French troops to cross Spain to conquer Portugal. In the end, however, the French occupied Spain itself. *Madrileños* blamed the royals and their hated counsellor, Godoy, and riots broke out in March 1808. The king was forced to abdicate in favour of his son, Fernando VII, though with the French occupying Madrid he ruled in name only.

On 2 May, *Madrileños* turned on the occupying troops in front of the Palacio Real. This popular uprising was met with bloody reprisals by the French the following day.

Goya's *The 3rd of May* (1814) with the French executing Spanish patriots

TIMELINE

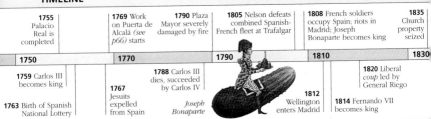

1755 Palacio Real is completed	1769 Work on Puerta de Alcalá *(see p66)* starts	1790 Plaza Mayor severely damaged by fire	1805 Nelson defeats combined Spanish-French fleet at Trafalgar	1808 French soldiers occupy Spain; riots in Madrid; Joseph Bonaparte becomes king	1835 Church property seized
1750	**1770**		**1790**	**1810**	**1830**
1759 Carlos III becomes king	1767 Jesuits expelled from Spain	1788 Carlos III dies, succeeded by Carlos IV	*Joseph Bonaparte*	1812 Wellington enters Madrid	1820 Liberal *coup* led by General Riego
1763 Birth of Spanish National Lottery				1814 Fernando VII becomes king	

After the May riots Napoleon, increasingly impatient with events in Spain, installed his brother Joseph Bonaparte (José I) on the Spanish throne. Spanish sentiment against the occupying French could not be stopped, however, and the country rose up in arms. In the face of organized, well-armed French troops, Spaniards resorted to terrorist tactics, with small bands mounting surprise attacks on the enemy before vanishing into mountain hiding places.

In 1810, the army of the British Duke of Wellington landed in Portugal and started the two-year campaign to drive the French from the Iberian Peninsula.

LIBERALS VERSUS CONSERVATIVES

A century of close contact with the French left its mark on Spain. Liberal ideas found fertile soil among the Spanish enlightened classes and, while the war was at its peak, delegates in Cádiz drafted Spain's first constitution. Yet when Fernando VII was restored to the throne in 1814, he rejected the Cádiz document and ruled as an absolute monarch. This rift between reactionary and progressive sides would plague the country for the next century and a half. When an army uprising headed by the liberal Rafael de Riego in 1820 forced the king to accept the constitution, the exercise ended with Riego's execution.

After Fernando VII's death in 1833, Spanish politics became a complicated succession of *coups d'état* and uprisings. To make matters worse, the choice of his young daughter Isabel II as successor angered supporters of his brother Carlos, leading to a civil war in which 140,000 died. During Isabel's 35-year reign, Spanish politics were dominated by military brass, conservative or liberal.

Isabel II

Against this background of instability, Madrid was slowly becoming a modern European capital with a growing middle class. It was expanding relentlessly with the *Ensanche* (widening), with fashionable residential areas replacing overcrowded working-class districts.

In 1868 liberals joined forces with disgruntled military to oust Isabel II under the pretext of her corrupt and lascivious behaviour. But Spaniards still favoured a monarchy, and placed Amadeo of Savoy, son of Italy's King Victor Emmanuel, on the throne. The king received the cold shoulder from *Madrileños*, however, and abdicated after two years, at which point the Cortes (parliament) proclaimed a republic. The First Republic lasted only 11 months. In 1874, General Manuel Pavia ended it all by riding up the steps of the Cortes, declaring support for Isabel II's son, Alfonso. Under Alfonso XII (1875–85) and, later, the regency of his wife, María Cristina, who reigned on behalf of her son Alfonso XIII until 1902, Madrid enjoyed a period of prosperity and unstoppable growth, culminating with the inauguration of the Gran Vía *(see p48)* by Alfonso XIII in 1910.

THE BATTLE OF MADRID

Alfonso XIII felt it his duty to meddle in political affairs. Ministers were sacked by the dozen, and there were 33 governments between 1902 and 1923. Finally, the king resorted to General Miguel Primo de Rivera, who installed a dictatorship. It was relatively benign and had support among much of the working class. Spain underwent a flurry of public works, but Primo de Rivera was a disaster when it came to economics.

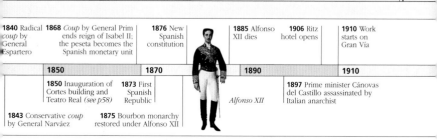

1840 Radical *coup* by General Espartero

1843 Conservative *coup* by General Narváez

1850 Inauguration of Cortes building and Teatro Real *(see p58)*

1868 *Coup* by General Prim ends reign of Isabel II; the peseta becomes the Spanish monetary unit

1873 First Spanish Republic

1875 Bourbon monarchy restored under Alfonso XII

1876 New Spanish constitution

Alfonso XII

1885 Alfonso XII dies

1897 Prime minister Cánovas del Castillo assassinated by Italian anarchist

1906 Ritz hotel opens

1910 Work starts on Gran Vía

1850　1870　1890　1910

Poster for the Nationalist cause in the Civil War

increasing territory, and by November 1936 the Nationalists had reached the outskirts of Madrid. The city was to be on the front line for the duration of the Civil War, suffering severe bombardment, until it finally fell in March 1939.

General Franco, who had manoeuvred himself into position as the uprising's *generalísimo*, was installed as dictator. Although Spain had remained nominally neutral during World War II, Franco's sympathies for Hitler and Mussolini were not forgotten, and for more than a decade the country was ostracized from the community of nations. Farms suffered a devastating drought, the black market thrived and Franco taught "autarchy" – his extreme form of isolationism and self-sufficiency. Yet the nation was starving, and millions were forced to emigrate to work in factories in France and Germany.

By the 1950s geopolitics came to the rescue. The US forgave Franco's past sins in return for support in the Cold War against the Soviet Union, in the form of US military bases in Spain. The door was open to foreign aid and investment. The first adventurous travellers soon followed.

General Francisco Franco

Within six years the country was bankrupt. After the dictator stepped down in 1930, Republicans forced Alfonso XIII to call elections. The vote went overwhelmingly to the Republicans, and the king headed for exile after an angry Madrid crowd demanded his abdication.

During the brief Second Republic, the bourgeoisie, landowners and military were increasingly alarmed by the spread of left-wing ideas. The assassination of conservative member of parliament, José Calvo Sotelo, in July 1936 precipitated events. On 18 July news reached Madrid that a military uprising had taken several Andalusian cities, including Seville. *Madrileños* flocked to the army barracks, demanding arms to defend the Republic, and within a day the working-class militia controlled the city. But, with much of the Spanish army's troops and weapons in the hands of insurgent Nationalists, the rebellion gathered

DICTATORSHIP TO DEMOCRACY
Franco's twilight years were devoted to securing the continuity of his regime. Alfonso XIII's grandson Juan Carlos was groomed as his nominal successor, while the real power was to be wielded by the hard-line prime minister, Admiral Luis Carrero Blanco. But in 1973, the militant wing of the Basque separatist group ETA assassinated Carrero Blanco.

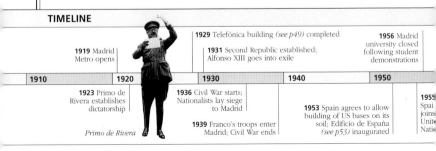

TIMELINE

1919 Madrid Metro opens

1929 Telefónica building *(see p49)* completed

1931 Second Republic established; Alfonso XIII goes into exile

1956 Madrid university closed following student demonstrations

1910	1920	1930	1940	1950

1923 Primo de Rivera establishes dictatorship

Primo de Rivera

1936 Civil War starts; Nationalists lay siege to Madrid

1939 Franco's troops enter Madrid; Civil War ends

1953 Spain agrees to allow building of US bases on its soil; Edificio de España *(see p53)* inaugurated

195 Spai joins Unite Nati

The Cortes being held at gunpoint in the _coup d'état_ on 23 February 1981

ferment, especially in Madrid. Under mayor Enrique Tierno Galván, the arts experienced a flurry of creativity, and the city revelled in a spirit of optimism and confidence, known as _La Movida (see p102)._

The party couldn't last forever. Creative verve can only go so far, and a series of scandals involving some people serving in high offices chipped away at the public's faith in the governing powers, ultimately costing the PSOE the 1996 elections.

When Franco died in November 1975, all eyes turned on his heir apparent, who was sworn in as king. Juan Carlos had been planning for Spain's reunion with the modern world while lending lip service to the Franco regime, and in a series of bold moves, he manoeuvred the country into its first post-Franco democratic elections in 1977. When die-hard supporters of the old regime seized the Cortes in 1981, the _coup_ failed largely due to Juan Carlos's intervention.

The next year the government passed bloodlessly from the centrists to the social democratic PSOE, under long-serving prime minister Felipe González. The first half of his tenure coincided with a period of economic buoyancy, crowned in 1992 with the Olympic Games in Barcelona, a world fair in Seville and Madrid's stint as the "European Capital of Culture". The 1980s were a time of euphoria and cultural

Like their counterparts in other European capitals, _Madrileños_ complain about traffic, never-ending public works and pollution. Yet despite this they retain a fiercely individualistic spirit, a refusal to conform to European hours and, above all, a sardonic sense of humour that sets them apart from other Spaniards. They are living in one of the world's most lively and attractive cities… and they know it.

Aerial image of present-day Madrid, a thriving metropolis

Rulers of Spain

Spain became a nation-state under Isabel and Fernando, whose marriage eventually united Castile and Aragón. With their daughter Juana's marriage, the kingdom was delivered into Habsburg hands. Carlos I and Felipe II were both capable rulers, but in 1700 Carlos II died without leaving an heir. After the War of the Spanish Succession, Spain came under the French Bourbons, who have ruled ever since – apart from an interregnum, two republics and Franco's dictatorship. The current Bourbon king, Juan Carlos I, a constitutional monarch, is respected for his support of democracy.

1665–1700 Carlos II

1479–1516 Fernando, King of Aragón

1474–1504 Isabel, Queen of Castile

1516–56 Carlos I of Spain (Holy Roman Emperor Charles V)

1598–1621 Felipe III

1400	1450	1500	1550	1600	1650
INDEPENDENT KINGDOMS			HABSBURG DYNASTY		
1400	1450	1500	1550	1600	1650

1469 Marriage of Isabel and Fernando leads to unification of Spain

1504–16 Juana la Loca (with Fernando as regent)

1621–65 Felipe IV

Fernando and Isabel, the Catholic Monarchs

UNIFICATION OF SPAIN

In the late 15th century the two largest kingdoms in developing Christian Spain – Castile, with its military might, and Aragón (including Barcelona and a Mediterranean empire) – were united. The marriage of Isabel of Castile and Fernando of Aragón in 1469 joined these powerful kingdoms. Together the so-called Catholic Monarchs defeated the Nasrid Kingdom of Granada, the last stronghold of the Moors (see p16). With the addition of Navarra in 1512, Spain was finally unified.

1556–98 Felipe II

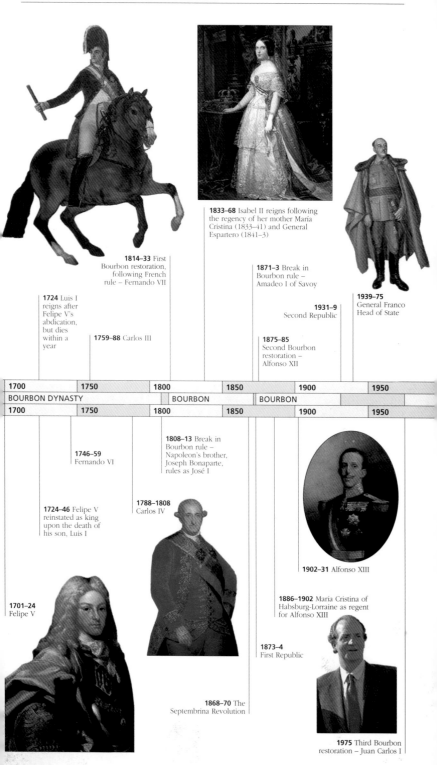

1833–68 Isabel II reigns following the regency of her mother María Cristina (1833–41) and General Espartero (1841–3)

1814–33 First Bourbon restoration, following French rule – Fernando VII

1724 Luis I reigns after Felipe V's abdication, but dies within a year

1759–88 Carlos III

1871–3 Break in Bourbon rule – Amadeo I of Savoy

1931–9 Second Republic

1875–85 Second Bourbon restoration – Alfonso XII

1939–75 General Franco Head of State

1700	1750	1800	1850	1900	1950
BOURBON DYNASTY		BOURBON		BOURBON	
1700	1750	1800	1850	1900	1950

1746–59 Fernando VI

1808–13 Break in Bourbon rule – Napoleon's brother, Joseph Bonaparte, rules as José I

1724–46 Felipe V reinstated as king upon the death of his son, Luis I

1788–1808 Carlos IV

1902–31 Alfonso XIII

1886–1902 Maria Cristina of Habsburg-Lorraine as regent for Alfonso XIII

1701–24 Felipe V

1873–4 First Republic

1868–70 The Septembrina Revolution

1975 Third Bourbon restoration – Juan Carlos I

MADRID AT A GLANCE

Over 100 places of interest are described in the *Madrid Area by Area* and *Beyond Madrid* sections of this book. The detailed catalogue of significant buildings and monuments traces the history of the city – beginning with the 16th- and 17th-century Habsburg Madrid ("Madrid de los Austrias"), as exemplified by the medieval Plaza de la Villa *(see p45)* and the Colegiata de San Isidro *(see p46)*. From here, it follows the development of Madrid from the Bourbon city of the 18th century with its Parque del Retiro and Plaza de Cibeles *(see p67)*, to the upmarket 19th-century Barrio de Salamanca and the modern skyscrapers in the Azca area. The list also includes recreational sights, such as Casa de Campo *(see p112)*. Pictured below are some attractions no visitor should miss.

MADRID'S TOP TOURIST ATTRACTIONS

Plaza Mayor
See p44.

Plaza de Toros de Las Ventas
See p108.

Parque del Retiro
See p77.

Museo Thyssen-Bornemisza
See pp70–73.

Museo Lázaro Galdiano
See pp98–9.

Museo Arqueológico Nacional
See pp94–5.

Centro de Arte Reina Sofía
See pp84–7.

Palacio Real
See pp54–7.

Museo del Prado
See pp78–81.

◁ The Edificio Metrópolis building on the corner of Calle de Alcalá and the Gran Via

Madrid's Best: Museums and Galleries

For a city of its size, Madrid boasts an exceptional number of world-class museums and galleries. Heading the list are the Prado, with the world's largest collection of Spanish art, the Thyssen-Bornemisza, which traces the development of Western art from the 14th century, and Reina Sofía, with its outstanding display of modern art. But there are many smaller, more intimate museums, too. Some, such as the Museo Lázaro Galdiano, are gems both for the sumptuous mansions housing the collections and for the untold treasures within. Note that many museums are closed on Mondays when planning your itinerary.

Museo Municipal
Anyone with an interest in Madrid's evolution, from prehistoric to present times, will be fascinated by this museum, which features a captivating scale model of 19th-century Madrid (see p101).

Museo Cerralbo
Entering this 19th-century mansion, with its eclectic array of artifacts, paintings and sculptures, gives an uncanny sense of stepping back in time and experiencing aristocratic life in Madrid at the turn of the 20th century (see p52).

Old Madrid

Real Academia de Bellas Artes
Goya's Entierro de la Sardina *is one of more than 1,000 paintings and sculptures, from the 16th–20th centuries, which can be seen at this arts academy (see p47).*

Museo Thyssen-Bornemisza
Sold to the nation in 1993, this vast private art collection traces Western art through the ages, with major works by Titian, Goya, Picasso and Rubens (see pp70–73).

Museo Lázaro Galdiano
The collection of the late José Lázaro Galdiano includes paintings, sculptures, jewellery, archeological finds and ceramics in his recently renovated Neo-Renaissance mansion (see pp98–9).

Around La Castellana

Museo Arqueológico Nacional
This museum, situated at the back of the Biblioteca Nacional, is second only to the Prado in terms of the importance of its collection. Exhibits date from prehistoric times to the 19th century (see pp94–5).

Museo del Prado
Recognized as one of the world's greatest art galleries, the Prado is particularly notable for its collections by Velázquez and Goya (see pp78–81).

Bourbon Madrid

| 0 kilometres | 0.5 |
| 0 miles | 0.5 |

Centro de Arte Reina Sofía
A former hospital, the Reina Sofía now houses an outstanding collection of 20th-century art (see pp84–7), including Retrato de Josette, by the Spanish Cubist Juan Gris (pictured), and Guernica, Picasso's famous depiction of the horrors of the Civil War.

Famous People of Madrid

Ever since Felipe II made Madrid the capital of Spain in 1561 *(see p17)*, the city has attracted the best artistic and literary talent in the country. Painters, writers, composers and architects in search of fame and fortune left behind their rural dwellings and migrated to Madrid, where they could take advantage of royal sponsorships and subsidies, publish their works and sell their wares to the city's ever-growing population. Thus Madrid became the cultural centre of Spain, a distinction that grew in times of political and economic stability, and flourished – as great art usually does – following times of turmoil and strife.

The prolific Golden Age dramatist, Félix Lope de Vega (1562–1635)

WRITERS

Spanish writers were the first to make their mark in Madrid, and throughout the 17th century the city acted as a magnet for the country's most famous scribes. The Barrio de las Letras (Writers' Quarter), or Huertas district, was where Spain's greatest literary figure, Miguel de Cervantes Saavedra (1547–1616), produced part of his comic master-piece, *Don Quixote*. In the local taverns he would argue with his rival, Félix Lope de Vega (1562–1635), Spain's most prolific dramatist. The Huertas area was also home to Cervantes' and Lope's 17th-century contemporaries,

José Zorrilla (1817–93)

writer Francisco de Quevedo y Villegas (1580–1645) and dramatist Pedro Calderón de la Barca (1600–81).

In the following centuries, this small area of Madrid continued to be the haunt of famous writers. The 18th-century Madrid native Leandro Fernández de Moratín was influenced by the French Enlightenment, as evidenced by his popular comedy *El Sí de las Niñas*. José Zorrilla y Moral (1817–93) was raised in the Huertas area, and his world-famous Romantic play, *Don Juan Tenorio* (1844), had its first showing in Madrid. In the same century, Madrid's most beloved writer, Benito Pérez Galdós (1843–1920), wrote his famous novel, *Miau* – a literary masterpiece that takes the reader on a journey through the streets and society of the Spanish capital during the city's most vibrant years. Madrid was at the centre of the "Generation of [19]27" writers that included poet and playwright Federico García Lorca (1899–1936) who, during his student years in Madrid, found inspiration as well as the theatres he needed to showcase his creations. The 20th century also produced Nobel Prize-winning novelist Camilo José Cela (1916–2002), whose novel *La Colmena*

Novelist Camilo José Cela (1916–2002), painted by Alvaro Delgado

depicted everyday life in hungry, postwar Madrid. And while 20th-century American writer Ernest Hemingway could not be mistaken for a *Madrileño*, his novels helped the world fall in love with Spain, and his antics in the city after long nights of sipping gin at the Ritz hotel *(see p68)* made him a local favourite. Today it is difficult to walk through Madrid's Plaza Mayor without imagining the writer swaggering down the narrow steps of the Arco de Cuchilleros on his way to a roast suckling pig dinner at Botín *(see p30)*.

PAINTERS

All of Spain's most famous artists had an impact, one way or another, on Madrid. But it was 17th-century artist Diego Velázquez (1599–1660) and 18th-century painter Francisco de Goya (1746–1828) who actually formed part of the city's history. Both were Spanish court painters whose works were inspired by their surroundings in the capital. Each weekend *Madrileños* brave traffic jams to escape the grey city in search of the blue skies made famous by Velázquez, many of whose works have been brought together by Madrid's Museo del Prado *(see pp78–81)*. There you can see his 1656 masterpiece, *Las Meninas*. Goya began his stint at the Spanish court in 1763 at the age of 17, and stayed on and off until 1826, two years before his death. He depicted life during one of the city's most violent times and was the painter of four kings – Carlos III, Carlos IV, José I (Joseph Bonaparte) and Fernando VII. While his works can be seen at several museums in Madrid, his masterpieces *The 3rd of May, Saturn Devouring One of his Sons* and *Naked Maja* are all displayed at the Prado.

Velázquez Bosco's Palacio de Cristal

Las Meninas (1656) by Diego Velázquez

ARCHITECTS

Architecture is an art form of which *Madrileños* are especially proud. Some of the best architects in the world have contributed to turning the capital into the "City of a Thousand Faces". Francesco Sabatini designed the Palacio Real *(see pp54–7)*, the grand Puerta de Alcalá *(see p66)* and the 18th-century extension wing to the Palacio de El Pardo *(see p138)*. Juan Gómez de Mora was the architect responsible for the Plaza Mayor *(see p44)*, which was

completed in 1619. Mora learned his trade from the masterful Juan de Herrera, the designer of Felipe II's monasterial palace El Escorial *(see pp126–9)*. In the 1640s, Mora designed the Monasterio de la Encarnación *(see p53)* and the *Ayuntamiento* (town hall) in the Plaza de la Villa. A balcony was added to the town hall by Juan de Villanueva, the architect of the Prado museum. In 1781 Villanueva and Sabatini, along with botanist Gómez Ortega, designed the Real Jardín Botánico, or Royal Botanical Gardens *(see p82)*. In the Parque del Retiro *(see p77)* there are two pavilions built by architect Velázquez Bosco: the Neo-Classical Palacio de Velázquez (1883) and the Palacio de Cristal (1887), constructed of glass and iron. Noteworthy contemporary architects include Rafael Moneo Valles, who designed the extension to the Museo del Prado *(see pp78–81)* and redesigned the 18th-century Palacio de Villahermosa, home to the Museo Thyssen-Bornemisza *(see pp70–73)*. Also notable are Luis Gutiérrez Soto for the Ministerio del Aire in the Plaza de la Moncloa and Antonio Lamela for the Torres de Colón in the Plaza de Colón *(see p96)*.

Although not an architect, the Marqués de Salamanca, a flamboyant banker and speculator, had a profound effect

on the design of the upmarket Barrio de Salamanca *(see p97)*. When investors shied away from much-needed expansion plans in the 1860s, the Marqués stepped in and began work on what is today a fashionable line of housing blocks along Calle de Serrano.

POLITICIANS

Since Madrid is the Spanish capital, there is a tendency here to claim or disclaim national figures as the city's own. Kings, dictators and prime ministers, while ruling from Madrid, did not always have a popular impact on the city. Felipe II *(see p17)*, for example, made Madrid the capital but then promptly left for his palace at El Escorial.

One of the best-loved political figures was the 18th-century *rey-alcalde* (king-mayor) Carlos III *(see p18)*. He took a personal interest in the city and set out to improve it with monuments, fountains, arches, street lighting and sewers. Another favourite politician was 20th-century (civilian) Socialist Mayor Enrique Tierno Galván, who became mayor in 1979, and died in 1986. He helped bring Madrid out of the grey dictatorial years by throwing his full support behind cultural events and progressive causes. He was instrumental in making Madrid's San Isidro festival *(see p34)* the popular cultural event it is today.

Enrique Tierno Galván, mayor of Madrid in the post-Franco era

Madrid's Best: Tabernas

It could be assumed that the first business establishment in Madrid was a *taberna* (tavern). In the 14th century, the area around Plaza Mayor and Plaza de la Villa was home to over 50 *tabernas*. Two hundred years later, their number had risen to 800. But, of the classical *tabernas* that took shape in the early to mid-19th century, only about a hundred remain. Although each is unique, they share common features, such as a large clock standing guard over a carved wooden bar with a zinc counter, and wine flasks cooled by water running through a polished filter on the bar. Table tops tend to be of marble, and ceramic tiles often line the façade or interior. To find out more about traditional *tapas* and the locations of these popular classical *tabernas*, see pages 158–161.

Bodega de Angel Sierra
Founded in 1818, this taberna *retains an authentic atmosphere and original decor, including the old ceramic tiles as advertisements.*

La Bola
This small, bright red taberna *was founded nearly 200 years ago. It has a beautifully carved wooden bar and, since 1873, it has been serving some of Madrid's best* cocido (see p159).

Old Madrid

Restaurante Botín
Established in 1725, this is one of the oldest restaurants in the world, and is considered by many to be one of Madrid's finest. It serves traditional Castilian fare, including roast suckling pig, and was, at one time, favoured by the writer Ernest Hemingway.

Taberna Antonio Sanchez
Madrid's tabernas *take their cue from this classical, 200-year-old watering hole, where the character of the place is just as important as the service. Many later* tabernas *have emulated its decor.*

0 kilometres 0.5

0 miles   0.5

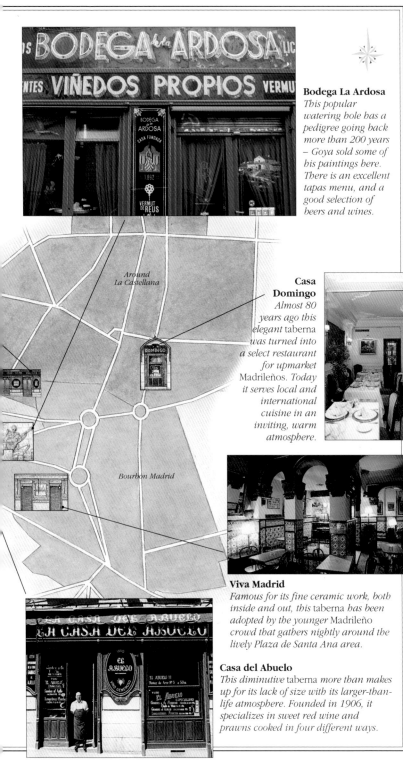

Bodega La Ardosa
This popular watering hole has a pedigree going back more than 200 years – Goya sold some of his paintings here. There is an excellent tapas menu, and a good selection of beers and wines.

Around La Castellana

Casa Domingo
Almost 80 years ago this elegant taberna was turned into a select restaurant for upmarket Madrileños. Today it serves local and international cuisine in an inviting, warm atmosphere.

Bourbon Madrid

Viva Madrid
Famous for its fine ceramic work, both inside and out, this taberna has been adopted by the younger Madrileño crowd that gathers nightly around the lively Plaza de Santa Ana area.

Casa del Abuelo
This diminutive taberna more than makes up for its lack of size with its larger-than-life atmosphere. Founded in 1906, it specializes in sweet red wine and prawns cooked in four different ways.

Madrid's Best: Architecture

Madrid has been described as the "city of a thousand faces", an image reflected in the diversity of its architectural styles. Among these are the rich and highly ostentatious buildings that mark the 16th-century areas of Old Madrid around the Plaza Mayor and the Plaza de la Villa. Northwest of Madrid, in El Escorial *(see pp126–9)*, the architecture of Felipe II's palace is characterized by unornamented severity of style. The 18th century brought with it the Bourbon urge to break with the previous mould, introducing new, ornate styles of Baroque architecture. In the mid-18th century, with the arrival of Carlos III *(see p18)*, more sedate Neo-Classical lines became fashionable. And, as the city expanded outwards, so did its love for new styles of architecture. Today Madrid's architects continue to experiment with adventurous building styles and techniques.

Modernism
The Puerta de Europa twin towers survived a financial scandal and now seem to defy gravity as they lean over Paseo de la Castellana.

Art Deco
This landmark building, at number 39 Gran Vía, was built by architect Luis Sainz de los Terreros between 1926–1928. It now houses the Allianz insurance company.

Old Madrid

Habsburg
Since 1560 the red brick and granite Monasterio de las Descalzas Reales (see p52) has been home to a society of cloistered nuns – the Royal Barefoot Sisters.

Baroque
Built in the 1720s by baroque architect José de Churriguera, this residence was stripped of its elaborate Baroque detail after being acquired by the Real Academia de Bellas Artes in 1773.

| 0 kilometres | 0.5 |
| 0 miles | 0.5 |

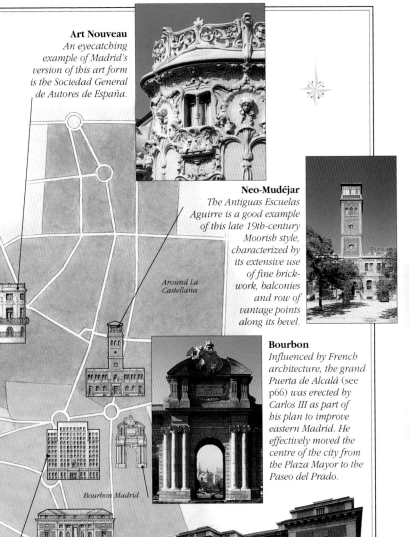

Art Nouveau
An eyecatching example of Madrid's version of this art form is the Sociedad General de Autores de España.

Around La Castellana

Neo-Mudéjar
The Antiguas Escuelas Aguirre is a good example of this late 19th-century Moorish style, characterized by its extensive use of fine brick-work, balconies and row of vantage points along its bevel.

Bourbon
Influenced by French architecture, the grand Puerta de Alcalá (see p66) was erected by Carlos III as part of his plan to improve eastern Madrid. He effectively moved the centre of the city from the Plaza Mayor to the Paseo del Prado.

Bourbon Madrid

Francoesque
The Instituto de Crédito Oficial is in the Neo-Herrerismo style, invented in the Franco years and named after 16th-century architect, Juan de Herrera.

Neo-Classical
Designed in 1785 by Juan de Villanueva, the Museo del Prado (see pp78–81) illustrates the Neo-Classical move towards dignity and away from the excesses of Baroque architecture.

MADRID THROUGH THE YEAR

A wide selection of fiestas, sports competitions and cultural events crowds the calendar in Madrid. Every neighbouring district, town and village also has its own fiestas, especially during the summer, with hair-raising bull runs, music and dancing until the early hours and spectacular fireworks which rank among the best

Matador with a cape playing a bull

in the world. There are vibrant street processions to celebrate Christmas and Easter, and at other times the capital's roads are completely taken over by bicycles, marathon runners and even sheep. Check with the tourist information office to see if your visit coincides with any public holidays, local festivals or special fairs.

Colourful tulips in a park, signalling the start of spring

SPRING

In late March the boulevards of the capital are lined with tulips, and on the first warm day in April the cafés open their terraces. But the weather is changeable, and it may be warm one day and cold the next. May's San Isidro fiestas, which herald the start of the bullfighting season, are often marred by rain, but the countryside also looks its best at this time. Many *Madrileños* leave town for the Easter Semana Santa holiday, and the deserted streets of Madrid resound with solemn religious processions.

MARCH

Cristo de Medinaceli *(first Fri)*, Iglesia de Medinaceli, Calle del Duque de Medinaceli. Thousands of people come to this church to make three wishes before the image of Christ, one of which will hopefully come true.

APRIL

Semana Santa *(Easter week)*. On Holy Thursday and Good Friday evening processions are held in Toledo *(see pp140–45)*

and all over Madrid. On Easter Saturday there are church services and a passion play in Chinchón *(see p139)*. Easter Sunday is marked in Tiermes by the symbolic burning of a tree and an effigy of Judas at noon.
Artisans & Ceramic Fair *(Easter week)*, Plaza de las Comendadoras.
El Día de Cervantes *(23 April)*, Alcalá de Henares. Book Day commemorates the death of Cervantes with a book fair and literary discussions in Alcalá de Henares and celebrations throughout Spain.
Madrid Marathon *(last Sun)*.

MAY

Labour Day *(1 May)*. Public holiday and rally held in the Puerta del Sol *(see p44)*.
Fiestas de Mayo *(1 May)*, Ajalvir, Casarrubuelos, Fresno de Torote and Torrelaguna. Local fiestas celebrating May.
Las Mayas *(first Sun)*, around Iglesia de San Lorenzo in the Lavapiés district *(see p61)*. Each street elects a May Queen *(maya)* who sits

in her best clothes surrounded by flowers in a spring fertility ritual.
La Maya *(2 May)*, Colmenar Viejo. Similar fiesta to above.
Día de la Comunidad *(2 May)*. Public holiday in Madrid and the surrounding area with a military parade in the Puerta del Sol and street festivals in Móstoles.
Fiestas de San Isidro *(15 May)*. Public holiday in Madrid and the feast of the city's patron saint. For a week either side of 15 May, the city vibrates with fiestas, music and dance, including the *chotis*. Bands play nightly in the Jardines de las Vistillas, Calle de Bailén.
San Isidro Corridas *(15 May–end Jun)*. Daily bullfight fiesta at Plaza de Toros de Las Ventas *(see p108)*.
Corpus Christi *(end May or beginning of Jun)*. Religious holiday with processions in Madrid and Toledo.
Romería Alpina *(last Sun)*, Lozoya. Country procession with La Virgen de la Fuensanta.
Feria del Libro *(end May–mid-Jun)*, Parque del Retiro *(see p77)*. Book fair.

Semana Santa *(Easter Week)* observed with solemn religious processions

AVERAGE DAILY HOURS OF SUNSHINE

Hours

12

9

6

3

0   Jan Feb Mar Apr May Jun Jul Aug Sep Oct Nov Dec

Sunshine Chart
Madrid is a sunny place and, even in the depths of winter when temperatures plummet, there are usually a few hours of sunshine to brighten the skies. At the height of the Madrid summer you can expect an average of 12 hours of blistering sun a day, so come prepared with a hat and a high-factor sun cream, and avoid the midday sun.

SUMMER

Madrid's outdoor swimming pools and aqua parks open in June *(see p188)*. By August, the fierce dry heat settles in and entire families escape to the cool of the mountains, the coast or outlying villages to visit relatives. Most offices work intensively from 8am to 3pm. Many bars and restaurants close in August, but those that stay open are thronged until the early hours. With a fraction of the usual traffic on the roads, it is a pleasant month in Madrid.

Madrileños in traditional *castizo* costume at the Fiesta de San Isidro

Madrid's terrace bars, great for cooling down in the summer heat

JUNE

Fiesta de San Antonio de la Florida *(13 Jun)*, Ermita de San Antonio, Paseo de la Florida. *Señoritas* throw pins in a font, dip in their hands and ask St Anthony for a boyfriend. If any pins stick to their hands they will have that many boyfriends in the year ahead.

JULY

Fiestas de la Virgen del Carmen *(around 16 Jul)*. District fiestas in Chamberí.
Concierto de las Velas *(first two Saturdays of Jul)*, Pedraza, Segovia. Candlelit fiesta.

Fiestas de Santiago Apóstol *(25 Jul)*. Public holiday for Spain's patron saint.
Romería Celestial *(26 Jul)*, Alameda del Valle, Lozoya. Procession climbs 3 km (2 miles) to La Ermita de Santa Ana. Bring your own picnic.

AUGUST

Castizo Fiestas *(6–15 Aug)*. Traditional *castizo* *(see p103)* fiestas in La Latina and Lavapiés. Traditional *Madrileño* fiestas of San Cayetano *(3 Aug)*, San Lorenzo *(5 Aug)* and La Virgen de la Paloma *(15 Aug)*.
Fiesta de San Lorenzo *(10 Aug)*, El Escorial *(see pp126-9)*.
Fiesta de San Roque, *(12–18 Aug)*, Chinchón. A bullfight in Plaza Mayor and *anís* tastings.
Asunción *(15 Aug)*. Assumption Day national holiday.
Encierros *(end Aug)*. Bull runs in San Sebastián de los Reyes.

Fiestas de San Bartolomé *(24 Aug)*, Alcalá de Henares. Fiestas with giants, classical theatre and bullfights.
Encierros *(last week)*, Cuellar, Segovia. Spain's oldest known bull run, dating back to 1546.
El Motín de Aranjuez *(end Aug or early Sep)*, Aranjuez. Carlos IV's abdication (1808), commemorated with bullfights, outdoor concerts and fireworks.

Decorations for La Virgen de la Paloma fiesta

AVERAGE MONTHLY RAINFALL

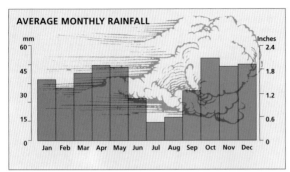

Jan Feb Mar Apr May Jun Jul Aug Sep Oct Nov Dec

Rainfall Chart
Madrid has two main rainy periods – one from March to May, and the other from October to December. During the autumn, the skies tend to open in short thundery bursts, bringing the year's highest rainfall. Summers are dry and hot, and you are very unlikely to see much rain from June to September.

View of the Plaza de España *(see p53)* **in autumn**

AUTUMN

With the onset of autumn, the first rains for months relieve the parched countryside and begin to replenish depleted reservoirs.

Madrileños love foraging in pine forests for the wild mushrooms produced by damp nights. **Wild mushrooms** The hunting season begins in October, and wild *níscalos* (fungi), boar, partridge and pheasant begin to appear on restaurant menus.

SEPTEMBER

Encierros *(first 12 days)*, Torrelaguna. Exciting bull runs and local celebrations.
Procesión Fluvial *(second Sat)*, Fuentidueña de Tajo. River procession with illuminated barges.

Procesión de la Virgen de la Ciguiñuela *(6 Sep)*, Fuente de Saz de Jarama. Procession honouring the Virgin of the Stork amid burning scrub.
Romería Panorámica *(second Sun)*, San Lorenzo de El Escorial. Procession with La Virgen de la Gracia (Grace) to a picnic in La Herrería woods.
Romería de la Virgen de los Hontanares *(10 Sep)*, Riaza, Segovia. Local pilgrimage and fiesta of the Virgin of Springs.

Virgen de la Fuencisla *(27 Sep)*. Segovia fiesta.

OCTOBER

Festival Taurino *(around 12 Oct)*, Chinchón. Bullfights.
Día de la Hispanidad *(12 Oct)*. Spanish National Day.
Virgen de Pilar *(12 Oct)*, Plaza Dalí, Salamanca. Various district fiestas are held.
Festival de Otoño *(mid-Oct to mid-Nov)*. Annual drama, ballet and opera festival.

NOVEMBER

Todos los Santos *(1 Nov)*. On All Saints' Day flowers are taken to graves of relatives.
La Almudena *(9 Nov)*. Old Madrid honours its patron saint La Virgen de la Almudena.
Romería de San Eugenio *(14 Nov)*. *Castizo* procession in open carriages to El Monte de El Pardo for picnics.
Expo/Ocio *(third week)*, Parque Ferial Juan Carlos I. Annual exhibition dedicated to sports and hobbies.
Procesión de San Andrés *(30 Nov)*, Rascafría. Procession in honour of the local saint.

Celebration of Mass in Plaza Mayor to honour La Virgen de la Almudena

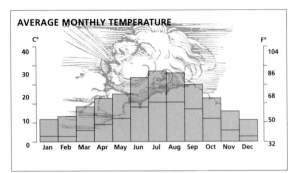

AVERAGE MONTHLY TEMPERATURE

Temperature Chart
Scorching hot summers and freezing winters make Madrid a place of extremes, with averages giving scant indication of the heights and depths of temperature the city can achieve. For many people, the most comfortable months to visit Madrid, in terms of milder temperatures, are June and October.

WINTER

The first snow usually falls in the Sierra de Guadarrama *(see p130)*, heralding the start of the skiing season, and traffic jams form on the way up to its small resorts. Madrid, and the higher parts of central Spain, can become very cold. Christmas is a special time of celebration – an occasion for families to reunite, share food and attend religious services. On New Year's Eve, crowds gather in the Puerta del Sol.

Skiers in the Sierra de Guadarrama, north of Madrid *(see p126)*

DECEMBER

Día de la Constitución *(6 Dec)*. Constitution Day.
Inmaculada Concepción *(8 Dec)*. Immaculate Conception.
Christmas Fair *(mid-Dec–5 Jan)*, Madrid's Plaza Mayor.
Nochebuena *(24 Dec)*. Christmas Eve – an important night of family celebrations.
Día de Navidad *(25 Dec)*. Christmas Day celebration.
Belén Viviente *(last eves Dec)*, Buitrago del Lozoya. Nativity play on horseback.
Nochevieja *(31 Dec)*. New Year's Eve. Crowds in Puerta del Sol eat a grape each midnight chime.

JANUARY

Cabalgata de Reyes *(5 Jan)*. Evening (6pm) procession from Parque del Retiro *(see p77)* to the Plaza Mayor *(see p44)* with floats, animals and celebrities.
Los Reyes Magos *(6 Jan)*. Epiphany is celebrated with the giving of gifts.
San Antón *(17 Jan)*, Calle de Hortaleza 63, Madrid. Animals blessed at Iglesia de San Antón.
Vaquillas *(20 Jan)*, Pedrezuela and Fresnedillas. Fiesta in which youths dress up as bulls.
San Sebastián *(20 Jan)*, Villaviciosa de Odón. Procession, fiestas and dancing.
FITUR Tourist Fair *(end Jan)*, Parque Ferial Juan Carlos I.

FEBRUARY

La Vaquilla Premiada *(2 Feb)*, Colmenar Viejo. Amateur bull-fighting contest and fiesta.
La Romería de San Blas *(3 Feb)*, Madrid and Miraflores. Costumed celebrations.
Alcadesas de Zamarramala *(around first Sun)*, Segovia. For a day village women boss their men around.
Semana Internacional de la Moda *(mid-Feb)*, Parque Ferial Juan Carlos I. International fashion week.
ARCO *(mid-Feb)*, Parque Ferial Juan Carlos I. International contemporary art fair.
Carnaval *(run up to Lent)*. Fancy-dress parties; parade in the city centre.

Entierro de la Sardina *(Shrove Tue)*, Casa de Campo. "Burial of the Sardine" parade to mark the changeover from *Carnaval* to Lent.

NATIONAL PUBLIC HOLIDAYS

Año Nuevo *(New Year's Day)* (1 Jan)
Los Reyes Magos *(Epiphany)* (6 Jan)
Jueves Santo *(Maundy Thursday)* (Mar/Apr)
Viernes Santo *(Good Friday)* (Mar/Apr)
Domingo de Pascua *(Easter Sunday)* (Mar/Apr)
Día del Trabajo *(Labour Day)* (1 May)
Asunción *(Assumption Day)* (15 Aug)
Día de la Hispanidad *(National Day)* (12 Oct)
Todos los Santos *(All Saints' Day)* (1 Nov)
Día de la Constitución *(Constitution Day)* (6 Dec)
Inmaculada Concepción *(Immaculate Conception)* (8 Dec)
Navidad *(Christmas Day)* (25 Dec)

Fuente de Cibeles *(see p67)* ▷

MADRID AREA BY AREA

OLD MADRID

When Felipe II chose Madrid as his capital in 1561, it was a small Castilian town with a population of barely 20,000. In the following years, it was to grow into the nerve centre of a mighty empire. Narrow streets with houses and medieval churches began to grow up behind the old Moorish fortress *(see p15)*, which was later replaced by a Gothic palace and eventually by the present-day Bourbon palace, the Palacio Real. By the end of the century the population had more than trebled.

The 16th-century city is known as the "Madrid de los Austrias", after the Habsburg dynasty. At this time, monasteries were endowed and churches and palaces were built. In the 17th century, the Plaza Mayor was added and the Puerta del Sol became the spiritual and geographical heart of Spain.

SIGHTS AT A GLANCE

Historic Buildings
Edificio Grassy ⑪
Muralla Arabe ㉖
Palacio de Santa Cruz ⑦
Palacio del Senado ⑱
Palacio Real pp54–7 ⑳
Teatro Real ㉒
Telefónica ⑫

Museums and Galleries
Museo Cerralbo ⑯
Real Academia de
  Bellas Artes ⑨

Churches and Convents
Basílica Pontificia de
  San Miguel ⑤
Catedral de la
  Almudena ㉔
Colegiata de San Isidro ⑥
Iglesia de San Nicolás ㉓
Monasterio de la
  Encarnación ⑲

Monasterio de las
  Descalzas Reales ⑭
San Francisco
  el Grande ㉗

Streets, Squares, Parks and Districts
Calle de Preciados ⑮
Campo del Moro ㉕
Gran Vía ⑩
La Latina ㉙
Plaza de España ⑰
Plaza de la Paja ㉘
Plaza de la Villa ④
Plaza de Oriente ㉑
Plaza de Santa Ana ⑧
Plaza del Callao ⑬

Plaza Mayor ②
Puerta del Sol ①

Markets
El Rastro ㉚
Mercado de San Miguel ③

GETTING THERE
Line 1 on the Metro goes to Gran Vía and Sol, while 2, 3, 5 and 10 are good for getting to the main sights. Useful buses include the 51, 52, 150 and 153 to the Puerta del Sol.

KEY

Street-by-Street map
pp42–3

Ⓜ Metro station

Main bus stop

🅘 Tourist information

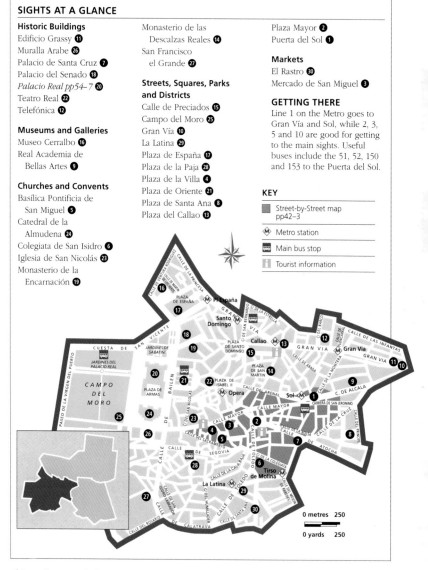

0 metres 250
0 yards 250

◁ Equestrian statue of Felipe III in the centre of the Plaza Mayor *(see p44)*

Street-by-Street: Old Madrid

Stretching from the charming Plaza de la
Villa to the busy Puerta del Sol, the
compact heart of Old Madrid is steeped
in history and full of interesting sights.
Trials by the Inquisition and executions
were once held in the Plaza Mayor. This
porticoed square is Old Madrid's finest
piece of architecture, a legacy of the
Habsburgs *(see p16)*. Other noteworthy
buildings include the Colegiata de San
Isidro and the Palacio de Santa Cruz. For
a more relaxing way of enjoying Old
Madrid, sit in one of the area's numerous
cafés or browse among the colourful
stalls of the Mercado de San Miguel.

★ Plaza Mayor
*This beautiful 17th
century square
competes with the
Puerta del Sol as
the focus of Old
Madrid. The arcades
at the base of the
impressive buildings
are filled with cafés
and craft shops* **②**

Mercado de San Miguel
*Housed in a 19th-century iron
structure, the market has a
variety of delicatessen stalls* **③**

**Palacio
Real**

CALLE MAYOR
PLAZA
MORENAS

PLAZA
DE LA
VILLA

CORDÓN

PUÑONROSTRO

CALLE DE SACRAMENTO

**Town hall
(ayuntamiento)**

Casa de Cisneros

CUCHILLE

**Arco de
Cuchilleros**

★ Plaza de la Villa
*The 15th-century Torre de
los Lujanes is the oldest of
several historic buildings
standing on this square* **④**

0 metres	100
0 yards	100

STAR SIGHTS

★ Plaza Mayor

★ Plaza de la Villa

★ Puerta del Sol

**Basílica Pontificia
de San Miguel**
*This imposing 18th-
century church has
a beautiful façade
and a graceful
Baroque interior* **⑤**

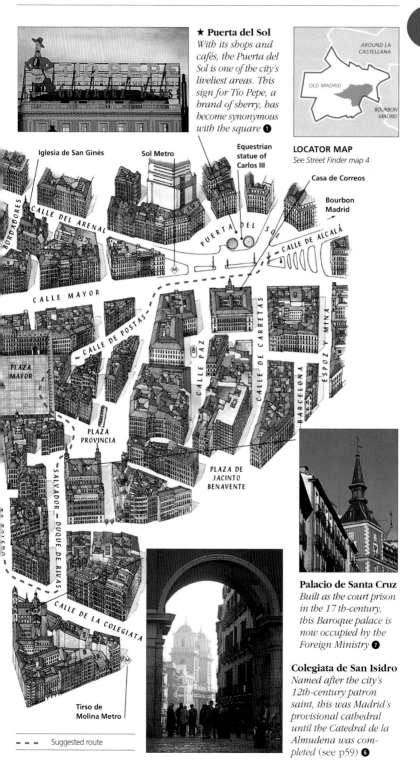

★ **Puerta del Sol**
With its shops and cafés, the Puerta del Sol is one of the city's liveliest areas. This sign for Tío Pepe, a brand of sherry, has become synonymous with the square ❶

LOCATOR MAP
See Street Finder map 4

AROUND LA CASTELLANA

OLD MADRID

BOURBON MADRID

Iglesia de San Ginés

Sol Metro

Equestrian statue of Carlos III

Casa de Correos

Bourbon Madrid

BORDADORES

CALLE DEL ARENAL

PUERTA DEL SOL

CALLE DE ALCALÁ

CALLE MAYOR

CALLE DE POSTAS

CALLE PAZ

CALLE DE CARRETAS

BARCELONA

ESPOZ Y MINA

PLAZA MAYOR

PLAZA PROVINCIA

PLAZA DE JACINTO BENAVENTE

SALVADOR — DUQUE DE RIVAS

CALLE DE LA COLEGIATA

Tirso de Molina Metro

- - - Suggested route

Palacio de Santa Cruz
Built as the court prison in the 17th-century, this Baroque palace is now occupied by the Foreign Ministry ❼

Colegiata de San Isidro
Named after the city's 12th-century patron saint, this was Madrid's provisional cathedral until the Catedral de la Almudena was completed (see p59) ❻

Kilometre Zero, the centre of Spain's road network, at the Puerta del Sol

Puerta del Sol ❶

Map 4 F2. Ⓜ *Sol.*

Noisy with traffic, chatter and policemen's whistles, the Puerta del Sol ("Gateway of the Sun") makes a fitting centre for Madrid. It is one of the city's most popular meeting places; huge crowds converge on this famous square on their way to the shops and sights in the old part of the city. Restoration work will affect the area until 2009.

The square marks the site of the original eastern entrance to Madrid, once occupied by a gatehouse and castle. These disappeared long ago and in their place came a succession of churches. In the late 19th century the area was turned into a square and became the centre of café society.

Today the "square" is shaped like a half moon. The equestrian statue of Carlos III in its centre is a recent addition. The square's southern side is occupied by the austere red-brick Casa de Correos, once the city's post office, built in the 1760s under Carlos III. In 1847 it became the headquarters of the Ministry of the Interior. In 1866 the clocktower, which gives the building much of its identity, was added. During the Franco regime *(see p20)*, the police cells beneath the building were the site of many human rights abuses. In 1963, Julián Grimau, a member of the underground Communist party, allegedly fell from an upstairs window and miraculously survived, only to be executed shortly afterwards.

The building is now home to the regional government and is the focus of many festive events. At midnight on New Year's Eve dense crowds fill the square and people swallow a grape on each stroke of the clock, a tradition supposed to bring good luck for the rest of the year. Outside the building, a symbol on the ground marks Kilometre Zero, considered the centre of Spain's road network.

The buildings opposite are arranged in a semicircle and contain modern shops and cafés. On the corner of Calle del Carmen is a bronze statue of the symbol of Madrid – a bear reaching for the fruit of a *madroño* (strawberry tree).

The Puerta del Sol has witnessed many important historical events. On 2 May 1808 the uprising against the occupying French forces began here, but the crowd was crushed *(see p18)*. In 1912 the liberal prime minister José Canalejas was assassinated in the square and, in 1931, the Second Republic *(see p20)* was proclaimed from the balcony of the Ministry of the Interior.

Plaza Mayor ❷

Map 4 E3. Ⓜ *Sol.*

The Plaza Mayor forms a splendid rectangular square, complete with balconies, pinnacles, dormer windows

Allegorical paintings on the Casa de la Panadería, Plaza Mayor

and steep slate roofs. The square, with its theatrical atmosphere, has a noticeably Castilian character. Much was expected to happen here and a great deal did – bullfights, executions, pageants and trials by the Inquisition *(see p17)* – all watched by crowds, often in the presence of the reigning king and queen.

The first great public scene in the Plaza Mayor was the beatification of Madrid's patron, San Isidro, in 1621. During the same year, the execution of Rodrigo Calderón, secretary to Felipe III, was held here. Although hated by the Madrid populace, Calderón bore himself with such dignity on the day of his death that the phrase "proud as Rodrigo on the scaffold" survives to this day. Perhaps the greatest occasion of all, however, was the arrival here – from Italy – of Carlos III in 1760.

Construction of the square started in 1617, and was completed in just two years, replacing slum houses on the site. Its architect, Juan Gómez de Mora, was successor to Juan de Herrera, designer of El Escorial *(see pp126–9)*, Felipe II's austere monastery-palace. Mora echoed the style of his master, softening it slightly. The square was later reformed by Juan de Villanueva. The fanciest part of the arcaded construction is the **Casa de la Panadería** (bakery). Its façade is decorated with allegorical paintings.

The **equestrian statue** in the centre is of Felipe III, who ordered the square to be built. Begun by the Italian Giovanni de Bologna and finished by his pupil Pietro Tacca in 1616, the statue was moved here in 1848 from the Casa de Campo *(see p112)*. Nowadays the square is lined with cafés and hosts a collectors' market on Sundays. The southern exit leads into the Calle de Toledo towards the streets where El Rastro, Madrid's famous flea-market *(see p61)*, is held. A flight of steps in the southwest corner of the square takes you under the Arco de Cuchilleros to the Calle de Cuchilleros, where there are a number of *mesones*, traditional restaurants.

Shopping in the 19th-century Mercado de San Miguel

Mercado de San Miguel ❸

Plaza de San Miguel. **Map** 4 D3.
Ⓜ *Sol.* ☐ *check times locally.*
⬤ *public hols.*

Although there are larger markets in Madrid, the Mercado de San Miguel this one is the last surviving example in the capital of a marketplace constructed from iron. The unique single-level, glassed-in market was built in 1914–15. It stands on the site of the former Iglesia de San Miguel de los Octoes, which was demolished in 1810 during the reign of Joseph Bonaparte. Following a refurbishment during 2008, the market now boasts excellent delicatessen stalls decorated with beautiful tiles, as well as a restaurant.

Plaza de la Villa ❹

Map 4 D3. Ⓜ *Ópera, Sol.*

This much restored and frequently remodelled square is one of Madrid's most atmospheric spots, surrounded by many historic buildings.

The oldest building is the early 15th-century **Torre de los Lujanes**, with its Gothic portal and Mudéjar-style horseshoe arches. France's François I was allegedly imprisoned in it following his defeat at the Battle of Pavia in 1525. The **Casa de Cisneros** was built in 1537 for the nephew of Cardinal Cisneros, founder of the historic University of Alcalá *(see p135)*. The façade on Calle de Sacramento is an excellent example of the Plateresque style – early Spanish Renaissance with fine detail.

Linked to this building by an enclosed bridge is the **town hall** *(ayuntamiento)*. Designed in the 1640s by Juan Gómez de Mora, architect of the Plaza Mayor, it exhibits the same combination of steep roofs with dormer windows, steeple-like towers at the corners and an austere brick-and-stone façade. Before construction was completed, more than 30 years later, the building had acquired handsome Baroque doorways. A balcony was later added by Juan de Villanueva, architect of the Prado *(see pp78–81)*, so that the Royal Family could watch Corpus Christi processions passing by.

Portal of the Torre de los Lujanes

Basílica Pontificia de San Miguel ❺

Calle de San Justo 4. **Map** 4 D3. *Tel 91 548 40 11.* 🚇 *Sol.* 🕐 *10am–2pm, 6–8:30pm Mon–Sat; 6–9pm Sun.* 📷

Standing on the site of an old Romanesque church dedicated to two local child-martyrs put to death by the Romans, this building is a rare example of Bourbon-inspired Baroque in the middle of old Madrid. It was built for Don Luis de Borbón y Farnesio, the youngest son of Felipe V and Archbishop of Toledo at only five years of age.

Several architects had a hand in its design and construction between 1739 and 1746. The pediment and twin bell towers topping its convex façade were, however, added later. Four allegorical statues, representing Charity, Fortitude, Faith and Hope, grace the elegant façade. There are also carvings depicting the two child-martyrs, Justo and Pastor.

Inside, there is a single nave, and the roof is supported only by the curved and crossing arches sprouting from the exterior walls. The decor is a curious mixture of old and new – the frescoes on the ceiling and the organ in the choir (above the entrance) date from the 18th century, but many of the paintings and

Statue of Charity gracing the façade of Basílica Pontífica de San Miguel

stained-glass windows are contemporary. Today the church is administered by the Catholic lay organization, Opus Dei, who use it as a base for some of their activities. One of the side chapels, which is dedicated to the organization's Spanish founder, Monsignor José María Escrivá de Balaguer (1902–75), houses an eerily lifelike statue of him.

Ornate altar in the Colegiata de San Isidro

Colegiata de San Isidro ❻

Calle de Toledo 37. **Map** 4 E3. *Tel 91 369 20 37.* 🚇 *La Latina.* 🕐 *8am–1pm, 6–8pm Mon–Sat; 9am–2pm, 6–8pm Sun.*

This twin-towered church was built in the Baroque style for the Jesuits in the mid17th century. It was used as Madrid's unofficial cathedral until 1993 when Nuestra Señora de la Almudena (see p59) was finally completed and consecrated by the pope.

After Carlos III (1759–88) expelled the influential Jesuit order from Spain in 1767 (see p18), he commissioned Ventura Rodríguez to redesign the church's interior. It was then re-dedicated to St Isidore, Madrid's patron saint and, two years later, the saint's remains were brought here from the Iglesia de San Andrés. The Colegiata was returned to the Jesuits during the reign of Fernando VII (1814–33).

Palacio de Santa Cruz ❼

Plaza de Santa Cruz. **Map** 4 E3. *Tel 91 379 97 00.* 🚇 *Sol.* 📷 *to the public.*

Constructed between 1629 and 1643, this building is one of the jewels of Habsburg architecture. Since 1901 it has been the Ministry of Foreign Affairs, but has also housed the Overseas Ministry, law courts and, originally, the Carcel de la Corte (city prison). It was here that the luckless participants in the *autos de fé* (Spanish inquisition trials), held in the nearby Plaza Mayor *(see p44)*, awaited their fate. Its more famous inmates include the playwright Lope de Vega (1562– 1635), imprisoned for libelling his former lover, the actress Elena Osorio. The English writer and travelling Bible salesman, George Borrow, who was accused of instigating liberal ideas, also spent three weeks here. General Rafael de Riego, who led an uprising against Fernando VII in 1820, and the famous bandit Luis Candelas spent their last hours in its cells. Candelas was a colourful Robin Hood-like character, educated in Greek and Latin, who rubbed shoulders with the aristocracy (and stole their jewels). He was executed on 6 November 1837; today one of Madrid's tourist restaurants, situated on nearby Cava de San Miguel, is named after him.

The palace underwent a restoration in 1846, following a fire, and again in the aftermath of the Spanish Civil War *(see p20)*, but its original architecture remains essentially intact. The style of the building is in keeping with the area around the Plaza Mayor, with spired towers on its corners and two interior courtyards. The building only became known as the Palacio de Santa Cruz

The 17th-century Palacio de Santa Cruz – a jewel of Habsburg architecture

after 1846, when it was made the headquarters of Spain's Overseas Ministry.

Plaza de Santa Ana **8**

Map 7 A3. Ⓜ *Sevilla, Antón Martin.*

This large pedestrian square, just four blocks southeast of the Puerta del Sol *(see p44)*, is a popular gathering place with a lively, at times rowdy, atmosphere. Built during the reign of Napoleon Bonaparte's brother Joseph (1808–13), the square took its name from the 16th-century Convent of Santa Ana that stood here. It was demolished to make way for the square.

Scene from a play by Calderón de la Barca adorning his statue

Monuments to two of Spain's most famous writers testify to the square's strong literary connections. At one end is the brooding marble figure of Pedro Calderón de la Barca (1600–81). Madrid-born, he was the leading playwright in the twilight years of Spain's *Siglo de Oro* (Golden Century) of arts. His best-known work is *La Vida es Sueño* (Life is a Dream). The monument, with scenes from four of Calderón's plays adorning the pedestal, was sculpted by Juan Figueras in 1878. At the other end of the square, a statue of the poet Federico García Lorca *(see p28)*, erected in 1998,

commemorates the centenary of his birth and faces the **Teatro Español** *(see p76)*. Built in 1745, the theatre was originally known as the Teatro del Príncipe. It had to be restored in 1980 after a devastating fire.

The square's theatrical links go back even earlier, as the theatre stands on the spot of the Corral del Príncipe, one of Madrid's popular, 16th-century *corrales de comedias* (open courtyards where plays were staged). These tended to be boisterous affairs, often culminating in fights between the actors and the audience. Across from the theatre are the glassed-in balconies of **ME Madrid Reina Victoria** *(see p151)*, one of Madrid's classic hostelries. Before the Tryp chain acquired it, the hotel's then modest lodgings were used by bullfighters who could not afford luxurious city rooms. Now, it's a luxury modern hotel.

The other two sides of Plaza de Santa Ana and adjoining streets are home to some of the city's most popular bars and restaurants. The classic **Cervecería Alemana**, built in 1904 and once frequented by author Ernest Hemingway, is always packed with customers.

Around the corner from the theatre is the **Viva Madrid** *(see p31)*. This well-known *taberna*, near Plaza de Santa Ana, is popular with the

young and fashionable and boasts extraordinary 19th-century ceramic tableaux. Tile landscapes also adorn the **Villa Rosa**, located on the corner of Plaza de Santa Ana and Calle de Núñez de Arce.

Real Academia de Bellas Artes **9**

Calle de Alcalá 13. **Map** 7 A2. *Tel* 91524 08 64. Ⓜ *Sevilla, Sol.* ◐ *9am–7pm Tue–Fri, 9am–2:30pm, 4–7pm Sat, 9am–2:30pm Sun.* ● *some public hols.* ● *(free Wed).* ● *by appointment.* ● **www**.rabasf.insde.es

Dalí and Picasso are among the former students of this arts academy, housed in an 18th-century building by Churriguera. Its art gallery displays a large selection of works, including drawings by Raphael and Titian. A superb collection of old masters includes paintings by Rubens and Van Dyck. Spanish artists from the 16th to the 19th centuries are particularly well represented, with magnificent works by Ribera, Murillo, El Greco and Velázquez. One of the highlights is Zurbarán's *Fray Pedro Machado*, typical of his paintings of monks.

An entire room is devoted to Goya, a former director of the academy. On show here are his painting of Carlos IV's chief minister, Manuel Godoy, the *Burial of the Sardine*, the grim *Madhouse*, and a self-portrait painted in 1815.

Fray Pedro Machado by Zurbarán

Gran Vía ❿

In the mid-1800s, Madrid's burgeoning middle class was pushing the city's limits outwards, destroying houses and poor districts to allow for the *Ensanche* (widening). The city fathers saw the need for a new thoroughfare – a *Gran Vía*. Departing from the haphazard growth of the past, this street was to follow a plan and be a symbol of modern Madrid. On the drawing board since 1860, with even a satirical *zarzuela (see p75)* devoted to it, the project was not approved until 1904. Inaugurated by Alfonso XIII in 1910 *(see p19)*, building was carried out in three stages, each segment bearing a different name, although they are no longer used. The first, and most elegant – Avenida Conde de Peñalver (after the Mayor) – ran from Calle de Alcalá to Red de San Luis. The second phase, to the Plaza de Callao, was completed in 1922, while the final segment, ending in the Plaza de España, was built between 1925 and 1929. The new street gave architects an opportunity to prove their skill, providing a survey of early 20th-century design trends, including some of the best examples of modern architecture in the city.

Brass detail on the Edificio Metrópolis

The Museo Chicote *cocktail bar, on the ground floor of Gran Vía No. 12, has an immaculately preserved Art Deco interior. It opened in 1932 and was patronized by Salvador Dalí, Frank Sinatra, Ava Gardner and Orson Welles.*

The rounded Art Deco *façade of this building, like many along the Gran Vía, displays a style and grandeur befitting the city's most impressive thoroughfare. Many Art Deco buildings were built as cinemas, several of which are clustered around Plaza del Callao.*

Behind La Gran Peña's *curved façade (No. 2) is a luxurious, increasingly popular men's club. In 1926, attempts to make Franco a member caused such a stir that the club was later taken over and used by the militia during the Civil War* (see p20).

Edificio la Estrella *(No. 10) is a good example of the eclectic mix of Neo-Classical design and ornamental touches evident in the first buildings to have appeared along Gran Vía.*

Today's Gran Vía *continues to be a throbbing main artery for the city of Madrid, lined with theatres and cinemas, hotels, shops and restaurants.*

The two-tiered colonnade of the Edificio Grassy on Gran Vía

Edificio Grassy ⑪

Gran Via 1. **Map** 7 B1. **Tel** *91 532 10 07.* Ⓜ *Banco de España, Sevilla.* **Museum** ◻ *11am–1:15pm, 5:30–8pm Mon–Fri, 11am–1:15pm Sat.*

Designed by Eladio Laredo on a small sliver of land between the Gran Vía and the Calle de Caballero de Gracia, the Grassy building boasts a circular end-tower similar to that of the nearby Edificio Metropolis *(see p74).* It is crowned by a round, two-tiered colonnade. It was built in 1917, but became known as the Grassy building in the 1950s, after the jewellery shop that has occupied the ground floor since then. The prestigious jewellery firm, which was established in 1923, specializes in watches and, in the basement, is the **Museo de Reloj Grassy**, a collection of around 500 timepieces, from the 16th to 19th centuries, including rare clocks which belonged to European royalty.

Clock at the Grassy museum

Telefónica ⑫

Gran Via 28. **Map** 4 F1, 7 A1. Ⓜ *Gran Via, Callao.* **Museum Tel** *91 522 66 45.* ◻ *10am–2pm, 5–8pm Tue–Fri, 11am–8pm Sat, 11am–2pm Sun & public hols.* ◪ *Aug.* Ⓧ ♿ ◻ *(call to arrange).* **www**.fundacion.telefonica.com

If the Telefónica building has an American look to it, it is because it was inspired by Manhattan's skyscrapers and designed by an American – Louis S Weeks – although the Spanish architect Ignacio de Cárdenas was made officially responsible in order to secure planning permission. Built between 1926 and 1929 to house the Spanish telephone company, it was Madrid's tallest building. Its façade consists of tapered setbacks, ending in a central tower 81 m (266 ft) tall. The little exterior ornamentation it has was added by Cárdenas so that the building would seem less out of place amid the neighbouring architecture. The clear view from the upper floors enabled the Republican defenders of the city to monitor the movements of besieging Nationalists in the Spanish Civil War *(see p20).*

A section of the lower floors, which is entered from Calle de Fuencarral, is used for exhibitions. There are temporary exhibitions on the ground floor and a permanent one of the evolution of telecommunications on the first floor. Displays range from old phones, including the one used by Alfonso XIII to inaugurate Madrid's automatic telephone service in 1926, to a bank of switchboards with 19 life-sized operators and sound effects. The exhibition rooms are arranged around a gallery that overlooks the main foyer. The gallery once housed a formidable collection of modern art, now on long-term loan to the Centro de Arte Reina Sofía *(see pp84–91).*

The Telefónica – a Manhattan-style skyscraper from the 1920s

Plaza del Callao ⑬

Plaza del Callao. **Map** 4 E1. Ⓜ *Callao.*

This city's passion for films is fed by more than 60 cinemas and Plaza del Callao, the movie mecca of Madrid, has seven of them. Situated at the junction of Gran Vía and Calle de Preciados, the square was named after a naval battle off Callao, Peru, in 1866. The cinemas are the Art Deco Cine Callao, Imperial, Rex, Capitol, Palacio de la Música (music hall) and Palacio de la Prensa (Madrid Press Association). Films are advertised on huge, hand-painted signs.

Housed in the Capitol building is the Capitol cinema, built in 1933. A superb example of Art Deco architecture, its features include a covered entrance and a vast, box-like interior, 35 m (115 ft) wide, adorned with simple lines and curves.

The Capitol cinema, a good example of Art Deco architecture

Chapel with ornate altar in the Monasterio de las Descalzas Reales

Monasterio de las Descalzas Reales ⓮

Plaza de las Descalzas 3. **Map** 4 E2. **Tel** 91 454 88 00. ⓜ Sol, Callao. ◯ 10:30am–12:30pm, 4–5:30pm Tue–Thu & Sat, 10:30am–12:30pm Fri, 11am–2:30pm Sun & public hols. ● 1 & 6 Jan, three days, a week after Easter, 1 & 15 May, 9 Nov, 24–25 & 31 Dec. 📷 (free Wed for EU residents). 🎫 **www**.patrimonionacional.es.

Madrid's most notable religious building is also a rare surviving example of 16th-century architecture in the city. Around 1560 Felipe II's sister Doña Juana converted the medieval palace which stood here into a convent for nuns and women of the royal household. Her rank, and that of her fellow nuns, accounts for the vast store of art and wealth of the Descalzas Reales (Royal Barefoot Sisters).

The stairway has a fresco of Felipe IV with his family, and a fine ceiling by Claudio Coello. It leads to a first-floor cloister, ringed with chapels containing paintings and precious objects. The main chapel houses Doña Juana's tomb. The Sala de Tapices (Tapestries Room) contains a series of 17th-century tapestries. There are also works by Brueghel the Elder, Titian, Zurbarán, Murillo and Ribera.

Calle de Preciados ⓯

Map 4 F2. ⓜ Sol, Callao.

This pedestrian street leading north from Puerta del Sol to the busy Plaza de Callao is now the domain of shoppers. It was originally a humble country path from the centre of old Madrid to the orchards and threshing floors of the Convent of San Martín which, until 1810, faced the Monasterio de las Descalzas Reales. In the 17th century two brothers, the Preciados, purchased land from the convent to build their homes. They were in charge of controlling official weights and measures used for trade in Madrid.

Calle de Preciados acquired its modern look during the *Ensanche* (urban renewal) of the mid-19th century. It is the birthplace of Spain's most successful department store chain, El Corte Inglés. Started by Ramón Areces as a modest clothes store in 1940, it now occupies an eight-floor site at the southern end of the street. At the northern end stands a modern building occupied by FNAC, the local branch of a French chain which is one of the city's best sources for music, videos and books. Between the two superstores, trendy boutiques share space with old-fashioned shops.

Museo Cerralbo ⓰

Calle de Ventura Rodríguez 17. **Map** 1 C5. **Tel** 91 547 36 46. ⓜ Plaza de España, Ventura Rodríguez. ◯ 9:30am–3pm Tue–Sat, 10am–3pm Sun. ● public hols. 📷 (free Wed & Sun). ♿ 🚫 **www**.museocerralbo.mcu.es

This 19th-century mansion is a monument to Enrique de Aguilera y Gamboa, the 17th Marquis of Cerralbo. He bequeathed his lifetime's collection of art and artifacts to the nation in 1922, which ranges from Iberian pottery to 18th-century marble busts. One of the star exhibits is El Greco's *The Ecstasy of Saint Francis of Assisi*. There are also paintings by Ribera, Zurbarán, Alonso Cano and Goya.

The focal point of the main floor is the ballroom, lavishly decorated with mirrors. The mansion underwent a major refurbishment during 2008.

Main staircase of the exuberant Museo Cerralbo

◁ **Nighttime traffic on the Gran Vía, seen from the Plaza de España**

Stone obelisk with statue of Miguel de Cervantes, Plaza de España

Plaza de España ⓱

Map 1 C5. Ⓜ *Plaza de España.*

One of Madrid's busiest traffic intersections and most popular meeting places is the Plaza de España. In the 18th and 19th centuries the square was occupied by military barracks, built here because of the square's proximity to the Palacio Real *(see pp54–7)*. However, further expansion of Madrid resulted in it remaining a public space.

The square acquired its present appearance during the Franco period with the construction of the massive **Edificio España**. Commissioned by the Metropolitana real estate developers, the 26-floor concrete structure was built between 1947 and 1953, when Spain was isolated from the western world and materials were scarce. It was seen as a triumph of "autarchy" *(see p20)*. The imposing main tower is flanked by two 17-floor wings. The building has been recently sold.

Metropolitana also built the 33-floor **Torre de Madrid** on the corner of Plaza de España and Calle Princesa. Completed in 1957 and nicknamed La Jirafa (the Giraffe), for a time it was the tallest concrete structure in the world.

The most attractive part of the square is its centre, with a massive stone obelisk built in 1928. In front of it is a statue of Cervantes *(see p135)*. Below him, Don Quixote rides his horse while Sancho Panza trots alongside on his donkey.

Palacio del Senado ⓲

Plaza de la Marina Española. **Map** 3 C1. *Tel* 91 538 1441. Ⓜ *Plaza de España, Ópera.* ◯ *tours by appointment (91 538 1441).* Ⓟ ♿ **www**.senado.es

The upper house of the Cortes (Spanish parliament) is installed in a 16th-century monastery, adapted in 1814 for the purpose. It became the Senate headquarters when a two-chamber system was introduced 23 years later.

The monastery's courtyards were covered to create more meeting rooms. Some, such as the Salón de los Pasos Perdidos (Hall of the Lost Footsteps), contain enormous paintings depicting great moments in Spanish history. Among these are the surrender of Granada and Queen Regent María Cristina swearing to uphold the Constitution in 1897.

The library is a magnificent example of English Gothic style, dating from the turn of the 20th century. Ornate tiers of black metal bookcases contain 14,000 volumes, including a copy of Nebrija's *Gramática*, the first Spanish grammar.

In 1991 a modern granite-and-glass circular wing was added at the back of the building to create more space.

The Palacio del Senado is open to the public for three days, free of charge, in early December each year, to mark the establishment of the 1978 Constitution on 6 December.

Old assembly hall of the Palacio del Senado, housed in the church of the monastery

Imposing entrance to the Monasterio de la Encarnación

Monasterio de la Encarnación ⓳

Plaza de la Encarnación 1. **Map** 3 C1. *Tel* 91 454 88 00. Ⓜ *Ópera, Santo Domingo.* ◯ *10:30am–12:45pm, 4–5:45pm Tue–Thu & Sat, 10:30am–12:45pm Fri, 11am–1:45pm Sun & public hols.* ● *1 & 6 Jan, three days, a week after Easter, 1 & 15 May, 27 Jul, 9 Nov, 24–25 & 31 Dec.* ✍ *(free Wed for EU residents).* ♿ Ⓟ **www**.patrimonionacional.es

Set in a lovely tree-shaded square, this Augustinian convent was founded in 1611 for Margaret of Austria, wife of Felipe III. The architect, Juan Gómez de Mora, also built the Plaza Mayor *(see p44)*.

Still inhabited by nuns, the convent has the atmosphere of old Castile, with its Talavera tiles, exposed beams and portraits of royal benefactors. It also contains a collection of 17th-century art, with paintings by José de Ribera and Vincente Carducho and a polychrome wooden statue *Cristo Yacente* (*Lying Christ*) by Gregorio Fernández. The main attraction is the reliquary chamber which is used to store the bones of saints. There is also a phial of St Pantaleon's dried blood which, according to legend, liquifies every 27 July, the saint's birthday. The church, rebuilt after a fire in 1767, has paintings by Francisco Bayeu and frescoes by González Velázquez.

Palacio Real ⓴

Statue of Carlos III

Madrid's vast and lavish Royal Palace was built to impress. The site, on a high bluff overlooking the Río Manzanares, had been occupied for centuries by a royal fortress but, after a fire in 1734, Felipe V commissioned a truly palatial replacement. Construction lasted 17 years, spanning the reign of two Bourbon monarchs, and much of the exuberant decor reflects the tastes of Carlos III and Carlos IV *(see p18)*. The palace was used by the royal family until the abdication of Alfonso XIII in 1931. The present king, Juan Carlos I, lives in the more modest Zarzuela Palace outside Madrid, but the Royal Palace is still used for state occasions.

★ Dining Room
This gallery was decorated in 1879. Its chandeliers, ceiling paintings and tapestries evoke the grandeur of Bourbon and Habsburg entertaining.

★ Porcelain Room
The walls and ceiling of this room, built on the orders of Carlos III, are entirely covered in royal porcelain from the Buen Retiro factory. Most of the porcelain is green and white, and depicts cherubs and wreaths.

First floor

The Hall of Columns, once used for royal banquets, is decorated with 16th-century bronzes and Roman imperial busts.

STAR FEATURES

- ★ Dining Room
- ★ Porcelain Room
- ★ Gasparini Rooms
- ★ Throne Room

★ Gasparini Room
Named after its Neapolitan designer, the Gasparini Room is decorated with lavish Rococo chinoiserie. The adjacent antechamber, with painted ceiling and ornate chandelier, houses Goya's portrait of Carlos IV.

Plaza de Armas
The square forms the entrance to the Pharmacy, the Palace and the Royal Armoury. At noon, on the first Wednesday of each month, visitors can see the changing of the guard.

Entrance Hall
A marble staircase by Sabatini, next to the statue of Carlos III as a Roman emperor, leads to the main floor. The painted Rococo ceiling by Giaquinto vividly depicts allegorical scenes.

Billiards room

Hall of the Halberdiers

Entrance

VISITORS' CHECKLIST

Calle de Bailén. **Map** 3 C2.
Tel 91 454 88 00. Ópera.
3, 25, 39, 148. Apr–Sep:
9am–6pm Mon–Sat, 9am–3pm
Sun & public hols; Oct–Mar:
9:30am–5pm Mon–Sat, 9am–
2pm Sun & public hols. for
functions & 1 & 6 Jan, 1 & 15
May, 12 Oct, 9 Nov, 24, 25 & 31
Dec. (Free Wed for European
Union residents.)
www.patrimonionacional.es

Pharmacy
This unique collection includes decorated Talavera pottery storage jars and herb drawers. The Pharmacy Museum has recipe books detailing medications pre-scribed for the royal family.

KEY TO FLOORPLAN

☐ Exhibition rooms

☐ Entrance rooms

☐ Carlos III rooms

☐ Chapel rooms

☐ Carlos IV rooms

Visitors' centre

Plaza de Armas

Royal Armoury

★ **Throne Room**
This room is unique in the palace as it retains the original decor from the days of Carlos III. The huge mirrors were made in the royal glass factory of La Granja.

Exploring the Palacio Real

This splendid Royal Palace stands on the site of the original Moorish fortress, or alcázar, which served as a residence for visiting royals after the Christian conquest of Madrid in 1085 *(see p15)*. Following extensive modifications in 1561, it became the residence of Felipe II until the completion of El Escorial *(see pp126–9)* in 1584. The alcázar was destroyed by fire on Christmas Eve, 1734, during the reign of Felipe V. This suited Spain's first Bourbon king well – his idea of a royal palace was the Versailles of his childhood, and so he commissioned a new royal palace decorated in the French style.

Stately façade of the Palacio Real, seen from the Plaza de Armas

THE PALACE

Most of the limestone and granite building is the work of Italian Giovanni Battista Sachetti, with later modifications by other architects like Sabatini. So vast was the plan that construction lasted from 1738 to 1755, by which time

Felipe V was dead. His son, Carlos III, became the first royal resident. The palace remained the official home of the Spanish royal family until Alfonso XIII left for exile in 1931. The distribution of rooms and the interior decoration were altered by successive monarchs. General Franco *(see p20)* also used the palace – known at the time as the Palacio de Oriente – for official business, and would address the crowds from the balcony overlooking the Plaza de Oriente *(see p58)*. Today it is used for state functions.

Visitors enter the palace from the **Plaza de Armas**. The main entrance is crowned by a pediment with a clock and two bells, one of which dates from 1637 and is a survivor of the fire which destroyed the old alcázar. The interior is remarkable for its size and for the exuberant decor, carpets, tapestries and antique furnishings in many of the rooms.

Grand entrance stairway with 72 steps in Toledo marble

ENTRANCE ROOMS

The Toledo marble in the main stairway, presided over by ceiling frescoes by Corrado Gialquinto, provides a regal taste of what is to follow. The first port of call is the **Salón de los Alabarderos** (Hall of the Halberdiers, or palace guards), decorated with a fresco by Tiépolo. Adjoining it is the **Salón de Columnas** (Hall of Columns), which served as the banquet hall until the new dining hall was incorporated in the 19th century. Today it is used for receptions and functions – the charter by which Spain joined the EU was signed here, on the 19th-century table supported by sphinxes. There are five tapestries of the Deeds of the Apostles, based on cartoons by Raphael and originally commissioned by the Vatican.

Finally, visitors enter the Carlos III rooms through the 18th-century Rococo **Salón del Trono** (Throne Room), whose decor has remained constant throughout generations of rulers. Completed in 1772, it has two rock crystal chandeliers, numerous candelabra and mirrors, and walls of crimson velvet with silver embroidery. The twin thrones are recent (1977), while the bronze lions that guard them date from 1651. The room is used for functions, such as the royal reception on 12 October (the Día de la Hispanidad) or the yearly reception for the diplomatic corps posted in Madrid.

Regal crimson-and-gold Throne Room with a rock crystal chandelier

CARLOS III ROOMS

Leading off from the throne room are three smaller halls named after Mattia Gasparini, the original decorator. These were the king's private chambers. He would take his meals in the **Sala de Gasparini** – lonely affairs considering the queen had her own dining room. The **Antecámara de Gasparini** contains four paintings by Goya of Carlos IV and María Luisa de Parma. In the **Cámara de Gasparini** the king would be dressed, usually in the presence of courtiers. This is the only room to retain its original decor – Rococo and oriental, with a stucco ceiling and embroidered silk walls.

A small room, the **Tranvía de Carlos III**, leads into the former bedroom of Carlos III. In the Baroque **Sala de Porcelana** (Porcelain Room), 18th-century porcelain from the Buen Retiro factory covers the walls. The **Salita Amarilla** (Yellow Room), named after the tapestry covering the walls, leads to the Gala Dining Hall.

The lavish dining room, formerly the queen's private chambers

Portrait of *Carlos IV* by Goya in the Antecámara de Gasparini

DINING ROOM

This 400-sq m (4,300-sq ft) banquet hall was formed in 1879 when the queen's private chambers were joined together, during the reign of Alfonso XII. It is richly adorned with gold plate decoration on the ceiling and walls, frescoes, chandeliers, Flemish tapestries, Chinese vases and embroidered curtains. The table can accommodate up to 160 diners.

The rooms leading off from the dining room house exhibits of royal household possessions. The room immediately off the dining hall is devoted to commemorative medals, and also contains the elaborate centrepiece used during banquets. Other rooms contain the silverware, china, crystal, and an extraordinary collection of musical instruments, including unique Stradivarius examples.

CHAPEL ROOMS

Built in 1749–57, the chapel is still used for religious services, and also for musical soirées. While the decor is luxurious, it is the dome, with its murals by Giaquinto, that immediately catches the eye.

Next, visitors pass through the **Salón de Paso** and into María Cristina's chambers (originally Carlos IV rooms). During the reign of Alfonso XII these four small rooms served as an American-style billiards room, Oriental-style smoking room, the **Salón de Estucos** (queen's bedroom), and the **Gabinete de Maderas de Indias**, used as an office.

PHARMACY AND ARMOURY

Returning to the Plaza de Armas, near the ticket office is the **Real Farmacia** (Royal Pharmacy) founded by Felipe II in 1594. The pharmacy is a warren of rooms, with jars and vials bearing the names of different potions and medicinal plants.

On the other side of the plaza is the **Real Armería** (Royal Armoury), housed in a pavilion built in 1897 after the original armoury was destroyed by fire. It contains weapons and royal suits of armour. On display is an elaborate suit of armour which once belonged to Carlos I, the Holy Roman Emperor Charles V. The armoury could be considered as Madrid's first museum because it has been open to the public since Felipe II inherited the collection from his father. It originally contained weapons used by Spanish kings and those from defeated enemy armies.

Armour of Carlos I

Equestrian statue of Felipe IV, by Pietro Tacca, Plaza de Oriente

Plaza de Oriente ㉑

Map 3 C2. Ⓜ *Ópera.*

During his days as king of Spain, Joseph Bonaparte (José I) carved out this stirrup-shaped space from the jumble of buildings to the east of the Palacio Real (see pp54–7), providing the view of the palace enjoyed today.

The square was once an important meeting place for state occasions: kings, queens and dictators all made public appearances on the palace balcony facing the plaza. The many statues of early kings which stand here were originally intended to adorn the roofline of the Palacio Real, but proved to be too heavy. The equestrian statue of Felipe IV in the centre of the square is by Italian sculptor Pietro Tacca, and is based on drawings by Velázquez.

In the southeast corner of the plaza is the **Café de Oriente** (see p166), with outdoor tables for enjoying the view.

Teatro Real ㉒

Plaza de Oriente. **Map** 4 D2. *Tel* 91 516 06 00 (info); 90 224 48 48 (tickets). Ⓜ *Ópera.* ⊘ ♿ 🚹 10:30am–1pm Mon, Wed–Fri, 11am–1:30pm Sat–Sun & some public hols. ⬤ mid-Jun–mid-Sep. 📷 🌐 www.teatro-real.com

Madrid's opera house stands opposite the Palacio Real (see pp54–7) on the Plaza de Oriente. It is an imposing six-sided grey building, made all the more impressive by the six floors below street level as well as the nine floors visible above ground.

It was originally built around 1850. However, much of the structure that exists today is the result of a massive project to renovate the theatre, which took place between 1991 and 1997. The horseshoe-shaped main theatre area, decorated in red and gold with seating on five levels, holds 1,630 spectators and the stage area measures 1,430 sq m (15,400 sq ft). This, together with the curtain and the magnificent crystal chandelier weighing 2.5 tonnes, are among the theatre's noteworthy features.

On the second floor, there are four large foyers arranged around the main hall. They contain tapestries, paintings, mirrors, chandeliers and antiques. All of them are laid with carpets produced especially for the theatre by the Manuel Morón workshop in Ciudad Real, south of Madrid.

The second-floor restaurant is also worth seeing. It has a ceiling representing Madrid's starlit sky as it was on the night of the theatre's inauguration. It is open from Tuesday to Sunday for tea (at 6:30pm) and dinner (at 9pm), but is reserved for theatre-goers on nights when there are performances. The restaurant is located in what was originally the ballroom, where Isabel II would often throw lively parties. On display are costumes from the operas *Aïda* and *Anne Boleyn*

Costume used in *Anne Boleyn*

On the sixth floor there is a pleasant cafeteria which has a good view overlooking the Plaza de Oriente and the Palacio Real (see pp54–7).

The site has always been associated with the stage. In 1708, an Italian company built a small theatre here, which was demolished in 1735 to be replaced by a more ambitious building. However, due to the presence of underground streams, this theatre suffered severe structural problems. In 1816, it was torn down to make way for a modern opera house instigated by Fernando VII. Construction dragged on in fits and starts for 32 years. The theatre was finally inaugurated in 1850 by Isabel II on her 20th birthday. A production

Awe-inspiring interior of Madrid's opera house, the Teatro Real

of Gaetano Donizetti's *La Favorita* marked the occasion, and the theatre became a centre of Madrid culture until the late 1920s. It appeared, however, that the new building was beset with problems just like its predecessor, and needed constant repair work to keep it upright. In the Spanish Civil War *(see p20)* it was used as a weapons depot and suffered further damage from an explosion. It was finally closed in 1988.

In 1991, an ambitious project to renovate the building was also plagued with problems. The architect died of a heart attack while inspecting the works and, when the theatre finally opened in October 1997 with a performance of Falla's *The Three-Cornered Hat*, it was way over budget and five years behind schedule.

Iglesia de San Nicolás ㉓

Plaza de San Nicolás 1. **Map** 3 C2. **Tel** 91 559 40 64. ⓜ Ópera. ⬜ 8:30am–1:30pm Mon, 6:30–8:30pm Tue–Sat, 10am–1:30pm Sun. 📷 by appointment.

The first mention of the church of San Nicolás de Bari is in a document written in 1202. Its brick tower, decorated with horseshoe arches, is

12th-century Mudéjar-style brick tower of the Iglesia de San Nicolás

View of the Catedral de la Almudena and the Palacio Real

the oldest surviving religious structure in Madrid. Thought to date from the 12th century, it is Mudéjar in style, and may originally have been the minaret of a Moorish mosque.

Catedral de la Almudena ㉔

Calle de Bailén 8 –10. **Map** 3 C2. **Tel** 91 542 22 00. ⓜ Ópera. ⬜ 9am–8:30pm daily (10am–2pm, 5–9pm Jul & Aug). ♿

The building of Madrid's cathedral began in 1879, but it was not until 1993 that it was completed and subsequently inaugurated by the Pope. The slow construction, which ceased completely during the Spanish Civil War, involved several architects. The cathedral's Neo-Gothic grey and white façade resembles that of the Palacio Real, which stands opposite. The crypt houses a 16th-century image of the *Virgen de la Almudena*. Further along, the Calle Mayor is the site of excavations which have unearthed remains of Moorish and medieval city walls.

Campo del Moro ㉕

Map 3 A2. ⓜ Príncipe Pío. ⬜ Oct–Mar: 10am–6pm daily; Apr–Sep: 9am–8pm daily. ⬤ for functions, 1 & 6 Jan, 1 & 15 May, 12 Oct, 9 Nov, 24–25 & 31 Dec. **www. patrimonionacional.es.**

The Campo del Moro (Field of the Moor) is a pleasing park, rising steeply from the Río Manzanares to offer one of the finest views of the Palacio Real *(see pp54–7)*. The park has a varied history. In 1109, a Moorish army, led by Ali ben Yusuf, set up camp here – hence the name. The park later became a jousting ground for Christian knights.

In the late 19th century, it was used as a playground for royal children and landscaped in what is described as the English style – with winding paths, grass and woodland, as well as fountains and statues. In 1931, under the Second Republic *(see p20)*, the Campo del Moro was opened to the public. Under Franco it was closed again and was not reopened until 1978.

The Muralla Árabe – archeological remains of Madrid's Moorish heritage

Muralla Árabe ㉖

Parque del Emir Mohamed I, Cuesta de la Vega. **Map** 3 C3. ⊛ *Opera.* ○ *dawn–sunset.*

Other than the city's name, which comes from the Arabic *Mayrit*, a small stretch of outer defence wall is all that is left of Madrid's Moorish heritage. The Muralla Árabe (Arab Wall) stands to the south of the Catedral de Nuestra Señora de la Almudena, down the steep Cuesta de la Vega street. It is believed that one of the main gateways to the Moorish town stood near this site (*see p15*). The wall, constructed from flintstone blocks of various shapes and sizes, rises over 3 m (10 ft) along one side of the Parque del Emir Mohamed I. The park is named after the Moorish leader who founded Madrid.

The site was discovered while excavations were being carried out in 1953. As well as Moorish ruins dating from the ninth century, there is also a segment of a 12th-century Christian wall. On the other side of the wall, and visible from Cuesta de la Vega, are examples of typically Moorish brick horseshoe arches.

Across the street, a plaque and an image of the Virgin identify this as the spot where the statue of the Virgen de la Almudena was discovered in 1085 (*almudena* is from the Arabic for "outer wall"), possibly hidden from the Moors.

During the summer, outdoor concerts and plays are held in Parque del Emir Mohamed I.

At other times, this treeless area is not well patrolled, and you should not visit the park on your own or after dark.

San Francisco el Grande ㉗

Plaza de San Francisco. **Map** 3 B4. **Tel** *91 365 38 00.* ⊛ *La Latina, Puerta de Toledo.* **Museum** ○ *Oct–Jun: 11am–12:30pm, 4–6:30pm Tue–Sat; Jul–Sep: 11am–12:30pm, 5–7:30pm Tue–Sat.* 🎫 **Capilla del Cristo de los Dolores** ○ *11am–1pm Sat.* 🎫

The site of this basilica was previously occupied by a Franciscan convent founded, according to legend, by St Francis of Assisi in 1217. When

Interior of San Francisco el Grande, a church richly endowed with the work of great artists

Felipe II made Madrid the capital of Spain in 1561 (*see p17*), the convent's wealth and status grew, and it was made custodian of the "Holy Places" conquered by the crusaders.

In 1760 Carlos III ordained that the convent be replaced by a Neo-Classical basilica. The architect, Francisco Cabezas, designed a dome to measure over 33 m (108 ft) in diameter. However, in 1768, work had to be halted due to complications with the size. It was finally completed in 1784 by Francisco Sabatini.

The basilica was taken over by the Foreign Ministry in 1835 and used as an army barracks. A few years later it was made into a national pantheon. The Franciscan friars had to leave, and they only returned in 1926.

In 1878, a renovation project was initiated and the church decorated extravagantly. The façade is dominated by the dome and twin towers, which house 19 bells, 11 of which form the church's carillon.

The seven main doors were carved in walnut by Juan Guas, under the direction of sculptor Antonio Varela. The central image above the doors is of Christ crucified with Faith and Hope at his feet. On either side are the two thieves who were crucified with him. The panels on the doors show biblical scenes.

Just inside the basilica, supported by bronze angels, are huge scallop-shaped marble bowls containing holy water.

The main chapel contains five large paintings executed by Manuel Domínguez and Alejandro Ferrant depicting the life of St Francis. The Four Evangelists, made from wood and plaster but imitating bronze, are by Sanmartí and Molinelli. The roof of the basilica and the frescoes inside have undergone restoration work.

On each side of the basilica are three chapels, the most famous being the one just to the left of the main entrance. This chapel boasts an early painting by Goya of San Bernardino de Siena, with the painter himself appearing on the right of the picture. Work by Andrés de la Calleja and Antonio González Velázquez is also featured here. As well as the chapels, the sacristy and old cloisters can be visited.

The adjoining Capilla del Cristo de los Dolores, dating from 1162, was designed by architect Hermano Francisco Bautista. In it is the remarkable sculpture of *Cristo de los Dolores*, with bleeding holes in Christ's hands from the nails on the cross. This polychrome statue was created in 1643 by Diego Rodríguez but is, in fact, a copy of Domingo de la Rioja's original sculpture. This statue, now in Serradilla, was venerated for its association with miracles and spent some time in the alcázar, taken there by Felipe IV *(see p22)*.

Plaza de la Paja ❷

Map 4 D3. Ⓜ *La Latina*.

Once the focus of medieval Madrid, the area around the Plaza de la Paja – literally Straw Square – is still atmospheric. Many interesting buildings are located around the square itself and the area is pleasant to walk around.

Climbing upwards from the Calle de Segovia, a glimpse left along Calle del Príncipe Anglona yields a view of the Mudéjar-style brick tower of the **Iglesia de San Pedro**, dating from the 14th century. Ahead is the **Capilla del Obispo** (Bishop's Chapel), which first belonged to the adjoining Palacio Vargas. The Baroque, cherub-covered dome of the **Iglesia de San Andrés** can also be seen.

Nearby is a cluster of inter-linked squares, ending in the Plaza Puerta de Moros, a reminder of the Muslim community which once occupied the area. From here, a right turn leads to the domed bulk of San Francisco el Grande, an impressive landmark.

La Latina ❷

Map 4 D4. Ⓜ *La Latina*.

The district of La Latina, together with the adjacent Lavapiés, is considered to be the heart of *castizo* Madrid *(see p103)*. This term describes the culture of the traditional working classes of Madrid – that of the true *Madrileño*.

La Latina runs along the city's southern hillside from the Plaza Puerta de Moros through the streets where El Rastro flea market is held. To the east it merges with Lavapiés.

La Latina's steep streets are lined with tall, narrow houses, renovated to form an attractive neighbourhood. There are a number of old-fashioned bars around the Plaza de la Cebada, which add to the charm of this part of Madrid. It is worth wandering through simply to savour its rich atmosphere and authenticity.

Shoppers taking a leisurely Sunday stroll around El Rastro flea market

El Rastro ❸⓪

Calle de la Ribera de Curtidores.
Map 4 E4. Ⓜ *La Latina, Embajadores*.
Ⓞ *10am–2pm Sun & public hols.*

Madrid's celebrated flea market *(see p173)*, established in the Middle Ages, has its hub in the Plaza de Cascorro and sprawls downhill towards the Río Manzanares. The main street is the Calle de la Ribera de Curtidores, or "Tanners' Riverbank", once the centre of the slaughterhouse and tanning industry.

Although some people claim that El Rastro has changed a great deal since its heyday during the 19th century, there are still plenty of *Madrileños*, as well as tourists, who shop here. They come in search of a bargain from the stalls which sell a huge range of wares – anything from new furniture to second-hand clothes. The wide range of goods and the lively crowds in El Rastro make it an ideal way to spend a Sunday morning.

The Calle de Embajadores is the market's other main street. It runs down past the dusty Baroque façade of the **Iglesia de San Cayetano**, designed by José Churriguera and Pedro de Ribera. Its interior has been restored since fire destroyed it in the Civil War *(see p20)*.

Further along is the former Real Fábrica de Tabacos (Royal Tobacco Factory), begun as a state enterprise in 1809. Its female workers had a reputation for taking an uncompromising stance in industrial disputes.

The atmospheric Plaza de la Paja, once the heart of medieval Madrid

BOURBON MADRID

To the east of Old Madrid, there once lay an idyllic district of market gardens known as the Prado – the "Meadow". In the 16th century a monastery was built here. The Habsburgs extended it to form a palace, of which only fragments now remain; the palace gardens are now the popular Parque del Retiro *(see p77)*. The Bourbon monarchs, especially Carlos III, expanded the area in the 18th century. Around the Paseo del Prado they built grand squares with fountains, a triumphal gateway, and what was to become the Museo del Prado, one of the world's greatest art galleries. More recent additions to the area are the Centro de Arte Reina Sofía, a collection of Spanish and international Modern art, and the Museo Thyssen-Bornemisza.

SIGHTS AT A GLANCE

Historic Buildings and Monuments
Ateneo de Madrid **17**
Banco de España **5**
Bolsa de Comercio **7**
Casa de Lope de Vega **20**
Círculo de Bellas Artes **13**
Congreso de los Diputados **16**
Edificio Metrópolis **15**
Estación de Atocha **30**
Hotel Palace **11**
Hotel Ritz **9**
Ministerio de Agricultura **27**
Observatorio Astronómico **28**
Palacio de Comunicaciones **3**
Palacio de Fernán Núñez **31**
Palacio de Linares **2**

Puerta de Alcalá **1**
Real Academia de la Historia **19**
Real Academia Española **23**
Teatro Español **18**

Museums and Galleries
Centro de Arte Reina Sofía pp84–7 **32**
Salón de Reinos **24**
Museo del Prado pp78–81 **21**
Museo Nacional de Antropología **29**
Museo Nacional de Artes Decorativas **8**
Museo Naval **6**
Museo Thyssen-Bornemisza pp70–73 **12**

Churches
Iglesia de San Jerónimo el Real **22**
Iglesia de San José **14**

Streets, Squares and Parks
Parque del Retiro **25**
Plaza Cánovas del Castillo **10**
Plaza de Cibeles **4**
Real Jardín Botánico **26**

GETTING THERE
The metro is the fastest and easiest way to get to and around Bourbon Madrid. Lines 1 and 2 serve all the main sights. Useful bus routes are 1, 2, 8, 14, 15, 27, 74 & 146 to the Plaza de Cibeles.

KEY

	Street-by-Street map *pp64–5*
Ⓜ	Metro station
🚉	Railway station
🚌	Main bus stop
🅗	Tourist information

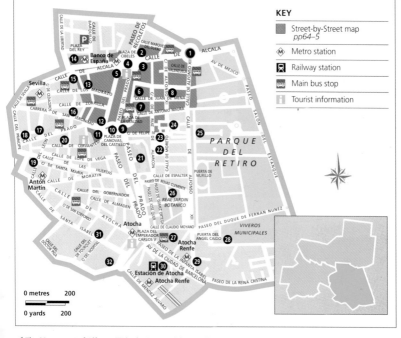

◁ **The Monument of Alfonso XII in the Parque del Retiro** *(see p77)*

Street-by-Street: Paseo del Prado

In the late 18th century, before the museums, sumptuous palaces and lavish hotels of Bourbon Madrid took shape, the Paseo del Prado was laid out and soon became a fashionable spot for strolling. Today the main attractions of the wide, tree-lined Paseo are its museums and galleries. Most notable are the Museo del Prado (just south of the Plaza Cánovas del Castillo) and the Museo Thyssen-Bornemisza, both displaying world-famous art collections. Among the grand monuments built under Carlos III are the Puerta de Alcalá, the Fuente de Neptuno and the Fuente de Cibeles, all at the centre of busy roundabouts.

★ Plaza de Cibeles
A fountain with a statue of the Greco-Roman goddess of nature, Cybele, stands in this square ❹

Banco de España Metro

Iglesia de San José
Designed by Pedro Ribera, this Baroque church was built from 1730 to 1748 ⓮

CALLE DE ALCALÁ

CALLE DEL MARQUES

Banco de España
Spain's central reserve bank is housed in this massive building with three façades at the Plaza de Cibeles ❺

Círculo de Bellas Artes
This cultural founda-tion, established in 1880, offers a theatre, library, artists' studios and a café overlooking Calle de Alcalá ⓭

CALLE DE LOS MADRAZO

DE CUBAS

ZORRILLA

★ Museo Thyssen-Bornemisza
This excellent art collection occupies the Neo-Classical Villahermosa Palace, completed in 1806 ⓬

PASEO

Westin Palace
A host of international artists, politicians and film stars have stayed at this elegant, centrally located hotel ⓫

PLAZA CÁNOVAS DEL CASTILLO

Museo del Prado

STAR SIGHTS

★ Plaza de Cibeles

★ Museo Thyssen-Bornemisza

★ Puerta de Alcalá

Plaza Cánovas del Castillo
In the middle of this large square stands a sculpted fountain of the god Neptune in his chariot ❿

0 metres   100
0 yards   100

★ **Puerta de Alcalá**
Sculpted from granite, this former gateway into the city is especially beautiful when floodlit at night ❶

Palacio de Comunicaciones
Spain's postal service and the city council are headquartered in this ornate building, often likened to a wedding cake ❸

LOCATOR MAP
See Street Finder maps 7 & 8

AROUND LA CASTELLANA

OLD MADRID

BOURBON MADRID

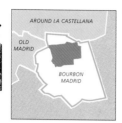

Palacio de Linares
This grandly decorated late 19th-century palace now houses the Casa de América, an organization that promotes Latin American culture ❷

Museo Nacional de Artes Decorativas
This museum, near the Retiro, was founded in 1912 as a showcase for Spanish interior design and ceramics ❽

PLAZA DE LA INDEPENDENCIA

CALLE DE ALCALÁ

CALLE DE ALFONSO X

CALLE DE ALFONSO XII

CALLE DE MONTALBAN

CALLE JUAN DE MENA

CALLE ANTONIO MAURA

PLAZA DE LA LEALTAD

RUIZ DE ALARCÓN

CALLE FELIPE IV

PLAZA DE CIBELES

Museo Naval
Part of the Ministry of Defence, this museum contains a wealth of navigational instruments, maps, models of ships and reconstructions of cabins ❻

Bolsa de Comercio
Madrid's stock exchange is housed in this attractive Neo-Classical building. Visitors can view events on the trading floor from a gallery ❼

Hotel Ritz
With its belle époque interior, the Ritz is one of the most elegant hotels in all of Spain ❾

KEY

– – – Suggested route

View through the central arch of the Puerta de Alcalá

Puerta de Alcalá ❶

Map 8 D1. 🚇 *Retiro.*

This ceremonial gateway is the grandest of the monuments erected by Carlos III *(see p23)* in his efforts to improve eastern Madrid. Designed by Francesco Sabatini, it replaced a smaller Baroque gateway which had been built by Felipe III *(see p22)* for his wife's entry into Madrid.

Construction of the gate was started in 1769 and lasted a total of nine years. It was built from granite in Neo-Classical style, with a lofty pediment and sculpted angels. It has five arches – three central and two outer rectangular ones.

Until the mid-19th century, the gateway marked the city's easternmost boundary. It now stands in the busy Plaza de la Independencia, and is best seen when floodlit at night.

Palacio de Linares ❷

Paseo de Recoletos 2. **Map** 8 D1. **Tel** 91 595 48 00. 🚇 *Banco de España.* ☐ *10am–2pm Sat & Sun for guided tours only.* ● *Aug.* **Exhibition Room** ☐ *11am–8pm, Mon–Sat, 11am–3pm Sun.* ● *Aug.* ♿ 🍴 www.casamerica.es

In 1873 Amadeo I *(see p23)* rewarded the Madrid banker, José de Murga, for his financial support by granting him the title of Marqués de Linares. The newly designated aristocrat quickly set about

building himself the most luxurious, palatial residence Madrid had ever known.

The rooms inside the palace are an extravaganza of ornate Rococo decor, resplendent with gold plate, inlaid wood and marble floors, glittering chandeliers, nubile nymphs and allegorical murals. The most striking rooms are on the first floor. They include the gala dining room, ballroom, the Salón China (Oriental Room), and Byzantine-style chapel. In the garden is the Pabellón Romántico, a wooden, fairy-tale-style pavilion which is also known as the Casa de Muñecas (Dolls' House).

After the Marqués died, the family fortunes declined. Many furnishings and decorations were sold, and the rest disappeared during the Spanish Civil War *(see p20)*. By 1977 the palace was almost derelict. However, it was saved by the Spanish government's decision to restore it for Madrid's year as European Capital of Culture in 1992. The main entrance to this French Baroque palace is on Plaza de Cibeles but it is used only for rare ceremonial occasions. General access is by a side entrance on Paseo de Recoletos. The building now houses the **Casa de América**, a cultural organization which promotes Latin American art, literature and cinema.

Mailbox at the Palacio de Comunicaciones

Palacio de Comunicaciones ❸

Plaza de Cibeles. **Map** 7 C2. 🚇 *Banco de España.* **Post Office Tel** 90 219 71 97. ☐ *8:30am–9:30pm Mon–Fri, 8:30am–2pm Sat.* **Museum Tel** 91 396 26 79. ☐ *9am–2pm, 4–6pm Mon–Fri, 9am–2pm Sat.* **www**.correos.es

Occupying one corner of the Plaza de Cibeles, this impressive building is the headquarters of Spain's postal service. Built between 1905 and 1917 by Antonio Palacios, its appearance – white with tall pinnacles – is often likened to a wedding cake. Its central hall is lined with counters providing services and, in the centre, are brass-and-wood lecterns where customers write their letters or fill out forms. You can still see the old-fashioned brass letterboxes with the names of different Spanish cities and provinces that are embedded in the wall to the right of the main entrance. The building also houses the offices of the Ayuntamiento, the City Council, which was formerly located in Plaza de la Villa. On special occasions such as Christmas and during the wedding celebrations of Prince Felipe in 2004, the building is used as a backdrop for special illuminations and projected images.

The height of Rococo extravagance in the Palacio de Linares ballroom

Plaza de Cibeles ❹

Map 7 C1. 🚇 *Banco de España*

In addition to being one of Madrid's best-known landmarks, the Plaza de Cibeles is also one of the most beautiful. The **Fuente de Cibeles** stands in the middle of the busy traffic island at the junction of the Paseo del Prado and the Calle de Alcalá. This fine, sculpted fountain is named after Cybele, the Greco-Roman goddess of nature, and shows her sitting in her chariot, drawn by a pair of lions. Designed in the late 18th century by José Hermosilla and Ventura Rodríguez, it is considered a symbol of Madrid.

Four important buildings rise around the square, the most impressive being the **Palacio de Comunicaciones**, mockingly known as "Our Lady of Communications". On the northeast side is the **Palacio de Linares**, built in 1873 about the time of the second Bourbon restoration. In the northwest corner, surrounded by attractive gardens, is the army headquarters, the **Cuartel General del Ejército de Tierra**, housed in the former Palacio de Buenavista. Commissioned by the Duchess of Alba in 1777, construction was twice delayed by fires.

Finally, occupying a whole block on the opposite corner, is the Venetian-Renaissance **Banco de España**, restored to its 19th-century magnificence.

The Fuente de Cibeles, with the Palacio de Linares in the background

Banco de España ❺

Calle de Alcalá 48. **Map** 7 C2. **Tel** 91 338 53 65 🚇 *Banco de España* ⏰ *by appointment only – write to Servicio de Protocolo.* 🚫
www.bde.es

Viewing this vast building, with façades facing Paseo del Prado, Plaza de Cibeles and Calle de Alcalá, you might wonder which is the main entrance. In fact it is the one on the Paseo del Prado, used only for ceremonial occasions nowadays. The original bank dates from 1882–91 and occupied the corner of Cibeles, while new wings were added later. The Bank of Spain itself was founded in 1856. The bank's vast main staircase, made of Carrara marble and overlooked by stained-glass windows with mythological and allegorical themes, leads to the Patio del Reloj, a glass-roofed central courtyard with the cashiers' windows. It is a striking example of Art Deco design. The library, which is open to researchers, is located in another large hall, the interior of which is made entirely of wrought-iron filigree, painted off-white. There is also an older, smaller library with glassed-in mahogany bookshelves.

The various meeting rooms and hallways are decorated with the bank's sizeable collection of tapestries, vases, antique furniture and paintings, including a first printing of Goya's series of etchings of bullfighting, the *Tauromaquia.* In the circular Goya room are eight further paintings by the Spanish master *(see p28)*, including portraits of Carlos IV and various governors of the Bank of Spain. In *Conde de Floridablanca in the Artist's Studio,* rather than looking out at the viewer, Goya is seen gazing at his companion.

Beneath the Patio del Reloj, 30 m (98 ft) below street level and off limits to visitors, is a chamber with an island-like structure ringed by a moat. On it is the vault containing the bank's gold. Prior to sophisticated security gadgetry, this chamber would immediately flood were there any threat of a bank robbery.

Museo Naval ❻

Paseo del Prado 5. **Map** 7 C2. **Tel** 91 523 87 89. 🚇 *Banco de España.* ⏰ *10am–2pm Tue–Sun.* 🚫 *Aug & some public hols.* 🚫 📷
www.museonavalmadrid.com

Added to the Ministry of Defence building in 1977, the copper-tinted-glass Naval Museum has 18 display halls charting Spain's centuries-old history of seafaring. As well as a large collection of scale models of ships throughout the ages, often dating from the same period as the ships themselves, there are numerous figureheads, amphorae, globes, astrolabes, sextants, compasses and maps. Weapons used in Spain's conquest of the New World *(see p16)* also feature here. One unusual exhibit is a map of the world dated 1500. It was drawn for Isabel and Fernando *(see p22),* and features the Americas for the first time. There is also a piece of the tree trunk upon which Hernán Cortés is said to have rested after *La Noche Triste* (The Sad Night) in 1520, when he and his men fled from Montezuma's Aztec capital, Tenochtitlán.

Astrolabe from the Museo Naval

View from the gallery – dealers at work in the grand Bolsa de Comercio

Bolsa de Comercio ❼

Plaza de la Lealtad 1. **Map** 7 C2.
Tel 91 589 22 64. Banco de
España. by appointment (2
months in advance). Jul, Sat, Sun
& public hols. by appointment.
www.bolsamadrid.es

The Madrid Stock Exchange
was established in 1831. It
operated in 11 different, generally inadequate venues – it was
once housed in a convent –
before moving in 1893 to the
headquarters it now occupies.
Designed by Enrique María
Repullés y Vargas, the building
took more than six years to
construct, at a cost of around
three million pesetas. Nearly
one third of this went on the
concave, Neo-Classical façade
and main entrance, with its six
giant columns topped by
Corinthian capitals.

Dealers occupy the **Sala de
Contratación** (trading floor).
This large, vaulted space of
970 sq m (10,400 sq ft) has an
ornate Neo-Baroque clock on
a marble plinth at its centre.
Visitors can watch the pro-
ceedings from the **Salón de**
los Pasos Perdidos (Hall of
the Lost Steps). This gallery is
often used for exhibitions on
the history of the institution.

Museo Nacional de Artes Decorativas ❽

Calle de Montalbán 12. **Map** 8 D2.
Tel 91 532 64 99. Retiro, Banco
de España. 9:30am–3pm Tue–Sat
(also 5–8pm Thu), 10am–3pm Sun &
public hols. (free Sun).
Sun. **www**.mnad.mcu.es

Housed in an aristocratic
residence built in the 19th
century and near the Parque
del Retiro (see p77), the
National Museum of Decorative
Arts contains an interesting
collection of furniture and
objets d'art. The exhibits are
mainly from Spain and date
back to Phoenician times.

On show are excellent
ceramics from Talavera de la
Reina, a town famous for the
craft, and a collection of
jewellery and ornaments from
the Far East. Note that
throughout 2009 the museum
will undergo refurbishment
and some rooms may be
closed.

Hotel Ritz ❾

Plaza de la Lealtad 5. **Map** 7 C3.
Tel 91 701 67 67. Banco de
España. **www**.ritz.es

A few minutes' walk from the
Prado (see pp78–81), this
hotel is said to be Spain's most
extravagant. It was commissioned in 1906, around the
time that Alfonso XIII (see p23)
was embarrassed by the lack
of luxury accommodation in
the city for his wedding guests.

At the start of the Civil War
(see p20), the hotel became a
hospital, and anarchist leader
Buenaventura Durruti died
here of his wounds in 1936.

The opulence of the Ritz is
reflected in its prices (see
p152). Each of the 158 rooms
is beautifully decorated in a
different style, with carpets
made by hand at the Real
Fábrica de Tapices (see p110).

Plaza Cánovas del Castillo ❿

Map 7 C3. Banco de España.

This busy roundabout takes
its name from Antonio
Cánovas del Castillo, one of
the leading statesmen of 19th-
century Spain, who was
assassinated in 1897.

Dominating the plaza is the
Fuente de Neptuno, a fountain with a statue of Neptune
in his chariot, being pulled by
two horses. The statue was
designed in 1780 by Ventura
Rodríguez as part of a grand
scheme by Carlos III (see p20)
to beautify eastern Madrid.

The Fuente de Neptuno

The relaxed elegance of the Westin's glass-domed Rotunda Hall lounge

Westin Palace ⓫

Plaza de las Cortes 7. **Map** 7 B3.
Tel 91 360 80 00. Ⓜ *Sevilla, Banco de España & Atocha.* 🚇 **www**.
palacemadrid.com

The former palace of the Duque de Medinaceli was torn down to build this hotel, which opened in 1912. Alfonso XIII wanted his capital to have elegant hotels to match those in other European cities, and actively encouraged the project. Its life as an elegant hostelry was interrupted only during the Civil War, when it housed a hospital and refuge for the homeless, as well as the Soviet Embassy.

For many years, the Westin and the Ritz were the only grand hotels in Madrid. However, while the Ritz was the exclusive reserve of its titled guests, none of whom would dare to venture from their rooms without a tie, the no less luxurious but more informal Westin was open to non-residents and was a lively meeting place for *Madrileños*. It was the first establishment in Madrid where ladies could take tea unaccompanied. It is still a favourite rendezvous and the wood-panelled **Palace Bar** and **Rotonda Hall** lounge, with its huge glass dome roof, are Madrid landmarks.

Statesmen, spies, literati and film stars have all stayed here. Past guests include Henry Kissinger, Mata Hari, Ernest Hemingway, Orson Welles, David Bowie, Richard Attenborough, Michael Jackson and Salvador Dalí, who once drew

lewd pictures on the walls of his hotel room. Unfortunately, an over-zealous maid scrubbed the walls clean the next day.

The hotel underwent extensive renovation in 1997, adding a Royal Suite, solarium and fitness centre, as well as a wine cellar for tastings and sales.

Museo Thyssen-Bornemisza ⓬

See pp70–73.

La Pecera café in the Círculo de Bellas Artes

Círculo de Bellas Artes ⓭

Calle del Marqués de Casa Riera 2.
Map 7 B2. *Tel* 91 360 54 00. Ⓜ
Banco de España, Sevilla. 🕙 10am–9pm (café closes 1am). 🚫 Aug. 📷
by appointment. 🎟 **Exhibitions**
Tel 90 242 24 42. 🕙 11am–2pm, 5–9pm Tue–Sat, 11am–2pm Sat–Sun.
www. circulobellasartes.com

The Círculo de Bellas Artes is a cultural foundation established in 1880. Since 1926, it has been housed in this building designed by Antonio Palacios, architect of the Palacio de

Comunicaciones *(see p66)*. The building has a vast ballroom, exhibition halls, a theatre, library and studios for use by artists and sculptors. As well as exhibitions, workshops and lectures, it hosts cultural and social events, such as the Carnival Masquerade Ball held every February.

Although the foundation is for members only, the token admission fee gives visitors access to parts of the building, including the café. Known as **La Pecera** (Fishbowl) for its large windows, it is a great place to observe life on the Calle de Alcalá. There is also a cinema at a separate entrance.

Iglesia de San José ⓮

Calle de Alcalá 43. **Map** 7 B1.
Tel 91 522 67 84. Ⓜ *Banco de España.* 🕙 7am–1:30pm,
6:30–8:30pm daily (Sun from 9am).

This church was once part of a Carmelite convent founded in 1605. The convent was demolished in 1863 to build a theatre, and the church itself was rebuilt during the reign of Felipe V *(see p22)*. When the Gran Vía *(see p48)* opened in 1908, the church was changed yet again. Adorning the façade, with its three arched entrances, is an attractive statue of the Virgen del Carmen. A number of the church's treasures are housed in the Prado *(see pp78–81)*, but a few interesting images remain on the Neo-Classical main altar and in the Baroque side chapels. Many are by French sculptor Robert Michel, who carved the Cibeles fountain's lions *(see p67)*. No. 41, next door, is still referred to as the **Casa del Párroco** (parish priest's house). On 4 April 1910, Alfonso XIII symbolically struck the church with a pickaxe to signal the start of demolition work which would make way for the Gran Vía.

Museo Thyssen-Bornemisza ⑫

This magnificent museum is based on the collection assembled by Baron Heinrich Thyssen-Bornemisza and his son, Hans Heinrich, the preceding baron. In 1992 it was installed in Madrid's 18th-century Villahermosa Palace, and was sold to the nation the following year. From its beginnings in the 1920s, the collection sought to illustrate the history of Western art, from Italian and Flemish primitives through to Expressionism and Pop Art. It is regarded by many as the most important privately assembled art collection in the world and includes masterpieces by Titian, Goya, Van Gogh and Picasso. In spring 2004 a new extension opened, displaying 250 more paintings, mainly Impressionist works acquired by Baroness Carmen Thyssen-Bornemisza.

★ Our Lady of the Dry Tree *(c.1450)*
This tiny painted panel is by Bruges master Petrus Christus. The letter A hanging from the tree stands for "Ave Maria".

★ Harlequin with a Mirror
The figure of the harlequin was a frequent subject of Picasso's. The careful composition on this 1923 canvas, which is thought by some to represent the artist himself, is typical of Picasso's "Classical" period.

STAR PAINTINGS

- ★ Our Lady of the Dry Tree by Christus
- ★ Harlequin with a Mirror by Picasso
- ★ The Toilet of Venus by Rubens

GALLERY GUIDE

The galleries are arranged around a covered central courtyard, which rises the full height of the building. The top floor starts with early Italian art and goes through to the 17th century. The first floor continues the story with 17th-century Dutch works and ends with German Expressionism. The ground floor is dedicated to 20th-century paintings.

Hotel Room *(1931)*
Edward Hopper's painting is a study of urban isolation. The solitude is made less static by the suitcases and the train timetable on the woman's knee.

Portrait of Baron Thyssen-Bornemisza
This informal portrait of the previous baron, against the background of a Watteau painting, was painted by Lucian Freud.

★ **The Toilet of Venus**
This reflection of ideal beauty was painted by the Flemish master Rubens between 1606 and 1611. The picture illustrates his luscious use of colour and form.

St Casilda *(c.1630)*
Francisco de Zurbarán, best known for his depiction of monks in white habits, also painted saints. Here, St Casilda's robe stands out against the plain background.

Second floor

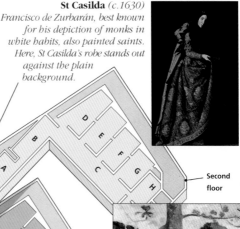

First floor

Main entrance

Ground floor

Mata Mua
Painted in 1892, during his stay on the Marquesas Islands, Gauguin's colourful depiction of a Tahitian paradise is one of his most highly regarded works of this period.

Autumn Landscape in Oldenburg
Karl Schmidt-Rottluff was a member of the Brücke Expressionist group, founded in Dresden in 1905. He painted this north German landscape two years later.

KEY TO FLOORPLAN

☐ Ground floor
☐ First floor
☐ Second floor
☐ Temporary exhibitions
☐ Non-exhibition space

Exploring the Museo Thyssen-Bornemisza

This collection provides a sweeping overview of Western art between the 14th and 20th centuries, touching on every school and trend in European art over the last 500 years. It is strong in areas where the Prado is weak, such as in Italian and Dutch primitives, 19th-century American painting, Impressionism and Expressionism. Portraiture from different periods is also well represented. The Carmen Thyssen Collection contains mainly landscapes, from 17th-century Dutch examples to Impressionist and Expressionist works.

Christ and the Samaritan Woman (1311) by Duccio

THE BIRTH OF THE RENAISSANCE

Early Italian art (room 1), while still influenced by medieval aesthetics and often overwhelmingly religious in subject matter, shows a gradual return to naturalism. Paintings become more three-dimensional and strive to tell a story, as in Duccio's *Christ and the Samaritan Woman* (1311).

The section on medieval art (room 2) illustrates how Italian influences combined with the Gothic style popular in Europe, such as Koerbecke's *Assumption of the Virgin* (c.1457).

Room 3 shows early Dutch art, including two jewels of the collection, Jan van Eyck's *The Annunciation* (c.1435–41) and Petrus Christus's *Our Lady of the Dry Tree* (c.1450). The stage is set for the aesthetic revolution of the Renaissance and a return to Classical forms, which began in Italy in the 1400s. The best example is Bramantino's *Resurrected Christ* (room 4).

Later, religion ceases to be the dominant theme, as seen in the outstanding series of early Renaissance portraits (room 5), including Holbein's detailed *Henry VIII* (c.1534–6).

RENAISSANCE TO BAROQUE

This section encompasses the height of the Renaissance, ending with Baroque art and 18th-century Italian painting. Outstanding examples of high Renaissance in Italy (room 7) include Carpaccio's *Young Knight in a Landscape* (1510) and Raphael's *Portrait of a Young Man* (c.1515).

Rooms 8–10 are dedicated to German and Dutch painters of the same period, including Dürer, with his *Jesus among the Doctors* (1506). Room 11 has works by Titian (*St Jerome in the Wilderness* c.1575), Tintoretto and El Greco.

Room 12 begins with early Baroque, when artists started to break with the rigid Classical rules of the Renaissance and introduce elements of drama and pathos into their work. This new trend flourishes in the art in rooms 13–15, with examples from Italy, France and Spain, where the period corresponded with the *Siglo*

Young Knight in a Landscape (1510) by Vittore Carpaccio

de Oro (Golden Century) of the arts. Included here is Murillo's *Madonna with Child with St Rosalina of Palermo* (c.1670).

Italy's continuing influence on European art is recognized in rooms 16–18, devoted to 18th-century Italian art, in which landscapes make an appearance. This is illustrated by two views of the *Canal Grande in Venice*, one by Canaletto (before 1723) and a later one by Francesco Guardi.

DUTCH AND FLEMISH PAINTING

The remarkable series of Dutch and Flemish art is a strong point of the collection. The first series (room 19) features 17th-century Flemish

Esau Selling His Birthright (c.1627) by Hendrick ter Brugghen

painting, with works by Jan Brueghel the Elder and Van Dyck, though the big attraction is *The Toilet of Venus* (c.1629), one of four Rubens on display.

The growing distinction between Flemish and Dutch works can be seen by comparing the preceding works with the Dutch art in rooms 20–21. The theme here is the Italian influence on Dutch portraiture and painting, for example in *Esau Selling His Birthright* (c.1627) by Brugghen.

Some of the most interesting works are in rooms 22–26, where everyday scenes, landscapes and informal portraits reveal the unique quality of Dutch art. Excellent examples are Frans Hals's *Family Group in a Landscape* (c.1645–8) and Nicholas Maes's *The Naughty Drummer* (c.1655). Dutch still lifes from the period are well represented in room 27.

Waverly Oaks (1864) by Winslow Homer

ROCOCO TO REALISM

Rococo to Neo-Classicism is the theme of this section, indicating a rapid shift in tastes over a relatively brief period. Rococo took Europe by storm at the beginning of the 18th century. It is best represented here in room 28 by Antoine Watteau's *The Rest* (c.1709) and *Pierrot Content* (c.1712), and by François Boucher's *La Toilette* (1742). However, the increasingly exaggerated forms of Rococo were eventually rejected in favour of more restrained and elegant lines.

Meanwhile, different developments were taking shape across the ocean. Rooms 29–30 display 19th-century American painting. Landscape art fulfilled a need to express America's romantic spirit and pride in the land, as seen in the paintings of Thomas Cole. American artists were increasingly interested in depicting everyday scenes, such as idyllic fishing trips and strolls through the woods.

The coming of age of American art at the end of the century is represented by the paintings of Winslow Homer, especially *Waverly Oaks* (1864), James Whistler and John Singer Sargent.

In Europe, the 19th century saw the dawn of Romanticism (room 31), a transition best illustrated here through three works by Goya. The series also demonstrates a growing trend towards Realism, a shift that is plainly depicted in Constable's *The Lock* (1824).

MODERN MASTERS

The year 1863 was pivotal in the evolution of modern art, because artists whose work was rejected by Paris's art salon were displayed in a parallel Salon des Refusés. This show of discarded art marked the birth of Impressionism, a revolution which broke ties with academic restraints. Some of the most highly regarded exponents of the movement are represented in rooms 32–33, including Manet, Degas with *Swaying Dancer* (1877–9), Renoir and Sisley. Impressionism freed the artist and led to further developments, such as Post-Impressionism and Symbolism, which centred on the artist as an individual. Such is the case with Vincent van Gogh, represented here by *Les Vessenots in Auvers* (1888), Toulouse-Lautrec with *Gaston*

Swaying Dancer (1877–9) by Degas

Bonnefoy (1891), Cézanne with his *Portrait of a Farmer* (c.1900) and Gauguin, whose *Mata Mua* (c.1892) is now part of the Carmen Thyssen-Bornemisza Collection. A series of works in room 34, belonging to the Fauve school, demonstrates this short-lived movement based on bright colours and simplified forms.

A name that did endure was Expressionism, which started in Germany. This school drew on the artist's emotions, and sought to precipitate an emotion in the viewer. Its earliest practitioners were centred around the Dresden group, "The Bridge", founded in 1905. Among its members was Karl Schmidt-Rottluf, whose *Autumn Landscape in Oldenburg* (1907) is shown here. The collection of Expressionist art in rooms 35–40 is one of the museum's highlights.

Eight ground-floor rooms (41–48) deal with modern and contemporary art, divided into three themes – "Experimental Avant-Garde", "The Synthesis of Modern" and "Surrealism, Figurative Tradition and Pop Art". Among the gems here are Picasso's *Harlequin with a Mirror* (1923) and Edward Hopper's *Hotel Room* (1931).

Parisian-inspired cupola of the Edificio Metrópolis

Edificio Metrópolis ⓯

Calle de Alcalá 39. **Map** 7 B1.
Ⓜ Sevilla. ◑ to the public.

Of unmistakable French inspiration, this building, jutting out like a ship's prow at the corner of Calle Alcalá and the Gran Vía *(see p48)*, is a Madrid landmark. Inaugurated in 1911, it was designed by Jules and Raymond Février for the Unión y el Fenix Español insurance company.

The restrained ground level is topped by ornate colonnaded upper floors, each pair of columns serving as a pedestal for allegorical statues representing Commerce, Agriculture, Industry and Mining. The rounded corner tower is crowned by a double-layered dome of dark slate with gilded ornaments. It used to hold the symbol of the Unión y el Fenix company – a bronze statue representing the mythological Phoenix and, astride it, a human figure with upraised arm representing Ganymede. In the early 1970s, the company sold the building to its present owners, the Metrópolis insurers. In a controversial move, they decided to take the statue – by then a familiar element of the Madrid skyline – to their ostentatious new headquarters on the Paseo de la Castellana. Eventually the statue was replaced by a new one, representing Winged Victory; the original Phoenix is in the garden of the Unión y el Fenix's modern building.

Almost unnoticed on the ground just in front of the circular tower of the Edificio Metrópolis is "La Violetera", a small statue of a young woman selling violets. It recalls a character from a popular *zarzuela* (Spanish light opera), which later inspired the film, *La Violetera*, starring Sara Montiel. The violet-sellers – Madrid's answer to Eliza Doolittle of *Pygmalion* – would sell their flowers to theatre-goers on the Gran Vía after each performance. An inscription at the base of the statue bears the first two lines of the song, *La Violetera*: *"Como ave precursora de primavera, en Madrid aparece la violetera"* ("The violet-seller appears in Madrid like a bird announcing spring").

Congreso de los Diputados ⓰

Plaza de las Cortes. **Map** 7 B2. **Tel** 91 390 60 00. Ⓜ Sevilla. ◑ by appt (fax 91 390 64 35) Mon–Fri, 10:30am– 12:30pm Sat. ◑ Aug & public hols. ⊘ ⓰ www.congreso.es

This imposing yet attractive building is home to the Spanish parliament, the Cortes. Built in the mid-19th century, it is characterized by Classical columns, heavy pediments and bronze lions. It was here, in 1981, that Colonel Tejero of the Civil Guard held the deputies at gunpoint, as he tried to spark off a military coup *(see p21)*. His failure was seen as an indication that democracy was firmly established in Spain.

Bronze lion guarding the Cortes

Ateneo de Madrid ⓱

Calle del Prado 21. **Map** 7 B2. **Tel** 91 429 17 50. Ⓜ Antón Martin, Sevilla. ◑ by appointment (Secretario Primero, C/ del Prado 21, Madrid 28014). www.ateneodemadrid.com

Formally founded in 1835, this learned association has strongly liberal political leanings. It is similar to a gentlemen's club in atmosphere, with a grand stairway and panelled hall hung with the portraits of famous fellows. Often closed down during past periods of repression and dictatorship, it is still a mainstay of liberal thought in Spain. Many leading Socialists, writers and other intellectuals are members.

LA TERTULIA – LITERARY GROUPS IN MADRID

Interior of the Café Comercial

The Ateneo de Madrid was one of many homes for the unique Madrid institution of *la tertulia*. Groups of people with common interests gathered to discuss everything from politics or the arts to the finer points of bullfighting. Not a formal club, yet more than a casual conversation among friends, *tertulias* were a major source of news, ideas and gossip in the 19th century, and more than one political plot was hatched over cups of coffee. They were usually held at Madrid's historic 19th-century cafés. Those which occupied choice bits of real estate, such as the Pombo, El Oriental and the Paix, have since disappeared, but there are a few survivors. The best known are the Café Comercial on Glorieta de Bilbao and the Café Gijón *(see p92)* on Paseo de Recoletos.

La Zarzuela - Spanish Light Opera

The *zarzuela*, a direct descendant of Italian light opera, started out as an amusement for kings, but was soon appropriated by the common people as Madrid's most characteristic performing art genre. The name is derived from the Palacio de La Zarzuela, current home of the Spanish royal family, outside Madrid. Zarzuelas were initially performed during the reign of Felipe IV, in the 17th century. With the ascendancy of the Bourbon kings (see p17), who preferred traditional Italian opera, the zarzuela left the royal palaces and was taken up in the corrales de comedias, the popular theatres of Madrid. It was here that it evolved into the lighthearted spectacle we know today, halfway between opera and musical comedy. Although no new zarzuelas have been written in decades, the genre has a tremendous following in Madrid, where there are regular performances and where record shops always have a section devoted to it. The best known title is La Revoltosa, a portrayal of the chemistry between the residents in a typical Madrid corral de vecinos, which were humble dwellings grouped around a central courtyard.

Statue of
"La Violetera"

Calderón de La Barca, *the famous 17th-century Spanish playwright, was one of the first great exponents of this type of opera. Others followed, most notably Tomás Breton (born 1850), who composed nearly 40 zarzuelas. His most famous is* La Verbena de la Paloma.

The central theme *of zarzuelas is life in castizo Madrid (see p103), with its streetwise majas (women) and cocky chulos (men) dressed in traditional costumes. It combines singing, spoken dialogue and a variety of dances, such as the Madrid jig, the chotis.*

By the middle *of the 19th century, zarzuela was so popular that a theatre was specially built for performances. Today, the 1,200-seat Teatro de la Zarzuela (see p182) continues to stage zarzuelas, as do others. In summer, outdoor shows are held at Jardines de Sabatini (see p115).*

A colourful *zarzuela* performance by the Compañía de Zarzuela J Tamayo

Sunlit balconies of the magnificent Teatro Español

Teatro Español ⓲

Calle del Príncipe 25. **Map** 7 A3.
Tel 91 360 14 80. Ⓜ *Sol, Antón
Martín & Sevilla.* ☐ *for performances from 7pm Tue–Sun.* 🎫 ♿
www.telentrada.com

Dominating the Plaza de
Santa Ana *(see p47)* is the
Teatro Español, one of the
oldest and most beautiful
theatres in Madrid. In the late
16th century many of Spain's
finest plays were performed in
the Corral del Príncipe which
originally stood here. Replaced
by the Teatro del Príncipe in
1745, it underwent extensive
restoration in the mid-19th
century and was renamed
Teatro Español. Engraved on
the Neo-Classical façade are
names of great Spanish drama-
tists, including that of Federico
García Lorca *(see p28)*.

Real Academia de
la Historia ⓳

Calle del León 21. **Map** 7 A3. **Tel** 91
429 06 11. Ⓜ *Antón Martín.*
☐ 4–7pm Mon–Fri, 11am–2pm Sat
& Sun (exhibitions). **www.**rah.es

This austere brick building,
housing the Royal Academy of
History, was built by Juan de
Villanueva in 1788 and is aptly
located in the Barrio de las
Letras (Writers' Quarter).
From 1898 to 1912, the great
intellectual and bibliophile,
Marcelino Menéndez Pelayo,
was director of the academy.
The library holds over 200,000

books and several important
manuscripts. The antiquities
owned by the academy will be
displayed in a new museum
scheduled to open during 2009.

Casa de Lope
de Vega ⓴

Calle de Cervantes 11. **Map** 7 B3.
Tel 91 429 92 16. Ⓜ *Antón Martín.*
☐ 9:30am–1:30pm Tue–Fri, 10am–
2pm Sat. ● *Aug, Xmas week.*
(free Sat). 🎫 **www.**munimadrid.es

Félix Lope de Vega, a leading
Golden Age writer *(see p28)*,
moved into this sombre
house in 1610 and lived here
until his death in 1635. It was
here that he wrote over two-
thirds of his plays, thought to
total almost 1,500. The house
was first opened to the public
in 1935 after a meticulous
restoration project, using some
of Lope de Vega's own
furniture, and gives a great
feeling of Castilian life in the

Félix Lope de Vega

early 17th century. A dark
chapel with no external
windows occupies the centre,
separated from the writer's
bedroom by only a barred
window. The small garden at
the rear, complete with the
original well, is planted with
the flowers and fruit trees
mentioned in the writer's plays.

Museo del Prado ㉑

See pp78–81.

Iglesia de San
Jerónimo el Real ㉒

Calle de Moreto 4. **Map** 8 D3. **Tel** 91
420 35 78. Ⓜ *Banco de España,
Atocha.* ☐ Oct–Jun: 10am–1pm,
5:30–8:30pm daily (6–8:30pm
Jul–Sep). ● *Easter Sat.* ♿

Built in the 16th century for
Isabel I *(see p22)*, but since remodelled, San Jerónimo is
Madrid's royal church. From
the 17th century it was virtually a part of the Buen Retiro
palace which once stood here.
Originally attached to the
Hieronymite monastery, which
today stands beside it in ruins,
the church was the location
for the marriage of Alfonso XIII
(see p23) and Victoria Eugenia
von Battenberg in 1906. The
church is still a popular venue
for society weddings. The cloisters and part of the atrium
form an annex of the Prado's
new extension.

Real Academia
Española ㉓

Calle de Ruiz de Alarcón 17. **Map** 8
D3. **Tel** 91 420 14 78. Ⓜ *Banco de
España, Retiro.* ● *to the public.*
www.rae.es

Spain's Royal Academy's
motto is "*Limpia, brilla y da
esplendor*" ("Cleans, polishes
and shines"). It describes the
function of the organization,
which is to preserve the purity
of the Spanish language. Founded in 1713, the academy only
moved to this Neo-Classical
building in 1894. The elegant
façade boasts a majestic
entrance with Doric columns
and a carved pediment. The 46

members include scholars, writers and journalists – the post, which is for life, is unpaid – who occupy seats identified by a letter of the alphabet. They meet regularly to assess the acceptability of any new trends in the language.

Salón de Reinos ㉔

Calle de Méndez Núñez 1.
Map 8 D2. Retiro, Banco de España. for refurbishment until 2015.

The Salón de Reinos (Hall of Kingdoms) is one of the two remaining parts of the 17th-century Palacio del Buen Retiro and gets its name from the shields of the 24 kingdoms of the Spanish monarchy, part of the decor supervised by court painter Velázquez *(see p28)*. In the time of Felipe IV, the Salón was used for diplomatic receptions and official ceremonies.

The Salón de Reinos is currently undergoing an extensive refurbishment to restore the interiors to their former glory. It will ultimately become part of the Prado *(see pp78–81)*. Among the exhibits to be housed in the new gallery will be five equestrian portraits by Velázquez, and Zurbarán's series of ten paintings on the life of Hercules, along with other 17th-century royal paintings. It is hoped that the building will be open by 2015.

Façade of Salón de Reinos (Hall of Kingdoms)

Despite this closure, the Palacio del Buen Retiro is worth visiting to admire its impressive facade. The original Palacio was built for King Felipe IV in 1637 on a large stretch of land situated next to the Monastery of San Jeronimo.

Parque del Retiro ㉕

Map 8 E3. **Tel** *91 409 23 36.*
Ibiza, Retiro, Atocha. **Park**
May–Sep: 6am–midnight; Oct: 6am–11pm; Nov–Apr: 6am–10pm.
Casa de Vacas *11am–8pm daily, till 9pm Jul & Aug.*

Retiro Park, in Madrid's smart Jerónimos district, was once the setting for Felipe IV's palace *(see p22)*, the Real Sitio del Buen Retiro. All that remains is the Casón del Buen Retiro *(see p81)* and the Museo del Ejército. In the 17th century the park was the private playground of the royal family, and only became fully open to the public in 1869. Today, it is a popular place for relaxing.

A short stroll from the park's northern entrance is the lake, where rowing boats can be hired. On one side, in front of a half-moon colonnade, a statue of Alfonso XII *(see p23)* rides high on a column. On the other, portrait painters and fortune-tellers ply their trade.

To the south of the lake are the Palacio de Velázquez and the Palacio de Cristal, both built by Ricardo Velázquez Bosco. His other work includes the grandiose Ministerio de Agricultura building *(see p82)*.

The Palacio de Velázquez was intended as a pavilion to stage the National Exhibition of Mining, Metal, Ceramics, Glass and Mineral Water industries in 1884. Today it is simply used for temporary exhibitions.

Nearby, the iron-and-glass Palacio de Cristal was modelled on the Crystal Palace built for London's Great Exhibition in 1851. Designed to stage an exhibition of tropical plants in the Philippines Exposition of 1887, the palace has become a forum for receptions and art displays. Its reflection in the lake remains one of the best known images of Madrid.

In the Paseo de Colombia, the Casa de Vacas puts on free exhibitions of Madrid art.

Monument of Alfonso XII (1901) facing the boating lake in the Parque del Retiro

Museo del Prado ㉑

The Prado Museum contains the world's greatest assembly of Spanish painting – especially works by Velázquez and Goya – ranging from the 12th to 19th centuries. It also houses impressive foreign collections, particularly of Italian and Flemish works. The Neo-Classical building was designed in 1785 by Juan de Villanueva on the orders of Carlos III, and it opened as a museum in 1819. The Spanish architect Rafael Moneo has constructed a new building, over the adjacent church's cloister, where the temporary exhibitions are located. Some galleries may be closed temporarily due to the ongoing expansion of the museum.

★ **Velázquez Collection**
The Triumph of Bacchus *(1629), Velázquez's first portrayal of a mythological subject, shows the god of wine (Bacchus) with a group of drunkards.*

The Adoration of the Shepherds
(1612–14)
This dramatic work shows the elongated figures and swirling garments typical of El Greco's style. It was painted during his late Mannerist period for his own funerary chapel.

The Three Graces
(c.1635) This was one of the last paintings by the Flemish master Rubens, and was part of the artist's personal collection. The three women dancing in a ring – the Graces – are the daughters of Zeus, and represent Love, Joy and Revelry.

STAR EXHIBITS

★ Velázquez Collection

★ Goya Collection

Ticket office

The Garden of Delights *(c.1505)*
Hieronymus Bosch (El Bosco in Spanish), one of Felipe II's favourite artists, is especially well repre-sented in the Prado. This enigmatic painting de-picts paradise and hell.

Second floor

GALLERY GUIDE

The museum's permanent collection is arranged over the three main floors, although some of the paintings may not be on show, or galleries may be closed due to ongoing renovation; check the website for more details. The permanent collection is accessed via the Velázquez entrance, however, visitors to the temporary exhibitions should use the Jerónimos entrance.

VISITORS' CHECKLIST

Paseo del Prado. **Map** 7 C2.
Tel 91 330 28 00.
Atocha, Banco de España.
10, 14, 19, 27, 34, 37, 45.
9am–8pm Tue–Sun &
public hols. 1 Jan, Good
Fri,1 May, 25 Dec. (free
6–8pm Tue–Sat, 5–8pm Sun).
www.museodelprado.es

First floor

★ Goya Collection

In The Clothed Maja *and* The Naked Maja *(both c.1800), Goya tackled the taboo subject of nudity, for which he was later accused of obscenity.*

Murillo entrance

Ground floor

The Martyrdom of St Philip
(c.1639) José de Ribera moved from his native Valencia to Naples as a young man. There he was influenced by Caravaggio's dramatic use of light and shadow, known as chiaroscuro, *as seen in this work.*

Velazques entrance

The Annunciation

Fra Angelico's work of c.1425–28 is a high point of Italy's Early Renaissance, as illustrated by the detailed architectural setting and deep perspective of the interior.

KEY TO FLOORPLAN

- Spanish painting
- Flemish and Dutch painting
- Italian painting
- French painting
- German painting
- Sculpture
- Temporary Exhibitions
- Non-exhibition space

Casón del Buen Retiro
Jerónimos Building
Underground link
Villanueva Building
CALLE DE MORETO
Jerónimos entrance
PASEO DEL PRADO
Salón de Reinos
CALLE DE FELIPE IV

CHANGES AT THE PRADO

The new Jerónimos Building is now partially open and houses temporary exhibitions and Renaissance sculptures, as well as a shop, café, restaurant, auditorium and cloakroom. In the future the Salón de Reinos will become part of the Prado.

- Museum Buildings
- Due to open in 2015

Exploring the Prado's Collection

The importance of the Prado is founded on its royal collections. The wealth of foreign art, including many of Europe's finest works, reflects the historical power of the Spanish crown. The Low Countries and parts of Italy were under Spanish domination for centuries. The 18th century was an era of French influence, following the Bourbon accession to the Spanish throne. The Prado is worthy of repeated visits, but if you go only once, see the Spanish works of the 17th century.

St Dominic of Silos Enthroned as Abbot (1474–7) by Bermejo

SPANISH PAINTING

Right up to the 19th century, Spanish painting focused on religious and royal themes. Although the limited subject matter was in some ways a restriction, it also offered a sharp focus that seems to have suited Spanish painters.

Spain's early medieval art is represented somewhat sketchily in the Prado, but there are some examples, such as the anonymous mural paintings from the Holy Cross hermitage in Maderuelo, which show a Romanesque heaviness of line and forceful characterization.

Spanish Gothic art can be seen in the Prado in the works of Bartolomé Bermejo and Fernando Gallego. The sense of realism in their paintings was borrowed from Flemish masters of the time.

Renaissance features began to emerge in the works of painters such as Pedro de Berruguete, whose *Auto-de-fé* is both chilling and lively. *St Catherine*, by Fernando Yáñez de la Almedina, shows the influence of Leonardo da Vinci, for whom Yáñez probably worked while training in Italy.

What is often considered as a truly Spanish style – with its highly-wrought emotion and deepening sombreness – first started to emerge in the 16th century in the paintings of the Mannerists. This is evident in Pedro Machuca's fierce *Descent from the Cross* and in the Madonnas of Luis de Morales, "the Divine". The elongation of the human figure in Morales' work is carried to a greater extreme by Domenikos Theotocopoulos, who is better known as El Greco (*see p143*). Although many of his masterpieces remain in his adopted

Saturn Devouring One of his Sons (1820–23) by Francisco de Goya

town of Toledo, the Prado has an impressive collection, including *The Nobleman with his Hand on his Chest*.

The Golden Age of the 17th century was a productive time for Spanish art. José de Ribera, who lived in (Spanish) Naples, followed Caravaggio in combining realism of character with the techniques of *chiaroscuro* (use of light and dark) and tenebrism (large areas of dark colours, with a shaft of light). Another master who used this method was Francisco Ribalta, whose *Christ Embracing St Bernard* is here. Zurbarán, known for still lifes and portraits of saints and monks, is also represented in the Prado.

This period, however, is best represented by the work of Diego de Velázquez. As Spain's leading court painter from his late twenties until his death, he produced scenes of heightened realism, royal portraits, and religious and mythological paintings. Examples of all of these are displayed in the Prado. Perhaps his greatest work is *Las Meninas* (*see p29*).

Another great Spanish painter, Goya, revived Spanish art in the 18th century. He first specialized in cartoons for tapestries, then became a court painter. His work went on to embrace the horrors of war, as seen in *The 3rd of May in Madrid* (*see p18*), and culminated in a sombre series known as *The Black Paintings*.

Still Life with Four Vessels (c.1658–64) by Francisco de Zurbarán

FLEMISH AND DUTCH PAINTING

Spain's long connection with the Low Countries naturally resulted in an intense admiration for the so-called Flemish primitives. Many exceptional examples of Flemish and Dutch art now hang in the Prado. *St Barbara*, by Robert Campin, has a quirky intimacy, while Rogier van der Weyden's *The Deposition* is an unquestioned masterpiece. Most notable of all, however, are Hieronymus Bosch's weird and eloquent inventions. The Prado has some of his major paintings, including the *Temptation of St Anthony* and *The Haywain*. Works from the 16th century include the *Triumph of Death* by Brueghel the Elder. There are nearly 100 canvases by the 17th-century Flemish painter Peter Paul Rubens, including *The Adoration of the Magi*. The most notable Dutch painting on display is Rembrandt's *Artemisia*, a portrait of the artist's wife. Other Flemish and Dutch artists featured at the Prado are Antonis Moor, Anton Van Dyck and Jacob Jordaens, considered one of the finest portrait painters of the 17th century.

ITALIAN PAINTING

The Prado is the envy of many museums, not least for its vast collection of Italian paintings. Botticelli's dramatic wooden panels telling *The Story of Nastagio*

David Victorious over Goliath (c.1600) by Caravaggio

degli Onesti, a vision of a knight forever condemned to hunt down and kill his own beloved, were commissioned by two rich Florentine families and are a sinister high point.

Raphael contributes the superb *Christ Falls on the Way to Calvary* and the sentimental *The Holy Family of the Lamb. Christ Washing the Disciples' Feet*, an early work by Tintoretto, is a profound masterpiece and reveals the painter's brilliant handling of perspective.

Caravaggio had a profound impact on Spanish artists, who admired his characteristic handling of light, as seen in *David Victorious over Goliath*. Venetian masters Veronese and Titian are also very well represented. Titian served as court painter to Charles V, and few works express the drama of Habsburg rule so deeply as his sombre painting *The Emperor Charles V at Mühlberg*. Also on display are works by Giordano and Tiepolo, the master of Italian

The Deposition (c.1430) by Rogier van der Weyden

Rococo, who painted *The Immaculate Conception* as part of a series intended for a church in Aranjuez.

FRENCH PAINTING

Marriages between French and Spanish royalty in the 17th century, culminating in the Bourbon accession to the throne in the 18th century, brought French art to Spain. The Prado has eight works attributed to Poussin, among them his serene *St Cecilia* and *Landscape with St Jerome*. The magnificent *Landscape with the Embarkation of St Paula Romana at Ostia* is the best work here by Claude Lorrain. Among the 18th-century artists featured are Antoine Watteau and Jean Ranc. *Felipe V* is the work of the royal portraitist Louis-Michel van Loo.

St Cecilia (c.1627–8) by the French artist Nicolas Poussin

GERMAN PAINTING

Although German art is not especially well represented in the Prado, there are several paintings by Albrecht Dürer, including his classical depictions of Adam and Eve. His lively *Self-Portrait* of 1498, painted at the age of 26, is undoubtedly the highlight of the small but valuable German collection in the museum. Lucas Cranach also figures, and works by the late 18th-century painter Anton Raffael Mengs include portraits of Carlos III.

Real Jardín Botánico

Plaza de Murillo 2. **Map** 8 D4. **Tel** 91 420 30 17. Atocha. 10am–dusk daily. 1 Jan, 25 Dec. www.rjb.csic.es

South of the Prado *(see pp78–81)*, and a suitable place to rest after visiting the gallery, are the Royal Botanic Gardens. The inspiration of Carlos III *(see p19)*, they were designed in 1781 by Gómez Ortega, Juan de Villanueva, architect of the Prado, and Francesco Sabatini.

Interest in the plants of the Philippines and South America was taking hold in Spain at this time, and the gardens offer a large variety of trees, shrubs, medicinal plants and herbs.

Statue of Bourbon King, Carlos III, in the Real Jardín Botánico

Ministerio de Agricultura ②

Paseo de la Infanta Isabel 1. **Map** 8 D5. **Tel** 91 347 53 48. Atocha. by appointment. **www**.mapa.es

This magnificent, imposing building was originally the home of the Ministry of Development, whose remit was to promote economic, industrial and scientific growth in Spain in the late 19th century. Today the enormous edifice houses the Ministry of Agriculture, and as such is frequently the target of protests by Spanish farmers and olive oil producers.

The elaborate but daunting face of Spain's Ministerio de Agricultura

The building itself is adorned with sculptures, friezes and painted tiles and brings together elements of both Neo-Classical and Romantic styles. It was constructed between 1884 and 1886 by Ricardo Velázquez Bosco, architect of the Palacio de Velázquez in the Parque del Retiro *(see p77)*. The artist Ignacio Zuloaga was later involved in its design.

Gigantic Corinthian columns line the exterior walls, with areas of coloured bricks and decorative glazed tiles enhancing the spaces between them. The pediment above the columns is decorated with the Spanish coat of arms. Crowning the building are allegorical sculptures created by Agustín Querol. The three central figures represent Glory personified bestowing laurels on Science and Art. On either side are statues of Pegasus. These were originally made of marble, but were replaced by bronze replicas when the stone deteriorated. The original statues are now at Plaza de Legazpi, south of the city.

Observatorio Astronómico ②

Calle de Alfonso XII 3. **Map** 8 E5. **Tel** 91 527 01 07. Atocha. only by appointment on Fridays. public hols. by appointment (fax 91 527 19 35). **www**.oan.es

When building began in 1790, this was one of only four observatories in Europe.

The Observatorio Astronómico was designed by Juan de Villanueva along Neo-Classical lines. The vertical slit window was used for telescopes, and the colonnaded roof cupola for weather observation.

There is one room open to the public where 18th- and 19th-century telescopes, as well as a Foucault pendulum, are on display. You will need to apply in writing to view the larger telescopes, a collection of English clocks and to peer through a telescope made in 1790 by Sir Frederick William Herschel, the astronomer who discovered Uranus.

Colonnaded roof cupola of the Observatorio Astronómico

Museo Nacional de Antropología ②

Calle de Alfonso XII 68. **Map** 8 D5. **Tel** 91 539 59 95. Atocha. 9:30am–8pm Tue–Sat, 10am–3pm Sun. public hols. (free Sat pm &Sun). book 15 days in advance. **www**.mnantropologia.mcu.es

Previously known as the Museo Nacional de Etnología, this three-floor museum, which is built around a grand open hall, was inaugurated by Alfonso XII *(see p23)* in 1875.

Through the displays, the anthropology and ethnology of geographical groups of people are studied. The ground floor houses an important collection from the Philippines. Originally shown in 1887 in the Palacio de Velázquez *(see p77)*, the centrepiece is a 10 m- (33 ft-) long dug-out canoe made from a single tree trunk. There are also some gruesome exhibits, such as deformed skulls from Peru and the Philippines, the mummy of a Guanche from Tenerife and the skeleton of Don Agustín Luengo y Capilla, a late 19th-century giant from Extremadura. He was 2.35 m (7 ft 4 in) tall and died aged 26.

The first floor is dedicated to Africa. As well as clothing, weapons, ceramics and utensils, there is a reproduction of a Bubi ritual hut from Equatorial Guinea, in which tribal members met the *boeloelo* (witch doctor). On the second floor is the American section, with exhibits on the lifestyles of indigenous groups.

Estación de Atocha ㉚

Entrance of Madrid's Estación de Atocha, busy with travellers

Plaza del Emperador Carlos V. **Map** 8 D5. **Tel** 90 224 02 02. Atocha RENFE. 6am–1am daily.

Madrid's first rail service, from Atocha to Aranjuez, was inaugurated in 1851 by Isabel II *(see p23)*. Forty years later, the original station at Atocha was replaced by the present one. The older part of the station was one of the first big constructions in Madrid to be built from glass and wrought iron. Now, it houses a palm garden. Next to it is the modern AVE terminus, providing high-speed links to various towns including Toledo, Seville, Córdoba, Zaragoza and Barcelona *(see p204)*. Outside, a monument commemorates those who died in the terrorist attack of 2004.

Palacio de Fernán Núñez ㉛

Calle de Santa Isabel 44. **Map** 7 B4. **Tel** 91 151 10 19. Atocha. to the public.

Also known as the Palacio de Cervellón, this building has a plain façade that gives scant indication of the riches within. Built for the Duke and Duchess of Fernán Núñez in 1847, the palace served as the family home until 1936. It was requisitioned by the Republican militia at the start of the Civil War *(see p20)*; the lower part served as a bomb shelter while the upper floor was occupied by a Socialist Youth organization. Amazingly, when the palace was returned to the duke's family, they found that none of its treasures had been damaged or stolen.

In 1941, the palace was sold and became the headquarters of the Spanish State Railway. It now houses the Foundation of Spanish Railways, which organizes exhibitions here.

That the palace was built in two phases is clear. The large, restrained rooms in the first section contrast sharply with the Rococo flourishes of the second. The older section has some interesting carpets from the Real Fábrica de Tapices *(see p110)*, as well as antique furniture, clocks and copies of paintings by Goya *(see p28)*. Attention, however, is inevitably drawn to the lavish gold-plated ornamentation of the later section, especially the ballroom with its mirrors, chandeliers and cherubs playing musical instruments. Rooms in this part are often used for official receptions.

Near the palace is the cloistered Convento Santa Isabel with its octagonal dome. It was founded in 1595 by Felipe II.

The sumptuously decorated ballroom of the Palacio de Fernán Núñez

Centro de Arte Reina Sofía ㉜

The highlight of this museum of 20th-century art is Picasso's *Guernica*. However, there are also other major works by influential artists, including Miró. The collection is housed in Madrid's former General Hospital, built in the late 18th century. Major extensions to the museum, designed by Jean Nouvel, were completed in 2005, allowing the permanent collection to extend to the first and third floors. The new glass buildings include two temporary exhibition rooms, a library, café-restaurant and an art shop.

Portrait II *(1938*
Joan Miró's huge
work shows eleme
of Surrealism, but
was painted more
than ten years aft
his true Surrealist
period ended.

Nouvel building

★ **Woman in Blue** *(1901)*
Picasso disowned this
work after it won only an
honourable mention in a
national competition.
Decades later it was
located and acquired
by the Spanish state.

Landscape at Cadaqués
Salvador Dalí was born
in Figueres in Catalonia.
He became a frequent
visitor to the town of
Cadaqués, on the Costa
Brava, where he painted
this landscape in the
summer of 1923.

Accident
Alfonso Ponce de León's disturbing work,
painted in 1936, prefigured his death
in a car crash later that same year.

STAR EXHIBITS

★ Woman in Blue
   by Picasso

★ Guernica by Picasso

★ La Tertulia del Café
   de Pombo by Solana

★ La Tertulia del Café de Pombo (1920)
*José Gutiérrez Solana depicts a gathering of
intellectuals (tertulia) in a famous café in
Madrid, which no longer exists.*

VISITORS' CHECKLIST

Calle Santa Isabel 52. **Map** 7 C5.
Tel *91 774 10 00.* Atocha.
6, 14, 19, 27, 45, 55, 86.
*10am–9pm Mon & Wed–Sat,
2:30pm Sun.* *1 Jan, 24, 25, 31
Dec & public hols.* *(free Sat pm
& Sun).*
www.museoreinasofia.es

GALLERY GUIDE

*The permanent collection is
in the Sabatini Building,
arranged around an open
courtyard. The displays of
20th-century art occupy four
floors, with individual rooms
allocated to significant artists
such as Dalí, Miró and
Picasso. However, there are
plans to rearrange the
collection in chronological
order, so visitors may
experience some disruption.
Two temporary exhibition
rooms are located in the new
Nouvel building.*

KEY TO FLOORPLAN

☐ Exhibition space

▨ Non-exhibition space

Glass elevator

Entrance

Visitors admiring *Guernica*

★ GUERNICA BY PICASSO

The most famous single work of the
20th century, this Civil War protest
painting was commissioned by the
Spanish Republican government in
1937 for a Paris exhibition. The artist
found his inspiration in the mass air
attack of the same year on the Basque
town of Gernika-Lumo, by German
pilots flying for the Nationalist air
force. The painting hung in a New
York gallery until 1981, reflecting the
artist's wish that it should not return
to Spain until democracy was re-
established. It was moved here from
the Museo del Prado in 1992.

**Toki-Egin
(Homenaje a San Juan de la Cruz)** (1952)
*In his abstract sculptures, Eduardo Chillida
used a variety of materials, such as wood,
iron and steel, to convey strength.*

Exploring the Centro de Arte Reina Sofía

The 20th century has undoubtedly been the most brilliant period in the history of Spanish art since the Golden Age of the 17th century. Many facets of the Spanish artistic genius are on show in the Centro de Arte Reina Sofía. Sculpture, paintings and even work by the Surrealist filmaker Luis Buñuel provide a skilfully arranged tour through an eventful century. Please note that the location of the artworks referred to below may be changing as a result of the extensive refurbishment taking place at the museum.

Guitar in Front of the Sea by Juan Gris (1925)

THE BEGINNINGS OF MODERN SPANISH ART

Following the storm of creativity that culminated with Goya in the 19th century, Spanish painting went through an unremarkable period. A few artists, such as Sorolla, managed to break the mould, hinting at the dawn of a new era of artistic brilliance. An emerging middle class, particularly in places like the Basque country and Barcelona, gave rise to a generation of innovative artists who constitute the introduction to this collection, including Zuloaga, Anglada-Camarasa and Nonell. Here also are p aintings by María Blanchard, one of the few women represented in the collection and a close friend of the Cubist artist, Juan Gris. Continuing round, you'll find the brooding, dark-coloured works of Gutiérrez Solana, whose favourite subjects are the *fiestas* and the people of his native Madrid. Influenced by the Spanish masters, especially Goya, his paintings include *La Tertulia del Café de Pombo* (1920) and the menacing *La Procesión de la Muerte* (1930).

There are also works by Blanchard, Delaunay and Lipchitz. Hinting at Cubism, they make a good introduction to the work of Juan Gris. Trained as a graphic designer, Gris moved to Paris in 1906 where, under the influence of Picasso, he produced *Portrait of Josette* (1916) and *Guitar in Front of the Sea* (1925). Also displayed are works in forged iron by Zaragoza-born sculptor Pablo Gargallo. His *Masque de Greta Garbo à la Meche* (1930), inspired by the actress, consists of delicate curves of iron hanging in space. Look out too for his slightly later work, *The Great Prophet* (1933).

The Great Prophet by Pablo Gargallo (1933)

PABLO PICASSO

The works on display span five decades in the life of Pablo Picasso. Born in the Andalusian city of Málaga, Picasso embraced a wide variety of styles in the course of his long career, including Realism, Cubism and Surrealism. He defied classification, creating some of the most important works of art of the 20th century. The first image the visitor notices is the haunting *Woman in Blue* (1901), one of Picasso's earliest works dating from his so-called "blue" period. In Room 6 is the most-visited piece in the collection – the vast *Guernica* (1937). Aside from its unquestionable artistic merits, the canvas has a deep historical significance for Spaniards, recalling one of the most harrowing episodes of the Spanish Civil War *(see p18)*. The painting is complemented by a series of sketches and preliminary studies completed in the week following the bombing of the Basque town of Gernika-Lumo.

It is interesting to see many of the symbols Picasso chose for *Guernica* appearing in his earlier work, the *Minotauromaquia* (1935). This painting is of the fearsome Minotaur of Greek legend – a bull-headed devourer of human flesh.

JULIO GONZÁLEZ

A friend and contemporary of Gargallo and Picasso, Julio González is known as the father of modern Spanish sculpture, chiefly because of

Minotauromaquia by Pablo Picasso (1935)

his pioneering use of iron as a raw material. Born in Barcelona, González began his career as a welder, learning to forge, cut, solder and bend the iron which had hitherto been considered an entirely industrial material. In the 1920s and 1930s he worked alongside Picasso and Gargallo in Paris, producing many three-dimensional pieces in the Cubist style. Look out for González' humorous self-portrait entitled *Tête dite "Lapin"* or *Head called "Rabbit"* (1930). In his work, you can also see many sketches that relate to the sculptures.

Girl at the Window by Salvador Dalí (1925)

MIRÓ, DALÍ AND THE SURREALISTS

Juan Miró turned his hand to many styles. His Surrealist experiments of the 1920s provide evidence of his love of the vivid colours and bold shapes of Catalan folk art. Similar elements remain in later pieces, such as *Portrait II* (1938).

His fellow Catalan, Salvador Dalí, is especially well known as a member of the Surrealist movement – the style of art inspired by the work of Sigmund Freud, which depended on access to subconscious images without censorship by the rational mind. Other prominent Surrealists whose work is displayed here are Benjamín Palencia (*Bulls*, 1933), Oscar Domínguez and Luis Buñuel.

Dalí's Surrealist masterpiece, *The Great Masturbator* (1929) hangs in contrast to the realistic portrait, *Girl at the Window* (1925). Like many of his contemporaries, Dalí embraced widely differing styles of working in the course of his career. *The Great Masturbator* was painted after he visited Paris, and came into contact with the French Surrealists. His work starts to reflect all the unfettered obses-

sions and fetishes that haunted this eccentric artist. Another product of this period are the films of Luis Buñuel whose 17 minute *Un Chien Andalou* (1929), in collaboration with Dalí, made a deep impression on the Surrealist movement.

Bulls by Benjamín Palencia (1933)

THE PARIS SCHOOL

The turbulent history of Spain in the 20th century *(see pp20–21)* has resulted in a steady stream of talented Spanish artists leaving their native land. Many of them, including Picasso, Dalí, Juan Gris and Miró, passed through Paris, some staying for a few months, others staying for years. Artists of other nationalities also congregated in the French capital, mainly from Eastern Europe, Germany and the United States, including the German abstract painter Hans Hartung and the Russian Nicholas de Staël. All of these artists were part of the Paris

School and it is possible to see the mutual influence of this closely-knit, yet constantly evolving group of young artists. On display are works by a wide range of less well-known Paris School painters, including Daniel Vázquez Díaz and Francisco Bores

FRANCO AND BEYOND

The Civil War (1936–9) had an enormous effect on the development of Spanish art. Under Franco, the state enforced rigid censorship; artists worked in an environment where communication with the outside world was sporadic, and where their work did not benefit from official approval. They sought mutual support in groups such as El Paso and Grupo 57, whose members included Antonio Saura, Manuel Millares and Eduardo Chillida. Painting mainly in black and white, Saura used religious imagery, such as the twisted crucifix in *Scream No. 7* (1959). Chillida's work includes the use of forged iron.

The best-known member was Antoni Tàpies. Concerned with texture, he used a variety of materials, including oil paint mixed with crushed marble, to explore the magical qualities of everyday objects.

Later works by the Equipo Crónica, Luis Gordillo and Eduardo Arroyo – such as *It's The Talk of the Town* (1982) – illustrate the transitional period that started even before the dictator's death in 1975 and culminated with the restoration of democracy in Spain.

It's The Talk of The Town by Eduardo Arroyo (1982)

AROUND LA CASTELLANA

The axis of modern Madrid is the tree-lined Paseo de la Castellana, a long, grand boulevard. A journey along it gives a glimpse of Madrid as Spain's commercial and administrative capital. The main north-south artery, it was first developed in the 19th century by the city's aristocracy with a string of summer palaces from Plaza de Colón northwards. The Museo Lázaro Galdiano, one of Madrid's best art museums, is housed in the former mansion of the financier José Lázaro Galdiano. To

Façade detail, Iglesia de Santa Bárbara

the east, La Castellana skirts the Barrio de Salamanca, an upmarket district of stylish boutiques and apartment blocks named after the 19th-century aristocrat who built it. To the southwest are Chueca and Malasaña, neighbourhoods offering a more authentic *Madrileño* atmosphere. The southern section of the boulevard is called Paseo de Recoletos. Nearby are the Museo Arqueológico Nacional, founded by Isabel II in 1867, and Café Gijón, an intellectuals' café founded in the early 20th century.

SIGHTS AT A GLANCE

Museums and Galleries
Fundación Juan March ⓫
Museo Arqueológico Nacional pp94–5 ❽
Museo de Cera ❻
Museo de Escultura al Aire Libre ⓮
Museo Lázaro Galdiano pp98–9 ⓬
Museo Municipal ⓰
Museo Romántico ⓯
Museo Sorolla ⓭

Churches
Iglesia de Santa Bárbara ❹

Streets, Squares, Parks and Districts
Calle de Serrano ❾
Calle del Almirante ❷
Malasaña ⓱
Plaza de Chueca ❸
Plaza de Colón ❼
Salamanca ❿

Historic Buildings
Café Gijón ❶
Cuartel del Conde Duque ⓲
Palacio de Liria ⓳
Tribunal Supremo ❺

GETTING THERE
The metro is the easiest way to get to and around this area. Lines 1, 4, 5, 6, 8, 9 and 10 serve the main sights. Useful buses include routes 27, which runs the length of La Castellana, and 5, 7, 12, 13, 40, 45 and 150. Bus 21 runs across the Salamanca district.

KEY
- Street-by-Street map pp90–91
- Ⓜ Metro station
- Main bus stop

0 metres 250
0 yards 250

Street: Paseo de Recoletos

is bordered by the fashionable shopping streets Calle de Serrano and Calle de Goya, the Museo Arqueológico Nacional, the Biblioteca Nacional (National Library) and Paseo de Recoletos, which is home to the classic Café Gijón. Between Calle del Almirante, another popular fashion street, and Calle de Génova is the Tribunal Supremo and the Iglesia de Santa Bárbara. Towards the Gran Vía are the narrow streets of Chueca with some interesting old taverns and eclectic bistros.

Iglesia de Santa Bárbara
Both Bárbara de Braganza and her husband, Fernando VI (see p19), are entombed in this fine Baroque church ❹

Tribunal Supremo
Spain's supreme court of law is located in the former convent and school of the adjoining Iglesia de Santa Bárbara ❺

Calle de Barquillo contains the best shops in the city for stereo equipment, mobile phones and other electronic goods.

CALLE DEL GENERAL CASTAÑOS

CALLE SAN LUCAS

CALLE LUIS DE GONGORA

PLAZA DE CHUECA

CALLE DE LA LIBERTAD

CALLE BARBARA DE

CALLE CONDE DE XIQUENA

CALLE DEL BARQUILLO

CALLE DEL ALMIRANTE

CALLE DE PRIM

CALLE AUGUSTO FIGUEROA

0 metres   100
0 yards   100

STAR SIGHTS

★ Museo Arqueológico Nacional

★ Plaza de Colón

Plaza de Chueca
The immaculate, exquisitely decorated Bodega de Angel Sierra bar in the Plaza de Chueca has hardly changed since it was built in 1897 ❸

Calle del Almirante
Originally a street of basket shops, Calle del Almirante now boasts several of the city's own-label fashion shops ❷

Museo de Cera
Madrid's wax museum has likenesses of many historical figures **6**

LOCATOR MAP
See Street Finder map 6.

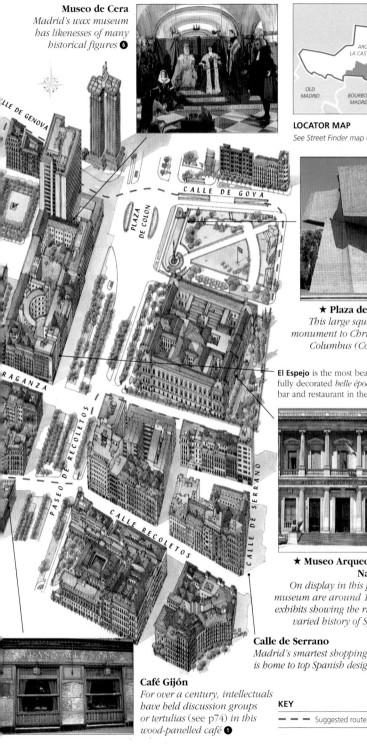

★ **Plaza de Colón**
This large square is a monument to Christopher Columbus (Colón) **7**

El Espejo *is the most beautifully decorated* belle époque *bar and restaurant in the city.*

★ **Museo Arqueológico Nacional**
On display in this palatial museum are around 100,000 exhibits showing the rich and varied history of Spain **8**

Calle de Serrano
Madrid's smartest shopping street is home to top Spanish designers **9**

Café Gijón
For over a century, intellectuals have held discussion groups or tertulias *(see p74) in this wood-panelled café* **1**

KEY

– – – Suggested route

Café Gijón ❶

Paseo de Recoletos 21. **Map** 5 C5.
Tel 91 521 54 25. Ⓜ Banco de
España. ⬭ 7:30am–1:30am Mon–
Fri, 8am–2am Sat, 8am–1:30am
Sun & public hols. ♿

Madrid's café life was one of
the most attractive features of
the city from the 19th century,
right up to the outbreak of the
Civil War. Many intellectuals'
cafés once thrived *(see p74)*,
but the Gijón is one of the
few that survives. It still attracts
a lively crowd of *literati*.
Although it is better known
for its atmosphere than its
appearance, the café has a
striking interior with cream-
painted wrought-iron columns
and black and white table tops.

Interior of the literary Café Gijón

Calle del Almirante ❷

Map 5 C5. Ⓜ Banco de España,
Colón & Chueca.

Running between the Paseo
de Recoletos and Calle
Barquillo, this street is famous
for its dozen own-label fashion
shops. For most of the 20th
century it was known as "Calle
de Cesterías" (basketwork
street). Now the only cane
shop left is that of Antonio
del Pozo, founded in 1891.
   In earlier days there were
five cane shops, where baskets,
chairs and other woven wares
were sold. There were also
several taverns where neigh-
bours gathered to pass the
time. Such was the fame of
the street that the wives of
both Winston Churchill and
the Shah of Persia visited the
del Pozo cane shop.

During the transition to democracy following Franco's death
in 1975, Calle del Almirante
gained a certain notoriety.
Fewer police patrolled the
area, and street crime rose.
Two gay bars opened in the
street and male prostitutes
touted openly for business.
   During this time Jesús del
Pozo – Antonio's brother and
a fashion designer – opened
the first boutique selling
clothes of his own design
next to the family cane shop.
However, it was not until
the 1980s, with the cultural
movement of *La Movida*
(see p102), that the area
became fashionable and
other clothes shops opened
here, along with a number
of chic furnishings and
decor outlets. Now Calle
del Almirante is a favourite
haunt of the wealthy and
business people from
neighbouring offices.
   Jesús del Pozo has become
famous, and his showrooms
on the first floor at No. 9 Calle
del Almirante sell outfits for
society weddings and events.
However, the street also retains
other original shops and
cafés. Manolo Huerta's family
have run the *panadería*
(bakery) since 1910 and the
Cafetería Almirante, which
serves *bocatas* (sandwiches) for
those in a hurry, has been run
by Juan Encinas since 1972.
   At No. 23 is the fascinating
Regalos Originales, a must-
see for browsers of antiques
and old curiosity shops.

View along the fashionable Calle del Almirante

Newsstand in the Plaza de Chueca

Plaza de Chueca ❸

Map 5 B5. Ⓜ Chueca.

The Plaza de Chueca is
situated between Calle Augusto
Figueroa and Calle Gravina.
The square was originally
called Plaza de San Gregorio
after a statue of the saint that
stood in Calle San Gregorio,
at the main gate to the manor
house of the Marqueses of
Minaya. In 1943 the square
was renamed after Federico
Chueca (1846–1908), a composer of *zarzuelas (see p131)*.
   Lining the plaza are small
shops, bars and apartment
buildings. On one side of the
square is the Bodega de Angel
Sierra *(see p90)*, a *taberna* full
of character that was founded
in 1897. On the outside there
are Andalusian-style tiles
advertising vermouth, beers
and wines, while
inside there is a
bar adorned with
finely polished
faucets (taps).
   The neighbour-
hood around the
plaza is an intricate
maze of little streets,
one of which,
Augusto Figueroa, is
full of wonderful,
yet inexpensive,
shoe shops. Also
called Chueca, by
night it is the main
focus of Madrid's
gay community,
with a good
selection of modish
bars and chic
restaurants.

Iglesia de Santa Bárbara ❹

Calle General Castaños 2. **Map** 5 C5.
Tel *91 319 48 11.* 🚇 *Alonso Martínez, Colón.* ⬜ *9am–1pm, 5–7:30pm Mon–Fri; 10am–1:30pm, 6:30–8:30pm Sat, Sun & public hols.*

No expense was spared on this fine Baroque church, which was built, along with an adjoining convent (now the Tribunal Supremo), for Bárbara de Braganza, wife of Fernando VI. To run the convent, which was to include a school for daughters of the nobility, Bárbara chose Las Salesas Reales – an order of nuns founded in 1610 by St Francis de Sales and St Jane Frances de Chantal in Annecy, France. The church is sometimes referred to as Las Salesas Reales.

François Carlier (1707–60), whose father worked on the gardens of La Granja de San Ildefonso *(see p131)*, was appointed architect. The first stone was laid in 1750 and, in 1757, the huge edifice was finished by builder Francisco de Moradillo. He added towers on the roof to Carlier's plans.

The main door is reached through pleasant gardens, added in 1930. The central medallion on the façade, by Doménico Olivieri, shows *The Visitation* of the pregnant Virgin to her cousin Elizabeth. The angels on either side hold the Cross and the two tablets of the Ten Commandments.

The extravagant interior decoration was assigned to Doménico Olivieri. To the right of the entrance is a painting of St Francis de Sales and St Jane de Chantal by Corrado Giaquinto. Opposite is *La Sagrada Familia* (The Holy Family), painted by Francesco Cignaroni.

To the right of the central aisle is the tomb of Fernando VI, adorned with tiers of angels crafted by Francisco Gutiérrez to a Neo-Classical design by Francesco Sabatini. Above the nearby altar is a painting of Francisco Javier and Santa Bárbara. It is by Francisco de Mora, as is *La Visitación* above the high altar. The high altar is decorated with sculptures of San Fernando and Santa

Elaborately decorated interior of the Iglesia de Santa Bárbara

Bárbara. To the left is the 19th-century tomb of General O'Donnell by sculptor Jerónimo Suñol. Alongside it is the *Surrender of Seville* by the French artist Charles Joseph Flipart. The tomb of Bárbara de Braganza is to the right of the altar in a separate chapel.

Tribunal Supremo ❺

Plaza de la Villa de Paris. **Map** 5 C5.
Tel *91 397 12 00.* 🚇 *Alonso Martínez, Colón.* ⬜ *by appointment in writing (Gabinete Técnico, Plaza de la Villa de Paris, Madrid 28071; fax 91 319 47 20).*

Built by François Carlier in the 1750s as a convent and school for the adjoining Iglesia de Santa Bárbara, this stately Baroque building was run by the Las Salesas Reales nuns. It was built on the orders of Bárbara de Braganza, wife of Fernando VI. After her death, the nuns were allowed to remain in the convent until 1870, when the building was expropriated by the secular government to become the Palace of Justice. The building fell into disrepair, which was made worse by fires in 1907

and 1915. Fortunately, the Iglesia de Santa Bárbara was unaffected. Later restoration work was undertaken by Joaquín Rojí in 1991–5. In the 1990s, the building became the country's supreme court.

In front of the palace is the Plaza de la Villa de Paris, a large French-style square. In the middle of it are statues of Fernando VI and Bárbara de Braganza. Across the square is the Audiencía Nacional (National Court). The surrounding roads are often lined with official cars and reporters.

Statue of Bárbara de Braganza in the Plaza de la Villa de Paris

Museo Arqueológico Nacional ®

With hundreds of exhibits, ranging from prehistoric times to the 19th century, this palatial museum is one of Madrid's best. It was founded by Isabel II in 1867 and contains many items uncovered during excavations all over Spain, as well as pieces from Egypt, ancient Greece and the Etruscan civilization. Highlights include items from the ancient civilization of El Argar in Andalusia, 7th-century gold votive crowns from Toledo province, Roman mosaics and Islamic pottery. Steps outside lead to a replica of the Altamira cave in Cantabria; the walls are covered with copies of Paleolithic paintings. Some rooms will be closed until 2010 due to a refurbishment project.

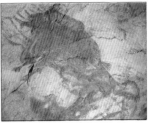

A bison, one of the wall paintings in the replica of the Altamira cave

Basement

★ Visigothic Crown
This 7th-century gold crown with pearls, sapphires and garnets was found at Guarrazar, Toledo. Letters spelling "RECCESVINTHVS REX OFFERET" hang from it, indicating it was a church offering from Visigoth King Recesvinto.

Moorish Arch
Constructed from plaster, this 11th-century arch was more decorative than functional. It formed part of the Palacio de Aljafería in Zaragoza (north central Spain).

STAR SIGHTS

★ Visigothic Crown

★ Dama de Baza

★ Roman Mosaic

Medieval religious paintings and icons

Carved Ivory Crucifix
Belonging to King Fernando I and Queen Sancha, this small Latin crucifix was made in 1063 and donated to the church of San Isidoro in León on its dedication. At the back is a recess for a relic of the True Cross.

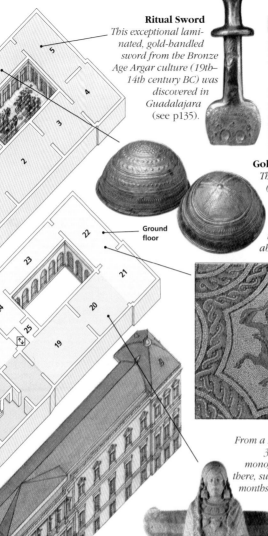

Ritual Sword
This exceptional laminated, gold-handled sword from the Bronze Age Argar culture (19th–14th century BC) was discovered in Guadalajara (see p135).

VISITORS' CHECKLIST

Calle de Serrano 13. **Map** 6 D5.
Tel 91 577 79 12. 🚇 Serrano,
Retiro. 🚌 1, 5, 9, 14, 19, 21, 27,
45, 51, 53, 74. ☐ 9:30am–8pm
Tue–Sat, 9:30am–3pm Sun. ☐
Holy Thu, Good Fri, 2 & 15 May,
25 Jul, 15 Aug, 12 Oct, 1 & 9 Nov,
6 & 8 Dec, 24, 25 & 31 Dec, 1 &
6 Jan. 🎟 Free during works. 🚻
📷 🍴 🛒 www.man.mcu.es

Gold Bowls
These late Bronze Age bowls (13th–12th century BC) have beaten patterns. They were found in Axtroki in the Basque country, where they had been hidden, probably by a sun-worshipping cult.

Ground floor

★ **Roman Mosaic**
From a Roman villa in Albacete, this 3rd-century mosaic shows the monogram of the family who lived there, surrounded by allegories of the months. This section represents April.

★ **Dama de Baza**
This ancient stone statue (4th-century BC) is from Granada. Covered in polychrome stuccowork, it has a niche at the left side for the ashes of the dead.

Main entrance

Replica of the Altamira cave

KEY

	Paleolithic to Iron Age
	Ancient Greece and Etruria
	Ancient Egypt, Africa and Orient
	Middle Ages
	Ancient Rome
	Visigothic, Romanesque and Mudéjar exhibits
	Non-exhibition space

GALLERY GUIDE
The museum's displays date from prehistory through to the 19th century. Outside the museum, in the garden, is the entrance to the replica Altamira cave. Until 2010 extensive refurbishment will result in room closures at alternate times. An exhibition, Masterpieces of the Museo Arqueológico, will be open for the duration of the works and will include many of the artifacts shown here. Entrance will also be free until the refurbishment is completed.

Museo de Cera ❻

Paseo de Recoletos 41. **Map** 6 D5.
Tel 91 319 26 49. Ⓜ Colón.
🕐 10am–2:30pm, 4:30–8:30pm
Mon–Fri, 10am–8:30pm Sat–Sun
& public hols. 🎦 ♿
www.museoceramadrid.com

Madrid's Wax Museum, off
Plaza de Colón, houses some
450 wax dummies of well
known Spanish and inter-
national figures, mostly set in
scenes. A wax likeness of
Miguel de Cervantes, author
of *Don Quixote*, sits at his
desk writing, with windmills
behind him. Another scene
imitates Goya's famous painting, *The 3rd of May*, depicting
French reprisals for the rebel-
lions of 2 May 1808 in Madrid
(see p18). Also shown is Christopher Columbus' return from
the New World. Other scenes
show navigators and scientists,
the Last Supper and the history
of the Spanish colonies.

More recent figures include
cowboys from the Wild West,
pop stars, Hollywood actors,
athletes and the Pope. There
is also a café scene where
visitors to the museum are
encouraged to try to identify
Spanish intellectuals, past and
present. Those with children
should bear in mind that
some of the scenes are quite
ghoulish. Particularly gruesome
is a bullfighting scene with a
horn piercing a matador's eye.

Upstairs is *Multivision*, a cinema where 27 projectors are
used simultaneously to show
a 60-minute history of Spain.

**Wax figure of Miguel de Cervantes
in the Museo de Cera**

**Modern monument to Christopher
Columbus, Plaza de Colón**

Plaza de Colón ❼

Map 6 D5. Ⓜ Serrano, Colón.

This large square, one of
Madrid's focal points, is
dedicated to Christopher
Columbus (Colón in Spanish).
It is overlooked by 1970s'
high-rise buildings, which
replaced the 19th-century
mansions that once stood
here. On the south side is
a palace housing the
National Library and
Archeological Museum
(see pp94–5). On the
north side, on the
corner of La Castellana,
the Post-Modernist sky-
scraper of the Heron
Corporation towers
over the square.

The real feature of the
square, however, is the
pair of monuments dedi-
cated to the discoverer of
the Americas. The oldest,
and prettiest, is a Neo-
Gothic spire built in 1885,
with Columbus at its
top, pointing west.
Carved reliefs on the
plinth give highlights
of his discoveries.
Across the square is
the second, more
modern monument –
a cluster of four large
concrete shapes in-
scribed with quotations
relating to Columbus'
historic journey to America.
Constantly busy with the
flow of traffic, the plaza may
seem an unlikely venue for

**Statue of
Columbus, Plaza
de Colón**

cultural events. Beneath it,
however, is an extensive
complex, the Centro Cultural
de la Villa de Madrid, which
includes the city's municipal
art centre, exhibition halls,
lecture rooms, a theatre,
renamed Fernán Gómez after
the famous actor, and a café.

Museo Arqueológico Nacional ❽

See pages 94–5.

Calle de Serrano ❾

Map 8 D1. Ⓜ Serrano.

Named after a 19th-century
politician, Madrid's smartest
shopping street runs north
from the triumphal Plaza
de la Independencia to the
Plaza del Ecuador, in the
well-heeled district of El
Viso. The street is lined with
shops *(see p172)* – many
specializing in luxury
items – housed in
old-fashioned mansion-
blocks. Several of Spain's
top designers, including
Adolfo Domínguez and
Roberto Verino, have
boutiques in the middle of
the street. Towards the
northern end are the ABC
Serrano mall *(see p173)* and
the Museo Lázaro Galdiano
(see pp98–9). A wide
selection of luxury goods
shops can be found on
Calle de José Ortega
y Gasset, including
branches of the Italian
shops Versace, Armani
and Gucci, as well as
Chanel, Calvin Klein
and Escada. Lower
down Calle de
Serrano, towards
Serrano metro station,
are two branches of
El Corte Inglés and
the stylish clothes
and leather goods
shop Loewe. On the
Calle de Claudio
Coello, which runs
parallel with Serrano, there
are several lavish antique
shops, in keeping with the
area's up-market atmosphere.

Statue of Salamanca's founder, the Marqués de Salamanca

Salamanca ⑩

Map 6 E3. 🚇 *Velázquez, Serrano, Núñez de Balboa, Lista, Príncipe de Vergara, Goya, Diego de León.*

Madrid's Salamanca district (Barrio de Salamanca) was developed in 1862–3 as an area for the bourgeoisie, and takes its name from its founder, José "Pepito" Salamanca, Marqués de Salamanca (1811–83). He was a lawyer who, by the age of 23, had already been elected as a deputy to the Cortes (Spanish parliament). The Marqués had a great flair for politics and business, and made his fortune from salt, railways and the building of Salamanca. He was also the founder of Banco de Isabel II, which was the forerunner of Banco de España *(see p67).*

The Marqués inaugurated his magnificent palace at Paseo de Recoletos 10, (now the BBVA Bank) in 1858, and by 1862 began developing his land behind it. The streets were planned to run north-south or east-west, and the area was to comprise apartment blocks, churches, schools, hospitals and theatres. He also built the first tramways in Madrid, connecting the Barrio de Salamanca with the centre of Madrid. A statue of the Marqués stands at the confluence of Ortega y Gasset and Príncipe de Vergara.

To this day the *barrio* consists mainly of six- to eight-floor apartment blocks, and is home to many well-to-do families. This is an area where just a hint of cool weather brings out the mink coats. Some of Madrid's best shops and markets can be found here, as well as a number of discreet restaurants. The *pijos* (rich spoilt children) gather at the *cervecerías* and bars around Calle de Goya and Calle de Alcalá.

The oldest church of the *barrio*, San Andrés de los Flamencos (Calle de Claudio Coello 99), built in 1884, now houses the Fundación Carlos de Amberes, a cultural centre maintaining links between Spain, Holland and Belgium. Behind the altar is a painting of St Andrew by Rubens. The unofficial parish church of Salamanca is the Iglesia de la Concepción (Calle de Goya 26), built between 1902 and 1914, with a notable white iron spire topped by a statue of the Virgin. At Calle de Hermosilla 45 is the charming Protestant Church of St George (1926).

The best preserved of the area's Neo-Classical palaces is Palacio de Amboage (1918) by Joaquín Roji on the corner of Velázquez and Juan Bravo. It is now the Italian Embassy, and features a lovely garden.

Modern and fascinating is the architecture inside Teatriz, an avant-garde restaurant at Calle de Hermosilla 15, designed by Philippe Starck. Diners sit in the auditorium of a former theatre and cinema, while on the stage is a back-lit onyx bar and steel stools, all reflected in a gigantic mirror.

Fundación Juan March ⑪

Calle de Castelló 77. *Tel 91 435 42 40.* 🚇 *Núñez de Balboa.* 🕐 *11am–8pm, Mon–Sat, 10am–2pm Sun & public hols.* 🗓 *Wed am, Fri pm (call to confirm times).* ♿ 🌐 www.march.es

Established in 1955 with an endowment from financier Juan March, this cultural and scientific foundation is best known for its art exhibitions and concerts. The marble-and-glass headquarters, in Madrid's Barrio de Salamanca, opened in 1975. The foundation has published over 380 books and collections. It also owns the Museo de Arte Abstracto in Cuenca and a gallery of Spanish art in Palma de Mallorca. The ground floor houses a shop, as well as the main exhibition area. Works by Kandinsky, Picasso and Matisse have been shown here, alongside some of the collection of over 1,300 contemporary Spanish pieces. There is a 400-seat auditorium in the basement where free concerts are held.

Sculpture by Chillida, Fundación Juan March

The second-floor library has a collection of contemporary Spanish music, with listening desks. There is also a library on contemporary Spanish theatre and entertainment.

Hidden away from the public are the Juan March Institute for Study and Investigation – one of the world's top forums in the field of biology – and the Centre for Advanced Study in the Social Sciences.

Sculpture by Barrocol, by the main entrance to the Fundación Juan March

Museo Lázaro Galdiano ⑫

This Neo-Renaissance mansion houses nearly 5,000 items from the private collection of financier and editor José Lázaro Galdiano (1862–1947). The exhibits, ranging from the 6th century BC to the 20th century, include archeological finds, religious artifacts, Limoges enamels, Old Masters, medieval ivory, jewellery and silver. In 1903 Lázaro Galdiano married Argentine heiress Paula Florido and they built the mansion to celebrate – and to show off the growing collection. By the time Lázaro Galdiano died, some 15,000 items were brought together in Madrid.

Second floor

19

15

16

G2

Atrium

7

14

13

First floor

Portrait of a Lady
Joshua Reynolds painted this portrait in the late 18th century. Other British artists represented in the museum include Constable, Romney and Hopper.

Marquetry Writing Desk
This elaborate, 16th-century German desk was among many exported to Spain by cabinet-makers in Augsburg and Nuremberg. Felipe II is known to have bought desks similar to this.

★ The Witches' Sabbath *(1798)*
This painting by Francisco de Goya is based on a legend from Aragón, the artist's birthplace. It shows two sisters who poisoned their children in order to attract the devil, represented here by a huge billy goat.

STAR EXHIBITS

- ★ The Witches' Sabbath
- ★ Tartessic Ewer
- ★ Crosier Head

GALLERY GUIDE

The ground floor houses archeological artifacts, Limoges enamels, 13th- and 16th-century religious items, jewellery and decorative bronzes from France and Italy. The first floor contains Spanish paintings, including a room devoted to Goya. Highlights on the second floor include works by Bosch.

Main entrance

St John the Baptist

Surrounded by the lamb of spiritual life and other allegorical animals and birds, Hieronymus Bosch's contemplative St John the Baptist (c.1485–1510) reclines in an almost pastoral landscape punctuated by grotesque plants.

VISITORS' CHECKLIST

Calle Serrano 122. **Map** 6 E1.
Tel *91 561 60 84.* Rubén
Darío, Gregorio Marañón.
*7, 9, 12, 14, 16, 19, 27, 40,
51, 150.* 10am– 4:30pm
Wed–Mon. Tue & public hols.
(free Sun).
www.flg.es

Inés de Zúñiga

This painting of the Countess of Monterrey was executed by Juan Carreño de Miranda in the late 17th century. She is dressed in a wide Spanish farthingale.

Ground floor

9
10
11

4
5
3
2
1

★ Crosier Head

This beautiful gilded and enamelled object was made in Limoges in the 13th century for the top of a bishop's staff (crosier). It is decorated with stylized plants to evoke the tree of life and a figure, believed to be St Matthew, holding a book.

★ Tartessic Ewer

One of the oldest and most interesting archeological items displayed in the museum is this Tartessic bronze jug, which has a fine feline head as its spout. It was made in the mid-6th century BC, in the Tartessic era.

KEY TO FLOORPLAN

☐ Ground floor
☐ First floor
☐ Second floor
☐ Non-exhibition space

Former studio of Impressionist Joaquín Sorolla in the Museo Sorolla

Museo Sorolla ⑬

Paseo del General Martínez Campos 37.
Map 5 C1. **Tel** 91 310 15 84.
Ⓜ *Rubén Dario, Iglesia, Gregorio
Marañón.* ◯ *9:30am–3pm Tue–
Sat (also 3–6pm Wed), 10am–3pm
Sun.* ◪ *(free Sun).* **www.**
museosorolla.mcu.es

The studio-mansion of
Valencian Impressionist
painter Joaquín Sorolla
is now a museum dis-
playing his art, left
virtually as it was when
he died in 1923.

Although Sorolla is
perhaps best known
for his brilliantly lit
Mediterranean beach
scenes, the changing styles of
his paintings are well represented here, with examples of his
gentle portraiture and works
depicting people from different
parts of Spain. Also on display
are objects amassed during
the artist's lifetime, including
tiles and ceramics. The house,
built in 1910, is surrounded
by an Andalusian-style garden,
designed by Sorolla himself.

Museo de Escultura al Aire Libre ⑭

Paseo de la Castellana. **Map** 6 E2.
Ⓜ *Rubén Dario.*

In the early 1970s J Antonio
Fernández Ordóñez and Julio
Martínez Calzón, the
architects of the Calle Juan
Bravo bridge, filled the space
underneath it with abstract
sculptures by 20th-century
Spanish artists. The space on
the east side of Paseo de la

Castellana is dominated by
*Sirena Varada, or Stranded
Mermaid* (1972–3), a concrete
sculpture hanging from four
rods by Eduardo Chillida,
the noted Basque sculptor.
Alberto Sánchez's *Toros
Ibéricos* is another dramatic
installation, and there is a
penguin by Joan Miró.
Other sculptors repre-
sented here are Andrés
Alfaro, Julio González,
Rafael Leoz, Mariel
Martí, José María
Subirachs, Francisco
Sobrino, Martín Chirino
and Eusebio Sempere.
On the west side are
two bronzes by Pablo
Serrano. Visitors should
take care when crossing the
busy Paseo de la Castellana.

*Toros Ibéricos,
Alberto Sánchez*

Museo Romántico ⑮

Calle de San Mateo 13. **Map** 5 A4.
Tel 91 448 1045. Ⓜ *Tribunal, Alonso
Martínez.* ⬛ *for refurbishment until
early 2009 (call for details).* ◪ *(free
Sun).* **www.**museoromantico.mcu.es

This small Neo-Classical
mansion was designed by
Manuel Martín in 1776 for
the Marqués de Matallana. By
1924 it had been turned into a
museum by the Marqués de la
Vega-Inclán, the founder of
Spain's fine network of state-
owned parador hotels (*see
p149*), who was an avid art
lover and collector. In 1921,
the Marqués donated his
hoard of 19th-century
paintings, books and some
furniture to form the nucleus
of a museum. Three years

later the museum was
acquired by the state, and
reorganized to look like the
home of a wealthy mid-19th-
century family, evoking the
epoch of the Romantic period.

The exhibits are housed in
20 rooms on the first floor of
the building. As well as a vast
array of 19th-century objects,
such as musical instruments,
photographs, dolls and ornaments, there are many
portraits by leading artists.
They include General Prim by
Esquivel, José de Madrazo's
Fernando VII and María
Cristina by Salvador Gutiérrez.
Several works by Leonardo
Alenza include the disturbing
Satire of a Romantic Suicide.

In the ballroom is a Pleyel
piano that belonged to Isabel
II (*see p23*). The ceiling is by
González, and the carpet
comes from the Real Fábrica
de Tapices (*see p110*).

The Museo Romántico
contains a fine collection of
works by the costumbristas –
artists who painted scenes
of everyday life in Andalusia
and Madrid. Many of their
works depict local festivals
and traditions.

Earlier works on display in
the museum include a painting of St Gregory the Great by
Goya (*see p28*), which can be
seen above the altar in the
intimate chapel.

The Mariano José de Larra
Room is dedicated to this
great satirical journalist and
writer. Among his personal
effects is the duelling pistol
he used to kill himself, after
being rejected by his lover.

Goya's *St Gregory the Great* in the
chapel of the Museo Romántico

Baroque façade of the Museo Municipal, by Pedro de Ribera

Museo Municipal 🔟

Calle de Fuencarral 78. **Map** 5 A4.
Tel *91 701 18 63.* Ⓜ *Tribunal.*
🕐 *9:30am–8pm Tue–Fri (9.30am–2.30pm Aug), 10am–2pm Sat & Sun (several areas closed for renovation during 2009).* 🌐 *public hols.* ♿
🚩 *by arrangement.* **www. munimadrid.es**

The Municipal Museum is worth visiting just for its majestic Baroque doorway by Pedro de Ribera, arguably the finest in Madrid. Housed in the former hospice of St Ferdinand, the museum was inaugurated in 1929. Upstairs is a series of maps showing how radically Madrid has been transformed. Among them is Pedro Texeira's 1656 map, thought to be the oldest of the city. There is also a meticulous model of Madrid, made in 1830 by León Gil de Palacio.

Modern exhibits include the reconstructed study of Ramón Gómez de la Serna, a key figure of the literary gatherings in the Café de Pombo *(see p85).* In the garden is the *Fuente de la Fama* (Fountain of Fame), also by Ribera.

Malasaña 🔟

Map 2 E4. Ⓜ *Tribunal, Bilbao, San Bernardo.*

Officially called *Barrio de Maravillas,* or District of Miracles, after a 17th-century church that once stood here, this area is more widely known as Malasaña. Thin streets slope down from Carranza and Fuencarral to its bohemian hub, the **Plaza del Dos de Mayo.**

In 1808, *Madrileños* made an heroic last stand here against Napoleon's occupying troops at the gate of Monteleón barracks. The arch in the square is all that is left of the barracks. In front of it is a memorial by Antonio Solá to artillery officers Daoiz and Velarde, who defended the barracks.

In the 1940s and '50s the area deteriorated, but residents fiercely fended off demolition threats. It acquired its bohemian atmosphere in the 1960s, when hippies were lured into the district by cheap rents. Later it became the centre of *La Movida (see p102),* the frenzied nightlife that began after the death of Franco.

Today Malasaña's streets combine the best of both worlds. Artists and writers have once again moved into the area, along with antiques sellers and yuppies. The charming streets have been cobbled, and boast pretty fountains and plenty of trees. At night, however, the streets are still thronged with people looking for a wild time.

Malasaña is rich in sites of historical and cultural interest. **Plaza de San Ildefonso,** one of many squares remodelled by José I (Joseph Bonaparte) *(see p19),* has an attractive central fountain with serpents entwined around conch shells. Near the Neo-Classical **Iglesia de San Ildefonso,** built in 1827, is the **Vaquería,** a

dairy shop opened in 1911 and hardly changed since. Outside decorative cows frame the door, while inside there are ageing oil paintings of the seasons in Art Deco style.

In Calle de la Puebla, the 17th-century **Iglesia de San Antonio de los Alemanes** is remarkable for its elliptical interior, swathed in frescoes by Juan Carreño, Francisco de Ricci and Luca Giordano.

Close by is the 17th-century **Iglesia de San Plácido** with a cupola painted by Francisco Rizi and the work of Claudio Coello adorning the altars.

The **Iglesia de San Martín,** in Calle de San Roque, was built in 1648. The painting above the altar depicts St Martin of Tours giving half his cloak to a naked beggar.

The main altar of Iglesia de San Plácido in Malasaña painted by Claudio Coello

---

MANUELA MALASAÑA

The daughter of Juan Manuel Malasaña, a craftsman and hero of the 1808 uprising *(see p18),* Manuela Malasaña died at the age of 16 in the struggle against Napoleon. She was a seamstress who, according to local legend, was caught carrying a pair of scissors by the French and was subsequently shot for possession of a concealed weapon. In 1961 Calle de Manuela Malasaña, which lies between Fuencarral and San Bernardo where the Monteleón artillery park had been, was named after this local heroine.

Ribera's sculptured door at the Cuartel del Conde Duque

Cuartel del Conde Duque ⑱

Calle del Conde Duque 9–11.
Map 2 D4. **Tel** 91 588 58 34.
Ⓜ Noviciado, San Bernardo.
🕐 10am–2pm, 6:30–9pm Tue–Sat,
10:30am–2pm Sun & public hols.
♿ www.munimadrid.es

This enormous rectangular complex is named after Gaspar de Guzmán (1587–1645), Conde Duque de Olivares. As a minister of Felipe IV (see p22), the count had a palace on this site. After his death, the palace was neglected and fell into ruin. Subsequently, the plot was divided into two distinct sections. On one section, the Palacio de Liria was built for the Duke of Alba. On the other, the barracks for Los Guardias de Corps were constructed between 1720 and 1754 by Pedro de Ribera, who adorned them with a Baroque façade. The three-floor barracks were in use for over a century but, in 1869, they suffered a major fire and eventually fell into a state of total dilapidation. A hundred years later, in 1969, Madrid's city hall made the decision to restore the old army barracks.

The building now houses the city's historical archives, several council offices, a municipal library, a cultural centre with four exhibition halls and the **Museo Municipal de Arte Contemporáneo**. This new museum of modern art exhibits the work of young Spanish

LA MOVIDA

With Franco's death in 1975 came a new period of personal and artistic liberty. For the young, this was translated into the freedom to stay out late, drinking and sometimes sampling drugs. The phenomenon was known as *la movida*, "the action", and it was at its most intense in Madrid. Analysts at the time saw it as having serious intellectual content and *la movida* has had a few lasting cultural results, like the emergence of satirical film director Pedro Almodóvar.

Poster for Almodóvar's *Women on the Verge of a Nervous Breakdown*

artists alongside that of better established names. The cultural centre is a venue for major concerts and in summer it runs an interesting programme of live music events, including jazz and flamenco festivals staged in a beautiful courtyard.

Palacio de Liria ⑲

Calle de la Princesa 20. **Map** 1 C4.
Tel 91 547 53 02. Ⓜ Ventura Rodríguez. 🕐 by appointment a year before (fax 91 541 03 77).

The lavish but much restored Palacio de Liria was completed by Ventura Rodríguez in 1780. It was once the

residence of the Alba family, and is still owned by the Duchess. The sumptuous palace rooms are home to the Albas' outstanding collection of art and Flemish tapestries. The walls are adorned with paintings by many famous masters, among them Titian, Rubens and Rembrandt.

Spanish art itself is particularly well represented, and the Albas' collection includes a number of major works by Goya (see p28). One such significant canvas is his 1795 portrait of the Duchess of Alba. Also featured are several interesting works by El Greco (see p143), Zurbarán and Velázquez (see p28).

Room adorned with paintings by Goya in the Palacio de Liria

Castizos of Madrid

The true working-class *Madrileños*, whose families have lived in the neighbourhoods of Old Madrid, Chamberí and Cuatro Caminos for many generations, are known as *castizos*. Around 1850, in their revolt against the bourgeoisie, who were basking in the Romantic and patriotic cultural revolution that followed the defeat of the French earlier in the 19th century, the *castizos* decided to reclaim their proud heritage. The Madrid equivalent of

Religious celebration – festivities on vehicle floats

London's Cockneys, *los castizos Madrileños* not only revived their district fiestas, one of the world's best neighbourhood-bonding traditions, but also reinvented costumes to go with them and formed numerous associations that still thrive today. At any of the traditional Madrid fiestas or *romerías* (processions) you will see the *castizos*, or *majos* (dandies) as they are known, with their *manolas*, or partners, attired in what is now their smart, traditional uniform.

Typical *manola* costume
consists of a flowery headscarf with at least one carnation in the front, an alfombra *(literally translated as carpet), which is actually a huge embroidered shawl, or* mantón de Manila, *worn over the shoulders, and a* falda vestida *(long dress), sometimes with an apron.*

Carnation on the headscarf

***Alfombra* – shawl with a long fringe**

Colourful dress (*falda vestida*)

Black-and-white *parpusa* (hat)

White *barbosa* (shirt)

Black *alares* (trousers)

Men's clothes are
referred to in castizo argot: *black or black-and-white check* parpusa *(cap), a white* barbosa *(shirt), a black* chupín *(waistcoat), a black or black-and-white check* chupa *(jacket), a* safo *(white handkerchief), a* peluco *(pocket watch), a red carnation in the buttonhole, black or black-and-white check* alares *(trousers),* picantes *(socks) and shining* calcos *(shoes).*

In May, *the* castizos *are out in force during the* Dos de Mayo *fiesta. On 15 May is the Fiesta de San Isidro, with a* romería *from the Puerta de Toledo down to the Río Manzanares. The next major fiestas are on 13 June at San Antonio de la Florida; and 15 August, with the Fiesta de la Virgen de Paloma, a* castizo *favourite.* Castizo *processions include the Romería de San Blas on 3 February, and the Romería de San Eugenio on 14 November.*

FURTHER AFIELD

Several of Madrid's best sights, including interesting but little-known museums, lie outside the city centre. The Museo de la Ciudad gives an overview of the development of the city, with models of buildings and districts, while the Museo de América displays arti-

Mosaic by Miró on the Palacio de Congresos y Exposiciones in Azca

facts from Spain's former colonies. There is a wealth of historic buildings outside the city centre, ranging from the Egyptian Templo de Debod to the Puerta de Toledo, a triumphal arch begun in 1813 on the orders of José I (Joseph Bonaparte), to the old-style apartment building of La Corrala.

There are a number of other attractions surrounding the centre of Madrid. To the north lies the modern commercial district of Azca, with skyscrapers, office blocks and upmarket shops. If you need to escape from the bustle of the city for a while, west of Old Madrid, across the Río Manzanares, is Madrid's vast, green recreation ground, the Casa de Campo.

SIGHTS AT A GLANCE

Historic Buildings
Arco de la Victoria ❷
La Corrala ⓫
Estación de Príncipe Pío ⓱
Puente de Segovia and Río Manzanares ⓭
Puerta de Toledo ⓬
Real Fábrica de Tapices ❾
Sala del Canal de Isabel II ❸
Templo de Debod ⓰

Churches and Convents
Ermita de San Antonio de la Florida ⓯

Museums and Galleries
Museo Casa de la Moneda ❽
Museo de América ❶
Museo de Ciencias Naturales ❺
Museo de la Ciudad ❻
Museo Nacional Ferroviario ❿

Squares, Parks & Districts
Azca ❹
Casa de Campo ⓮
Plaza de Toros de Las Ventas ❼

0 kilometres 1
0 miles 1

KEY

▮ Main sightseeing area
▯ Parks and open spaces
🚆 Railway station
═ Highway/Motorway
▰ Major road
═ Minor road

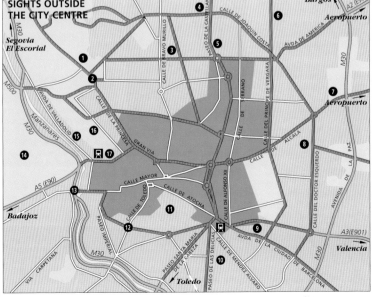

SIGHTS OUTSIDE THE CITY CENTRE

◁ Mudéjar arches and tilework on the exterior of the Plaza de Toros de Las Ventas

Old and new – the Mirador del Faro alongside the Museo de América

Museo de América ❶

Avenida de los Reyes Católicos 6.
Tel 91 549 26 41. ⓜ *Moncloa.*
⬜ 9:30am–3pm Tue–Sat, 10am–3pm Sun & public hols. ⬤ some public hols. 🎟 (free on Sun). ♿
www.museodeamerica.mcu.es

A unique collection of artifacts relating to Spain's colonization of the Americas is housed in this fine museum. Many of the exhibits, which range from prehistoric to more recent times, were brought to Europe by the early explorers of the New World *(see p16)*.

The collection is arranged on the first and second floors, and individual rooms are given cultural themes such as society, religion and communication. Documentation is given about the Atlantic voyages made by the first explorers.

For many visitors, the highlight of the museum is the rare Mayan *Códice Tro-cortesiano* (AD 1250–1500) from Mexico. This is a type of parchment illustrated with hieroglyphics of scenes from everyday life.

Also worth seeing are the Treasure of the Quimbayas, a collection of pre-Columbian gold and silver objects from around AD 500–1000, and the collection of contemporary folk art from some of Spain's former American colonies.

Arco de la Victoria ❷

Avenida de la Victoria. **Map** 1 A1.
ⓜ *Moncloa.*

Erected in 1956, this white arch was designed to celebrate the Nationalist victory in the 1936–9 Spanish Civil War *(see p20)*. General Franco would have passed by it each time he came to Madrid from his home in the Palacio de El Pardo *(see p138)*. Topped by a green sculpture of a chariot with horses, the arch stands 39 m (128 ft) tall – one of the city's highest commemorative *puertas* (gateways). The architects, Pascual Bravo and Modesto López Otero, built a room high up inside the arch. It contains a 25-sq m (270-sq ft) model of the neighbouring university and the plans for the arch itself. However, it is not open to the public.

Nearby is the **Faro de Moncloa** observation tower. Opened in 1992, it measures 92 m (300 ft). The tower offers excellent views of Madrid and the Guadarrama mountains.

The imposing Arco de la Victoria

Sala del Canal de Isabel II ❸

Calle de Santa Engracia 125.
Tel 91 545 10 00. ⓜ *Rios Rosas.*
⬜ 11am–2pm Tue–Sat, 11am–2pm Sun & public hols.
⬤ 1 Jan & 25 Dec. ♿ **www**.cyii.es

This renovated water tower is used to great effect as a venue for photographic exhibitions but, on the whole, most visitors come to marvel at its

Sala del Canal de Isabel II, a water tower turned exhibition centre

complex construction. In the late 19th century the water supply for Madrid was based on a project patronized by Isabel II *(see p23)* in 1851 and known as Canal de Isabel II, the name given to Madrid's water company. The first dam was built in the Lozoya Valley, about 80 km (50 miles) north of Madrid in the Guadarrama mountains, and a duct carried the water south to a reservoir.

More reservoirs were built to cope with the capital's ever-increasing needs but, in 1903, the development of the high-lying suburbs of Chamberi and Cuatro Caminos dictated the need for a water tower to supply new pipes by gravity. Martín y Montalvo was the engineer enlisted to carry out the task. He designed a polygonal tower of brick and iron, 36 m (118 ft) high, surmounted by a 1,500-sq m (16,145-sq ft) tank resting on an iron ring. Work started in 1908, and by 1911 the water tower was finished at a cost of nearly 350,000 pesetas. It was in service until 1952.

The regional government of Madrid decided to restore the tower in 1985, taking out the water works but retaining the huge tank. Access to the exhibition floors within the tower has been made possible by hydraulically driven elevators (lifts) and steel staircases.

Bordering the tower are the busy Calle de Santa Engracia and the gardens and turf that form a roof over one of the major underground reservoirs of the Canal de Isabel II.

Azca ❹

Nuevos Ministerios, Santiago Bernabeú.

In 1969, work began on the development of this "mini-Manhattan" along the west side of the Paseo de la Castellana. It stretches from the **Nuevos Ministerios** complex in the south to the **Palacio de Congresos y Exposiciones** in the north. The idea was to create a modern commercial area away from the congested city centre. Today, some 30,000 people work here.

By day Azca is a mecca for shoppers. A branch of the department store El Corte Inglés (*see p172*) runs alongside Nuevos Ministerios metro and railway station, and there is a Moda shopping mall served by Santiago Bernabeú metro. Across from the Plaza de Lima is the **Estadio Santiago Bernabéu**, home of Real Madrid Football Club. It was built in 1950, but has had a few facelifts since, especially for the 1982 World Cup Finals.

Major companies operate in the tower blocks, alongside hotels, apartments, cinemas, restaurants and bars. The elderly are drawn by bingo halls, while the young throng the discos at the weekends.

In the centre of Azca is the multi-level pedestrian **Plaza Pablo Ruíz Picasso** with trees, benches, fountains and walkways. If driving, do not try to negotiate the maze of roads underneath the complex unless you are very sure about where you intend to park or emerge.

Azca is dominated by the aluminium-clad **Torre Picasso**, Madrid's tallest office building. Completed in 1989, it has 46 floors, bronzed windows and a heliport. It was designed by Minoru Yamasaki, architect of the twin towers of New York's World Trade Centre, which were destroyed in the terrorist attack of 2001.

The **Torre Europa** on Plaza de Lima is another notable building. Designed by Miguel Oriol e Ybarra and completed in 1982, its exterior concrete supports incorporate a clock. As well as 28 floors of offices, it has three commercial floors below street level.

The rust-coloured **Banco Bilbao Vizcaya** on Azca's south corner was designed by Francisco Javier Sáenz de Oiza. Built in 1980, it stands over the underground rail line between Chamartín and Atocha.

Inside the modern Origins of Life section of Madrid's Museo de Ciencias Naturales

Museo de Ciencias Naturales ❺

Calle José Gutierrez Abascal 2.
Tel 91 411 13 28. *Gregorio Marañón.* 10am–6pm Tue–Fri, 10am–8pm Sat, 10am–3pm Sat (Jul & Aug only), 10am–2:30pm Sun & public hols. 1 Jan, 1 May, 25 Dec. by arrangement.
www.mncn.csic.es

This museum, built in 1887, contains 16,400 minerals, 220 meteorites, 30,000 birds and mammals and many more items in its archives. The entrance on the left leads to the Rhythm of Nature section. This is an ecological display of numerous examples of wildlife, from exotic birds to rare animals, insects and butterflies. Lions, tigers and deer stare out from the walls, while the shelves are heavy with bottled lizards, fish and snakes. An interactive computer display room provides valuable insight into the sounds and habitats of animals and birds.

A recent addition to this part of the museum is a cross-section of the Atapuerca site near Burgos, north of Madrid, where Europe's earliest human remains (some 780,000 years old) were discovered in 1997. There is also a huge African elephant. Shot by the Duke of Alba in the Sudan in 1916, the elephant's skin was sent back to Spain and reassembled.

The right entrance to the museum, by the gift shop, leads to a modern two-floor section, with displays on the origins of the earth and of life. The star of the show is the 1.8-million-year-old skeleton of *Megatherium americanum*, a bear-like creature from the late Cenozoic period found in Argentina in 1788. Nearby is a Glyptodon (giant armadillo), also from Argentina, and a life-size reproduction of a Diplodocus dinosaur skeleton found in the United States.

The Industrial Engineers' School is also housed in the museum building and behind are the headquarters of Spain's state scientific institute, CSIC. Opposite the entrances is a pleasant terrace bar which looks out over a small park with a fountain and a statue of Isabel I (*see p22*).

The Torre Europa rising above the commercial centre of Azca

Interior of the Museo de la Ciudad arranged around a central atrium

Museo de la Ciudad ❻

Calle del Príncipe de Vergara 140. *Tel* 91 588 65 99. Ⓜ *Cruz del Rayo.* ◻ *9:30am–8pm Tue–Fri, 10am–2pm Sat & Sun.* ◉ *public hols.* ♿ www.munimadrid.es

This modern museum in the northeast of Madrid shows how the city has evolved since the earliest settlement, using detailed panoramic models.

The museum consists of five floors built around an octagonal atrium. Here stands a copy of the Mariblanca statue in the Puerta del Sol *(see p44).* Right of the entrance is a bookshop. The ground and first floors house temporary exhibitions.

The displays on the second floor concern Madrid's utility companies. A subject that fascinates visiting schoolchildren is how Madrid gets its water from the mountains. Also on this floor is a huge model of the city, from Barajas Airport to Cuatro Vientos airfield.

The third floor deals with the history of Madrid from prehistory to Bourbon times. As well as books, charts and maps, there are models of Old Madrid, some monuments and the Palacio Real *(see pp54–7).*

The fourth floor is devoted to the 19th and 20th centuries, and has a superb model of the new part of the city from Plaza de Colón *(see p96)* to Torre Europa *(see p107).* Nearby there is also an impressive model of Plaza de Toros de Las Ventas, Madrid's bullring.

Plaza de Toros de Las Ventas ❼

Calle de Alcalá 237. *Tel* 91 356 22 00. Ⓜ *Ventas.* ◻ *10am–1:30pm Tue–Sun.* **Museo Taurino** *Tel* 91 725 18 57. ◻ *Mar–Oct: 9:30am–2:30pm Tue–Fri, 10am–1pm Sun; Nov–Feb: 9:30am–2pm Mon–Fri.* ♿ **www**.las-ventas.com

Whatever your opinion of bullfighting, Las Ventas is undoubtedly one of the most beautiful bullrings in Spain. Built in 1929 in Neo-Mudéjar style, it replaced the city's original bullring, which stood near the Puerta de Alcalá *(see p66).* Its horseshoe arches around the outer galleries and elaborate tilework decoration make it an attractive venue for the *corridas* (bullfights), held from May to October. The statues outside the bullring are of two Spanish bullfighters, Antonio Bienvenida and José Cubero.

Adjoining the bullring is the **Museo Taurino.** This contains a varied collection of bullfighting memorabilia, including portraits and sculptures of famous matadors, as well as the heads of several bulls killed during fights at Las Ventas. Visitors can examine bullfighters' capes and *banderillas* – sharp darts used to wound the bull. The gory highlight of the exhibition, for some people, is the blood-drenched *traje de luces* worn by Manolete during his fateful bullfight at Linares in Andalusia in 1947. Also on display is a costume which belonged to Juanita Cruz, a

female bullfighter of the 1930s who was forced, in the face of prejudice, to leave Spain. In September and October the bullring is used as a venue for a season of rock concerts.

Museo Casa de la Moneda ❽

Calle del Doctor Esquerdo 36. *Tel* 91 566 65 44. Ⓜ *O'Donell.* ◻ *10am–5:30pm Tue–Fri, 10am–2pm Sat & Sun.* ◉ *1 & 6 Jan; 1 May; Thu–Sun in Easter; 24, 25 & 31 Dec.* ♿ www.fnmt.es/museo

The Spanish mint and stamp factory is located in a vast granite building. The recently renovated museum, in the north side of the building, traces the history of currency, from early trading in salt, shells and bracelets up to the Euro – the monetary unit of the European Union.

Coins feature prominently, with maps and photographs complementing displays of Greek and Roman coins. The earliest coins have images of mythical gods; the picture of Cybele, mother of the gods, on a Roman coin from 78 BC is similar to the sculpture in the Plaza de Cibeles *(see p67).*

As well as later Roman coins endowed with more symbolic images, there are Visigothic and Moorish coins. Early Moorish coins are inscribed in Latin and later ones in Arabic.

There are also engravings for currency notes, stamps, medals and official documents.

Plaza de Toros de Las Ventas, Madrid's beautiful Neo-Mudéjar bullring

The Art of Bullfighting

Bullfighting is a sacrificial ritual in which men (and a few women) pit themselves against an animal bred for the ring. In this "authentic religious drama", as poet Federico García Lorca *(see p28)* described it, the spectator experiences the same intensity of fear and exaltation as the matador. There are three stages, or tercios, in the corrida (bullfight). The first two are aimed at progressively weakening the bull. In the

Poster for a bullfight

third, the matador moves in for the kill. Despite opposition on the grounds of cruelty, bullfighting is still very popular. For many Spaniards, talk of banning bullfighting is an assault on the essence of their being. For them, the toreo, the art of bullfighting, is a noble part of their heritage. However, fights today can be debased by practices designed to disadvantage the bull, in particular shaving its horns to make them blunt.

The toro bravo (fighting bull), *bred for courage and aggression, enjoys a full life prior to its time in the ring. Bulls must be at least four years old before they can fight.*

Manolete *is regarded by most followers of bullfighting as one of Spain's greatest ever matadors. He was finally gored to death by the bull Islero at Linares, Jaén, in 1947.*

The matador wears a *traje de luces* (suit of lights), a colourful silk outfit embroidered with gold or silver sequins.

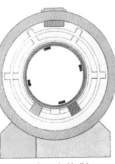

Banderillas (barbed darts) are thrust into the bull's back muscles to weaken them.

Joselito *was a leading matador, famous for his purist style and his superb skill with the* capa *(red cape) and the* muleta *(matador's stick). He has now officially retired from the* ruedos *(bullring).*

THE BULLRING

The *corrida* audience is seated in the *tendidos* (stalls) or in the *palcos* (balcony), where the *presidencia* (president's box) is situated. Opposite are the *puerta de cuadrillas*, through which the matador and team arrive, and the *arrastre de toros* (exit for bulls). Before entering the ring, the matadors wait in a *callejón* (corridor) behind *barreras* and *burladeros* (barriers). Horses are kept in the *patio de caballos* and the bulls in the *corrales*.

Plan of a typical bullring

KEY

- ☐ Tendidos
- ☐ Palcos
- ☐ Presidencia
- ☐ Puerta de cuadrillas
- ☐ Arrastre de toros
- ☐ Callejón
- ☐ Barreras
- ☐ Burladeros
- ☐ Patio de caballos
- ☐ Corrales

Real Fábrica de Tapices ⑨

Calle de Fuenterrabía 2. **Map** 8 F5.
Tel 91 434 05 51. ⓜ Menéndez
Pelayo. ◻ 10am–2pm Mon–Fri. ◼
public hols, Aug. ◪
www.realfabricadetapices.com

Founded by Felipe V in 1721, the Royal Tapestry Factory alone survives from the factories opened by the Bourbons in the 18th century. In 1889 the factory was moved to this building, just south of the Parque del Retiro *(see p77).*

Visitors can see the making by hand of the carpets and tapestries, a process which has changed little since the factory was built. Goya *(see p28)* and his brother-in-law Francisco Bayeu drew cartoons on which the tapestries for the royal family were based. Some of the cartoons are on display here, in the newly opened museum; others are in the Prado *(see pp78–81).* Several tapestries can be seen at the Palacio de El Pardo *(see p138)* and at El Escorial *(see pp126–9).* Today the factory makes and repairs the beautiful carpets decorating the Hotel Ritz *(see p68).*

Cafeteria of the Museo del Ferrocarril, set in a 1930s dining car

Museo del Ferrocarril ⑩

Paseo de las Delicias 61. **Tel** 90 222
88 22. ⓜ Delicias. ◻ 10am–3pm
Tue–Sun. ◼ 1 & 6 Jan,1 May, Aug,
25 Dec. ◪ (free on Sat). ♿ ▯ ▯
www.museodelferrocarril.org

Although railways had existed in the country since 1848, it was only in 1880 that Madrid's first proper railway terminus opened – the station of Delicias. This was the main station for Portugal, and it remained in use until 1971.

In 1984 the station re-opened as a railway museum. The majority of exhibits, in the form of trains, are located in the main terminus on tracks next to the original platforms. There are

1950s Talgo locomotive at the railway museum

more than 30 locomotives – steam, diesel and electric – as well as rolling stock. Explanatory plaques give details and describe the routes of the locomotives. You can explore some of the carriages, including a 1930s dining car that now serves as the site's cafeteria.

One of the most interesting engines is "La Pucheta", a steam locomotive built in 1884 by Sharp Stewart in Britain. Its water supply was on top of the boiler, in a container that resembles a bowler hat.

A 1931 electric locomotive, built in Spain, earned itself the nickname "The Lioness" because of its weight – more than 150 tonnes. This was the heaviest engine ever used by the Spanish state railways (RENFE), and the longest, measuring approximately 25 m (82 ft).

Also of special interest is a 1950s Talgo. These Spanish-designed express trains revolutionized railway transport in the country, and this model was in service until 1971. The train was light, with a very low centre of gravity, reduced height, and an articulated system, all of which enabled it to travel much faster than conventional carriages.

The 1928 wooden-sided carriage, the ZZ-307 Coche Salon, was the most luxurious the West Railway Company had to offer. Peering through the windows, you can still see an elegantly laid table in the dining room, the sleeping compartments and a tiny galley.

One of the popular sights on show is the Mikado, a steam locomotive built in 1960, which has been cut away to reveal the mysteries of steam propulsion. This engine was in service until 1975, when the use of regular steam-hauled services came to an end in Spain.

To one side of the station are four large halls that house detailed model train layouts, scale models of train stations and railway memorabilia, including signals, lights, telegraphs and photographs.

La Corrala ⓫

Calle de Mesón de Paredes, between Calle Tribulete & Calle del Sombrerete. **Map** 4 F5. Ⓜ *Lavapiés*. 🚇 *to the public.*

Corralas are timber-framed apartment blocks, or tenements, built during the 19th century mainly in poorer parts of the city, especially in the neighbourhood of Lavapiés. The buildings were arranged around an interior courtyard; balconies overlooked the courtyard and provided access to individual apartments.

La Corrala exemplifies this type of housing. Construction began in 1872, but some of the building permits were not in order, which may explain why only half of the building seems to exist. The courtyard, rather than being completely surrounded by the building, opens out on to a plaza. Its exposure means that there are good views of the building, and of the ubiquitous laundry hanging from the balconies.

In 1977, La Corrala was declared a monument of historic interest, and two years later it underwent complete restoration. In the past,

A *zarzuela* performance, using La Corrala as a backdrop

zarzuela (light opera) performances *(see p75)* have been staged at the site, a fitting backdrop since *La Revoltosa*, the best known *zarzuela*, is set in a corrala.

Nearby are several other corralas – one on the corner of Calle de Miguel Servet with Calle del Espino, one at Calle de Provisiones 12 and another at Calle de la Esperanza 11.

Puerta de Toledo ⓬

Glorieta de Puerta de Toledo. **Map** 4 D5. Ⓜ *Puerta de Toledo.*

The construction of this triumphal arch began in 1813 on the orders of French-born Joseph Bonaparte, José I *(see p19)*. It was intended to

commemorate his accession to the Spanish throne after the 1808 rout of Madrid. But in 1814, after a short-lived reign, José I fled Spain and was replaced by Fernando VII *(see p19)*. By the time the arch was completed in 1827, by the architect Antonio López Aguado, it had to be dedicated to Fernando VII.

The Puerta de Toledo is one of Madrid's two remaining city gates, and is topped by a group of sculptures that represent a personification of Spain. On either side of these are the allegorical figures of Genius and the Arts. All were carved in their entirety from Colmenar stone by Ramón Barba and Valeriano Salvatierra, and are flanked by sculptures based on military themes.

The majestic form of the Puerta de Toledo, one of Madrid's two remaining triumphal arches

Puente de Segovia and Río Manzanares ⑬

Calle de Segovia. Ⓜ *Puerta del Angel.*

Puente de Segovia, a grand granite bridge over the Río Manzanares, was commissioned by Felipe II *(see p22)* not long after he had decided to establish his court in Madrid. The bridge was to be a main entry point to Madrid and he chose Juan de Herrera, his favourite architect, to build it. Construction began in 1582. The bridge, with its nine arches topped with decorative bosses, was rebuilt in 1682.

Further downstream is the magnificent pedestrian bridge, **Puente de Toledo**, built between 1718 and 1732 for Felipe V *(see p23).* The architect was Pedro de Ribera.

The Manzanares, which is more of a stream than a river, never deserved such splendid bridges. It was the butt of many jokes; a German ambassador by the name of Rhebiner once said the river was the

best in Europe because it had the advantage of being "navigable by horse and carriage". Alexandre Dumas (1802–70), author of *The Three Musketeers*, wrote of the Manzanares during his visit to Madrid that "however hard I looked for it, I could not find it".

The river now has several dams, and the introduced fish and ducks have been able to survive, proving that the water is fairly clean. Rising in the Sierra de Guadarrama and eventually joining the River Tagus, the river forms a link between Spain's capital and Lisbon, the capital of Portugal.

Casa de Campo ⑭

Avenida de Portugal. **Tel** *91 463 63 34.* Ⓜ *Batán, Casa de Campo, Lago, Príncipe Pío.*

This former royal hunting ground of pine forests and scrubland extends over 17.5 sq km (6.7 sq miles) of south-

western Madrid. Its range of amenities and proximity to the centre make it a popular recreation area for *Madrileños*. Among its attractions are tennis courts, swimming pools, a boating lake, funfair – the **Parque de Atracciones** with over 50 rides – and the **Zoo-Aquarium**. In summer the park also stages concerts. One way to visit the park and take in the city's sights is to ride the **Teleférico** (cable car), which connects the Parque del Oeste with the Casa de Campo.

Tiger from the zoo at Casa de Campo

🐾 **Zoo-Aquarium**
Tel *91 512 37 70.* Ⓜ *Batán.*
◯ *11am–dusk daily.* 🅿️ 🅰️
www.zoomadrid.com

🎡 **Parque de Atracciones**
Tel *90 234 50 01.* Ⓜ *Batán.* ◯ *Sep–Easter: from noon Sat &Sun; Easter–Sep: from noon daily. Closing times vary from month to month, check locally.* 🅿️ **www**.parquedeatracciones.es

🚠 **Teleférico**
Paseo del Pintor Rosales. **Tel** *91 541 74 50.* Ⓜ *Argüelles.* ◯ *noon–dusk Sat, Sun & public hols; Apr–Sep: noon–dusk Mon–Fri.* 🅰️ 🅱️

Ermita de San Antonio de la Florida ⑮

Glorieta San Antonio de la Florida 5. **Tel** *91 542 07 22.* Ⓜ *Príncipe Pío.* ◯ *9:30am–8pm Tue–Fri, 10am–2pm Sat & Sun.* ◯ *public hols.* 🚫 🅱️
www.munimadrid.es/ermita

Goya enthusiasts should not miss this remarkable Neo-Classical church, built during the reign of Carlos IV *(see p23).* Standing on the site of two previous churches, the present building is dedicated to St Anthony and is named after the pastureland of La Florida, on which the original churches were built.

It took Goya *(see p28)* just four months in 1798 to paint the cupola's immense fresco. It depicts St Anthony raising a murdered man from the dead so that he can prove innocent

The buttressed arches of Puente de Segovia over the Río Manzanares

Egyptian temple of Debod, with two of its original gateways

Guadarrama mountains. The park is the site of the former Montaña barracks. In 1936, they were stormed by the people of Madrid in their hunger for weaponry. It was a desperate bid on their part to arm themselves against General Franco's encroaching army at the start of the Spanish Civil War *(see p20)*. It is also a place where many lost their lives to Napoleon in 1808.

Nearby is the **Paseo del Pintor Rosales**, popular for its pavement (sidewalk) cafés.

Estación de Príncipe Pío ⑰

Paseo de la Florida 2. **Map** 3 A1.
Tel 90 224 02 02. 🚇 *Príncipe Pío.*

Also known as Estación del Norte, this railway station was opened in 1880 to supply train services between Madrid and the north of Spain. Built by French engineers Biarez, Grasset and Mercier, iron from French and Belgian foundries was its main component. In 1915, the station's look was enhanced by Mudéjar-style pavilions designed by Demetrio Ribes. The entrance façade was added by architect Luis Martínez Ribes in 1926.

In the main building of the former station there are bars, restaurants, cinemas and a shopping centre. Another part of the station is a major transport interchange. Above the platforms is a splendid latticework canopy. Looking out along the tracks, it is possible to see the Sierra de Guadarrama.

the saint's falsely accused father. Ordinary characters from late 18th-century Madrid are also featured in the painting. They include low-life types and lively *majas* – shrewd but elegant women. The fresco is considered one of Goya's finest works. The artist lies buried under the dome of this church.

Templo de Debod ⑯

Paseo del Pintor Rosales.
Map 1 B5. ***Tel*** 91 366 74 15.
🚇 *Plaza de España, Ventura Rodríguez.* ◯ *10am–2pm Sat & Sun; Apr–Sep: 10am–2pm, 6–8pm Tue–Fri; Oct–Mar: 9:45am–1:45pm, 4:15–6:15pm Tue–Fri.* ● *public hols.*
📷 *Sat, by arrangement.*
www.munimadrid.es/templodebod

The authentic Egyptian temple of Debod was built in the 2nd century BC. It was given to Spain in 1968 by the Egyptian government as a tribute to Spanish engineers involved in rescuing ancient monuments from the flood-waters of the

Aswan Dam on the River Nile. The temple's carvings depict Amen, a Theban god with a ram's head, symbolizing life and fertility, to whom the temple is dedicated.

Situated on high ground above the Río Manzanares, and surrounded by the landscaped gardens of the **Parque del Oeste**, the temple stands in a line with two of its original three gateways. From here there are sweeping views stretching as far as the

The elegant main entrance to the Estación de Príncipe Pío

THREE GUIDED WALKS

Madrid is an excellent city for walkers: the contrast between the wide, majestic boulevards, grand squares and narrow back streets make for a continually varied experience.Compared to many capitals, Madrid is not a large city and most of the main tourist attractions are fairly close to each other.

Flamenco dancer, Corral de la Morería

Each of the three central areas described in the *Area-by-Area* section of this book has a short walk marked on its *Street-by-Street* map. These walks have been designed to take you past many of the most interesting sights in that particular area. On the following five pages, however, are routes for three walks that take you through areas of Madrid not covered in detail elsewhere. These range from the remnants of Moorish Madrid and vestiges of Spanish royalty in the Bailén district, to the capital's bustling gay district of Chueca, best undertaken at night to get the most out of the area *(see pp116-117)*, to the historic contrast between rich and poor in the Lavapiés and Letras districts *(see pp118-119)*. Along each of the walks suggestions are given for refreshment and dining stopping off points to make each route a more leisurely experience.

Sociedad General de Autores near Chueca *(see p116)*

CHOOSING A WALK

The Three Walks
This map shows the location of the three guided walks in relation to the main sightseeing areas of Madrid.

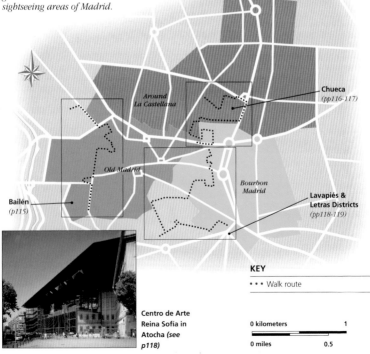

Around La Castellana

Chueca *(pp116-117)*

Old Madrid

Bourbon Madrid

Bailén *(p115)*

Lavapiés & Letras Districts *(pp118-119)*

Centro de Arte Reina Sofía in Atocha *(see p118)*

KEY

• • • Walk route

0 kilometers   1

0 miles   0.5

A 90-Minute Walk in the Bailén District

Old Madrid was mostly built on a plateau, and because of its superb vantage point the Moors built their Alcázar fortress on the ridge. The magnificent Palacio Real now stands on the site. This walk follows the ridge and Calle de Bailén past monuments such as the Arab city walls, two cathedrals, the royal palace, a Habsburg convent, and an incongruous Egyptian temple.

Café de Oriente
in Plaza de Oriente ⑦

Basilica de San Francisco el Grande to Plaza del Oriente

Start at the Basilica de San Francisco el Grande ① in Plaza de San Francisco (see pp60–61), a few minutes' walk from La Latina station. St Francis of Assisi visited Madrid in 1217 and founded the order that built this 18th-century church, which features the largest dome in Madrid. Follow Calle de Bailén and just before the bridge on the left is the Ventorillo Café & Terraza de las Vistillas ② at Bailén 14. In summer many watch the sunset here with views across the Manzanares River to the Guadarrama Mountains and the Casa de Campo (see p112). Nearby is the flamenco venue Corral de la Morería ③ at Calle de Morería 17.

Cross the viaduct over Calle de Segovia, continue up and turn left at the lights at the junction with Calle Mayor for the remains of a 9th-century Arab wall, the Muralla Arabe ④ (see p60). Back on Bailén, turn left to the Catedral de la Almudena ⑤. Built between 1883 and 1993, Carlos V had proposed a cathedral here 475 years earlier (see p61). Alongside it

is the visitors' entrance to the Palacio Real ⑥, built in 1764 on the site of a Moorish Alcázar destroyed by fire (see pp54–5). Cross Bailén to the Plaza de Oriente (see p58). A good refreshment stop is the Café de Oriente ⑦ (see p165).

Plaza del Oriente to Plaza de España

At the top of the plaza is Teatro Real ⑧, the city's opera house (see p58). Turn left down Calle de Felipe V and left into Calle de Arrieta to reach the Monasterio de la Encarnación ⑨, whose severe exterior belies the riches within (see p53). Go along Calle de la Encarnación

to reach the Palacio del Senado ⑩. The 16th-century building was once a university and convent, but was rebuilt in 1814 as the Spanish parliament, later to become the senate (see p53). On your left is the La Mi Venta *tapas* bar ⑪. At the bottom of the street turn left and left again to arrive at the Jardines de Sabatini ⑫. Exit northwards to Cuesta de San Vicente and walk up to Plaza de España ⑬ and the monument to Cervantes (see p53). Leave by the northern corner into Calle de Ferraz towards the Museo de Cerralbo ⑭, with its fine collection of paintings, furniture and porcelain (see p52).

Continue up Ferraz to the Templo de Debod ⑮, a 2nd-century BC Egyptian temple presented to Spain in 1968 (see p115). Return to Plaza de España for the nearest metro.

KEY

• • Walk route

Ⓜ Metro station

0 meters	400
0 yards	400

A 90-Minute Walk in and around Chueca

After the death of Franco in 1975 *(see p20)* Spain experienced a revolutionary transformation, which exploded in the *Movida* cultural movement of the early 1980s *(see p106)* when the innovative and the shocking were all the rage. The rundown Chueca area emerged as the new capital of hip fashion and was colonized by the gay community. Now all are welcome to its myriad of trendy shops, restaurants, *tapas* bars and discos packed into its maze of streets. To make the most of this walk, do it in early evening.

Iglesia de Santa Bárbara ②

Plaza de Santa Bárbara to Plaza de Chueca

Start near Plaza de Santa Bárbara outside the Sociedad General de Autores de España on Calle de Fernando VI ①, one of the finest Modernist buildings in Madrid *(see p33)*. The SGAE collects royalties of writers, one of whom was the composer Federico Chueca

(1846–1908), creator of many comic operas and *zarzuelas* and after whom this area of the city is named.

Walk down Calle de Fernando VI to the Iglesia de Santa Bárbara ② beside Plaza de Las Salesas, named after the Salesian order *(see p95)*. The church was built in the 18th century for Bárbara de Braganza and she is buried with her husband, Fernando VI, in the Baroque tombs here. Walk up to Plaza Villa de Paris ③. On one side is Spain's Tribunal Supremo ④, built between 1750–58 by Bárbara de Braganza as a school and monastery adjoining her church, but used as a court since 1870 *(see p95)*.

Leave the plaza by Calle de García Gutiérrez opposite the court and pass on your left the Audiencia Nacional ⑤. This modern complex witnesses trials for terrorism and other major Spanish crimes. Turn right

into Calle de Génova and walk down to Plaza de Colón ⑥ with its Christopher Columbus column *(see p98)*. The Jardines de Descubrimiento are dedicated to the discovery of America. On the right is the large 19th-century National Library with the Museo Arqueológico Nacional *(see pp96–7)* behind.

Turn right into Paseo de Recoletos and reach, on the right, the lovely *belle époque*-style bar and restaurant El Espejo ⑦. Across the road is its pavilion and summer terrace *(see p167)*. Further down Paseo de Recoletos is the venerable Café Gijón ⑧. For

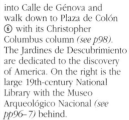

TIPS FOR WALKERS

Starting point: *Sociedad General de Autores, Fernando VI 6.*
Length: *2 km (1 mile).*
Getting there: *The start of this walk is on the 3, 21 and 37 bus routes or 200 m (220 yd) from Alonso Martínez metro station.*
Stopping off points: *Paseo de Recoletos is a long street with a central pedestrianised strip and is lined with restaurants and cafés, including the famous Café Gijon. Plaza de Chueca is also a good stopping off point for a drink, especially in early evening. Calle de la Libertad and Gran Vía are also good places to find good value bars and cafés where you can ease tired feet.*

El Espejo restaurant pavilion ⑦

Casa de Ángel Sierra on Plaza de Chueca ⑫

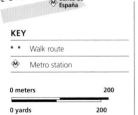

KEY

• • Walk route

Ⓜ Metro station

0 meters	200
0 yards	200

more than a century intellectuals frequented here but now you are just as likely to see a banker or a fellow tourist *(see p96)*. Just before Café Gijon is Calle del Almirante ⑨ with a host of fashion shops *(see p96)*.

Continue down Calle del Almirante passing Calle de Barquillo and its hi-fi shops ⑩, and you will reach Plaza de Chueca ⑪. This is the nerve centre of the gay area with outdoor café tables in summer *(see p96)*.

Plaza de Chueca to Gran Via
Overlooking the plaza is Casa de Ángel Sierra, an old *bodega* with lots of character ⑫. Leave the plaza opposite this bar, turn right into Calle de Augusto Figueroa and left into Calle de San Bartolomé. The Restaurante El Armario at San Bartolomé 7 ⑬ has a good reputation, as does the intimate disco alongside, Why Not, at San Bartolomé 6 ⑭.

Walking straight on you reach Plaza de Vázquez de Mella ⑮. The entrance to the underground car park includes a huge red anti-AIDS ribbon cast in steel. Walk through the

plaza and turn left down Calle de las Infantas. Turn back to Calle de la Libertad, named after local nuns whose main task was to get Christians released from the Moors in the 11th century. Bocaíto ⑯ at Libertad 4-6 is a renowned *tapas* bar *(see p170)*. Further up, also on the right, is Café Libertad 8 ⑰, a relaxed Bohemian bar with live music in the back room.

Turn right down Calle de San Marcos and then right again into Calle de Barquillo to reach Plaza del Rey on your right. Here the Casa de las Siete Chimeneas ⑱ is easy to see with its seven tall chimneys. Built in the 16th century, legend has it that a beautiful but wayward *señorita* lived here, "protected" by the king. The king was forced to arrange a marriage for her and gave her seven gold coins, signifying her seven deadly sins. She died a mysterious death in the mansion and her ghost is said to materialize at night between the seven chimneys. The building is now home to the Ministry of Culture.

Across the plaza is Liquid ⑲ at Barquillo 8, a minimalist techno bar popular with the gay set. Walk down Barquillo to Calle de Alcalá, turn right and continue until you reach the bar known as Museo Chicote ⑳ at Gran Vía 12. Sit back after your walk and enjoy a cocktail in its lovely Art Deco interior.

Entrance portal of the Casa de las Siete Chimeneas ⑱

A Two-Hour Walk in the Lavapiés & Letras Districts

Central Madrid is divided into *barrios* (districts) each with their own identity, and the contrasts you will encounter on this walk are fascinating. The cobbled streets of Lavapiés, the old Jewish Quarter, slope up towards the city centre, and the 19th-century *corralas* (tenements) here testify to the original working-class population. Today immigrants from Morocco, India and China inhabit the area, and Arab tearooms, Indian restaurants and Chinese stores abound. In contrast Letras is so called because many giants of Spanish literature lived here, close to theatres and other cultural centres.

Taberna Antonio Sánchez ⑩

writers. Return to the plaza and turn into Calle de Tribulete ⑤ with its Arab tearooms, Indian shops and the specialist comic shop El Coleccionista ⑥.

On the corner of Calle del Mesón de Paredes is La Corrala ⑦, one half of a typical 19th-century tenement block *(see p113).* Another *corrala* is nearby at Tribulete 25 ⑧. Retrace your steps passing Chinese-run clothes shops and the Biblioteca Esculeas Pías ⑨ and walk up Mesón de Paredes. At No. 13 is the Taberna Antonio Sánchez ⑩, run by a matador named Antonio Sánchez from 1870. His son also became a

New wing of the Centro de Arte Reina Sofía ①

The Lavapiés District

Start near the Atocha metro station, at the Centro de Arte Reina Sofía ① which was opened in 1992 in a former 18th-century hospital to display Spanish art from 1900 to the present day *(see pp84–7).* You reach the modern Jean Nouvel-designed extension, opened in 2005, by turning

TIPS FOR WALKERS

Starting point: *Centro de Arte Reina Sofía.*
Length: *3 km (2 miles).*
Getting there: *The Atocha metro station and bus routes 6, 10, 14, 19, 27, 34, 37 and 45 will take you to the starting point of this walk.*
Warning: *Petty crime is rife in Lavapiés so make sure you do this walk in daylight.*
Stopping off points: *Calle de Tribulete is a good stop for a cup of Arab tea, or, for something more substantial, stop at the Taberna Antonio Sánchez on Mesón de Paredes.*

left outside the museum and walking up Calle de Santa Isabel. On your right is Calle de Doctor Mata where Madrid's premier music school, the Real Conservatorio Superior de Música is situated ②.

Turn left down Calle del Hospital then right up Calle de Argumosa towards Plaza de Lavapiés, the old Jewish area. On the left is the rebuilt Teatro Olimpia ③. Crossing the plaza to Calle de Ave María, you reach the Barbieri café ④, an old haunt for artists and

KEY

••• Walk route

Ⓜ Metro station

0 meters   250

0 yards   250

bullfighter, but after a serious goring he retired to run the bar and his victims and paintings adorn the walls.

Carry on up Mesón de Paredes and turn right into Calle de Soler y González which becomes Calle de la Cabeza. On the corner with Calle de Lavapiés is Bar

Banco de España Ⓜ

Cine Doré exterior ⑬

Avapiés ⑪, once a medieval prison and part of an ancient *corrala*. Further up, on the corner with Calle del Olivar is Casa Lastra ⑫, which has been serving Asturian cuisine for decades. Follow Cabeza to Calle de Rosa and ahead is the charming Cine Doré cinema building ⑬ at Calle de Santa Isabel, which opened in 1923, and is one of the National Film archive sites.

1635 *(see p76)*. Turn right into Calle de San Agustín to reach the burial place of Cervantes ⑮ in the Convento de las Trinitarias, although there is no marked grave. Turn left then left again to Plaza de Jesús; at No. 2 is Los Gatos *tapas* bar ⑯ with a collection of memorabilia. Nearby is the Basílica Jesús de Medinaceli ⑰ where kissing a 17th-century sculpture of Jesus is said to redeem one's sins. Walk up Duque de Medinaceli, pass the Hotel Palace ⑱ on your right *(see p71)* and enter Plaza de las Cortes ⑲. The Congreso de los Diputados ⑳ is flanked by bronze lions *(see p78)*.

Take Calle Fernanflor to Calle de los Jovellanos to view the Teatro de la Zarzuela ㉑, where light operas are performed *(see p186)*. Turn right into Calle de los Madrazo, then left into Calle de Marqués de Casa Riera, and finish at the Círculo de Bellas Artes ㉒ art complex *(see 69)* near Banco de España metro station.

The Letras District

Head to Plaza de Antón Martín and cross Calle de Atocha to reach the start of Calle del León. You are now in Letras where the authors of the Spanish Golden Age lived. On the corner of León and Calle de Cervantes is a plaque to show that Cervantes *(see p28)* lived in the house. Walk down Cervantes to the Casa de Lope de Vega ⑭. The playwright lived here from 1610 to

Eclectic decor at Los Gatos tapas bar and restaurant ⑯

Elegant glass-domed lounge of the famous Hotel Palace ⑱

View across the landscape towards El Escorial (see pp126–9) ▷

BEYOND MADRID

BEYOND MADRID

Spain's vast central plateau consists mainly of wheat fields and awesome expanses of sienna and ochre plains which exude an empty beauty. Yet it also has mountains, gorges, forests and lakes filled with wildlife, while the towns and cities are permeated with history, reflected in some stunning architecture – Toledo's Gothic cathedral, Segovia's alcázar and the 15th-century castle at Manzanares el Real.

It is surprising how quickly one can escape past Madrid's dormitory towns and industrial estates to the real countryside. There is plenty of superb scenery and good walking country in the sierras to the north – a refuge for city dwellers who go there to ski in winter or sail and windsurf during the torrid summers. The Sierra Norte offers a paradise for birdwatchers, especially around the Moorish town of Buitrago del Lozoya.

In the western foothills of these mountains stands El Escorial, the royal monastery-palace built by Felipe II, from which he ruled his empire. Close by is the Valle de los Caídos, the war monument erected by Franco. The smaller royal palace of El Pardo is on the outskirts of Madrid, and south of the city is the 18th-century Aranjuez summer palace, set in lush parkland.

Historic towns include Alcalá de Henares – the birthplace of Cervantes, Sigüenza, with its impressive castle-parador, and Chinchón, where local garlic, wine and anis are sold beneath the creaking wooden balconies of its medieval plaza. Segovia, from where Felipe II's predecessors ruled Castile, is packed at weekends as visitors sample the famous roast lamb and suckling-pig and stop to admire its aqueduct – the largest Roman structure in Spain.

Toledo, which was the capital of Visigothic Spain, is an outstanding museum city. Its rich architectural and artistic heritage derives from a coalescence of Muslim, Christian and Jewish cultures with medieval and Renaissance ideas.

The picturesque Monasterio de El Parral in Segovia

◁ Celebration of Mass in the church of the Monasterio de Santa María de El Paular

Exploring Beyond Madrid

Stretching along the northern horizon of the province of Madrid are the peaks of the Sierra de Guadarrama. Reaching to 2,430 m (7,972 ft), they are often capped with snow until June. There are many hiking and even skiing opportunities in these mountains. Below, in the pine-scented southern folds of the Guadarrama, basks the monolithic monastery of El Escorial.

To the south lies the *meseta*, Spain's vast central plateau. Thanks to the mountains, rivers flow towards the arid plains, creating fertile valleys where olives grow. The historic towns of Castile nestle amid the rocky promontories. The River Jarama joins the Tagus *(Tajo)* near the 18th-century Royal Summer Palace and gardens in Aranjuez. Downstream it curls around ancient Toledo.

The 15th-century Casa de los Picos *(see p128)* in Segovia

Vast, fertile plain of the Spanish meseta

SIGHTS AT A GLANCE

Exterior of Casa-Museo de El Greco *(see p143)* in Toledo

SEGOVI **7**
LA GRANJA DE **6** SAN ILDEFONSO
Lagunas de Peñalara
SIERRA CENTRO DE **4** GUADARRAMA
    Cerceo
Ávila   NVI   Navacerrada
    Guadarra
SANTA CRUZ DEL **2** VALLE DE LOS CAÍDOS
   A6   AP6
    Torrelod
EL ESCORIAL **1**   Galápa
    Robledo de Chavela
Embalse de San Juan   Brunete
   Chapinería
   Aldea del Fresno
   Navalcarnero
Méntrida
    El Álamo
   A5
Santa Cruz del Retamar
   Fuensalida
CASTILLA LA MANCH
Torrijos
    Mo
Bargas
TOLEDO **18**

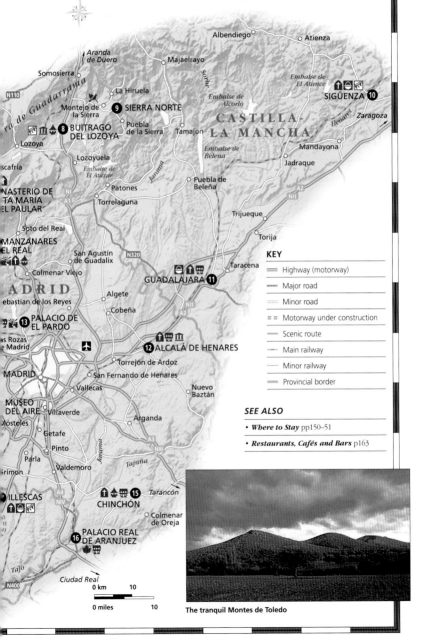

GETTING AROUND

The best way to explore sites beyond Madrid is with a car and a good map reader. Six toll-free dual carriageways (the A1 to A6), four toll motorways (the R2, R3, R4 and R5) and the free motorway to Toledo (the A42) fan out from the city, linked by the M30 and M40 ring roads. Be aware that as Spain is in the process of changing its road numbering system some of the roads featured here may differ from new road signs. Scheduled bus services can be slow. Railways serve the historic cities.

Albendiego
Atienza
Aranda
de Duero
Majaelrayo
Somosierra
N110
Embalse de
El Atance
SIGÜENZA ⑩
La Hiruela
Embalse de
Alcorlo
CASTILLA-
LA MANCHA
Zaragoza
Montejo de
la Sierra
⑨ SIERRA NORTE
Henares
⑧ BUITRAGO
DEL LOZOYA
Puebla
de la Sierra
Tamajón
Lozoya
Mandayona
scafría
Lozoyuela
Embalse de
El Atazar
Embalse de
Belena
Jadraque
NASTERIO DE
TA MARIA
L PAULAR
Patones
Torrelaguna
Puebla de
Beleña
Soto del Real
Trijueque
MANZANARES
EL REAL
San Agustín
de Guadalix
N320
Torija
ADRID
Colmenar Viejo
Taracena

KEY

▬▬▬	Highway (motorway)
▬ ▬	Major road
▬▬▬	Minor road
= =	Motorway under construction
▬	Scenic route
▬·▬	Main railway
▬	Minor railway
▬▬▬	Provincial border

GUADALAJARA ⑪
ebastian de los Reyes
Algete
Cobeña
⑬ PALACIO DE
EL PARDO
s Rozas
e Madrid
⑫ ALCALÁ DE HENARES
MADRID
Torrejón de Ardoz
San Fernando de Henares
Vallecas
Nuevo
Baztán
MUSEO
DEL AIRE
Villaverde
Arganda
Móstoles
Getafe
Pinto
Parla
Valdemoro
Tajuña
rimon
Tarancón
ILLESCAS
⑮
CHINCHÓN
Colmenar
de Oreja
⑯ PALACIO REAL
DE ARANJUEZ
Tajo
Ciudad Real
N400

SEE ALSO

• **Where to Stay** pp150–51

• **Restaurants, Cafés and Bars** p163

0 km   10
0 miles   10

The tranquil Montes de Toledo

El Escorial ❶

Fresco by Luca Giordano

Felipe II's imposing grey palace of San Lorenzo de El Escorial stands out against the foothills of the Sierra de Guadarrama to the northwest of Madrid. It was built between 1563 and 1584 in honour of St Lawrence, and its unornamented severity set a new architectural style which became one of the most influential in Spain. The interior was conceived as a mausoleum and contemplative retreat rather than a splendid residence. Its artistic wealth, which includes some of the most important works of art of the royal Habsburg collections, is concentrated in the museums, chapterhouses, church, royal pantheon and library. In contrast, the Royal Apartments are remarkably austere.

★ Royal Pantheon
The funerary urns of Spanish monarchs line the marble mausoleum

Tourist entrance

Bourbon Palace

Architectural Museum

Sala de Batallas

Patio de los Reyes

Main entrance

Basílica
The highlight of this huge, decorated church is the lavish altarpiece. The chapel houses statues of Felipe II and Carlos I (Holy Roman Emperor Charles V) at prayer.

The Alfonso XII College
was founded by monks in 1875 as a boarding school.

★ Library
This impressive library held Felipe II's personal collection. At its peak it boasted 40,000 volumes and an exceptional number of precious manuscripts. The long Print Room has beautiful 16th-century ceiling frescoes by Tibaldi.

STAR FEATURES

★ Royal Pantheon

★ Library

★ Museum of Art

The Royal Apartments, on the second floor of the palace, consist of Felipe II's modestly decorated living quarters. His bedroom opens directly on to the high altar of the basilica.

★ **Museum of Art**
Flemish, Italian and Spanish paintings are on display in this ground floor museum. One highlight is The Calvary, by 15th-century Flemish artist Rogier van der Weyden.

The Patio de los Evangelistas is a temple by Herrera.

Chapterhouses
On display here is Carlos I's portable altar. The allegorical ceiling frescoes are grotesque in style.

VISITORS' CHECKLIST

Paseo de Juan de Borbón y Batemberg. *Tel* 91 890 59 04. 🚉 from Atocha or Chamartin. 🚌 661, 664 from Moncloa. ⏰ 10am–6pm Tue–Sun (till 5pm Oct–Mar). 🔴 1 & 6 Jan, Easter week, 1 May, 10 Aug, 12 Sep, 24, 25 & 31 Dec. 🎫 (Free Wed for European Union residents.) ✝ 9:30am daily; 7pm, 8pm Sat & Sun 🎦 📷 🛍
www.patrimonionacional.es

Felipe II commissioned the monastery in 1558. Since 1885, it has been run by Augustinian monks.

***The Glory of the Spanish Monarchy* by Luca Giordano**
This fresco above the main staircase depicts Carlos I, Felipe II, and the building of the monastery.

The Building of El Escorial
When chief architect Juan Bautista de Toledo died in 1567 he was replaced by Juan de Herrera, royal inspector of monuments. The plain architectural style of El Escorial is called desornamentado, *literally, "unadorned".*

Exploring El Escorial

Felipe II built this palace as the final resting place of his revered father, Carlos I of Spain – Holy Roman Emperor Charles V – whom he succeeded in 1556. The gigantic building, with around 2,600 windows, was sited on the slopes of the Guadarrama and offered a stunning view that stretched away to the Spanish Empire. Felipe II, as King of Naples, Sicily, Milan, The Netherlands, Spain and the New World, used the finest talent available in the realm to decorate the austere monastery. The official tour goes through the Royal Apartments and Royal Pantheon in 45 minutes, leaving you to explore the rest by yourself.

Infanta Isabel Clara by Bartolomé González in the Royal Apartments

ROYAL APARTMENTS

The Palacio de los Austrias, or Royal Apartments, are built around and adjoining the basilica. From her bed, the Infanta Isabel Clara (Felipe II's daughter) could see the high altar and the officiating priest. On the right wall are paintings of her and her sister Catalina by Bartolomé González (1564–1627); between them is a portrait of Felipe II by Sánchez Coello (1531–88).

The **Sala de Retratos** is full of portraits, beginning above the fireplace with *Carlos I* by Juan Pantoja de la Cruz (1553–1608) – a copy of the original painting by Titian lost in a fire in 1604. Moving anti-clockwise, the next portrait is of *Felipe II* by Antonio Moro (1519–76), then *Felipe III* by Pantoja de la Cruz, young *Felipe IV* by Bartolomé González and young *Carlos II* by Juan Carreño de

Miranda (1614–85). In a corner of the room, in a glass case, is the folding chair that Felipe II, afflicted by gout, used during the last years of his life.

At both ends of the **Salas de los Paseos** are magnificent German marquetry doors. Blue Talavera tiles cover the lower part of the walls, while the upper parts are decorated with 16th-century maps and paintings of famous Spanish military victories. Inlaid in the floor of this room and the next-door dining room are solar adjusters made in 1755 for setting clocks.

In the king's chamber, the bed stands where Felipe II died in September 1598, with a view of the basilica's high altar. In his study is the last portrait of the king from Pantoja's studio.

PANTHEONS

Directly beneath the high altar of the basilica is the **Royal Pantheon**, where almost all Spanish monarchs since Carlos I are laid to rest. This pantheon, with Spanish black

Altar in the Royal Pantheon, where most of the Spanish monarchs are laid to rest

marble, red jasper and Italian gilt bronze decorations, was finished in 1654. Kings lie on the left of the altar and queens on the right. The most recent addition to the pantheon is the mother of Juan Carlos I.

Of the eight other pantheons, one of the most notable is that of **Juan de Austria**, Felipe II's half-brother, who became a hero after defeating the Turks at the Battle of Lepanto. Also worth seeing is **La Tarta**, a white marble polygonal tomb that resembles a cake, where royal children are buried.

CHAPTERHOUSES

The Salas Capitulares, or Chapterhouses, in the monastery's southeast corner, contain wooden benches for the monastery's 100 monks. These four light and spacious rooms with their fine vaulted ceilings are decorated with numerous paintings.

Enamelled and gold-plated retable in the Chapterhouses

Among the highlights are some by Titian (1490–1576), who painted many scenes for El Escorial. Here can be seen his *St Jerome at Prayer* and *The Last Supper*, the latter unfortunately trimmed to fit its place. Diego de Velázquez (1599–1660) is also represented, with *Joseph's Tunic* (1630), painted while the artist was in Italy.

A collection of paintings by Hieronymus Bosch (1450–1516), known as "El Bosco", is found here. A version of *The Haywain* – the original hangs in the Prado *(see p78)* –was executed by the Bosch school. This painting is said to originate from the Flemish proverb, "The world is like a hay-cart and everybody takes what he can". Felipe II kept it in his bedroom, along with Bosch's *The Garden of Earthly Delights*, also in the Prado. A copy of one panel is displayed here. Nearby is the beautiful enamelled and gold-plated wooden retable of Carlos I, Holy Emperor Charles V. The king took this portable altar with him on military campaigns.

The Martyrdom of St Maurice and the Theban Legion by El Greco

THE MUSEUMS

Within El Escorial are several small museums. The north façade entrance leads to St Maurice's Hall, home of *The Martyrdom of St Maurice and the Theban Legion* by El Greco (1541– 1614). Nearby stairs lead down to the small **Architectural Museum**, which contains plans, models and engravings of the palace.

Upstairs, the **Museum of Art** covers mostly 16th- and 17th-century works. The first room is dedicated to Italian masters, while the next two contain Flemish art. Michel Coxcie (1499–1592), known as the "Flemish Rafael", is featured here. Most notable is *The Martyrdom of St Philip* triptych.

The long fourth room is dominated by the superb *Calvary* by Rogier van der Weyden (c. 1400–64), and copies of the Flemish master's *Virgin* and *St John* by Juan Fernández Navarrete (c. 1538– 79), on either side.

In the fifth room is *St Jerome Doing Penance* by José de Ribera (1591–1652). In the last room are 16th- and 17th-century Spanish and Italian paintings.

THE LIBRARY

Established by Felipe II, this was the first public library in Spain, and boasts a vaulted ceiling and a marble floor. In 1619 the king issued a decree that a copy of each new publication in his empire should be sent to him. At its zenith, it contained some 40,000 books and manuscripts, mainly from the 15th and 16th centuries.

The long **Print Room** has a marble floor and glorious vaulted ceiling. The ceiling frescoes by Pellegrino Tibaldi (1527–96) depict Philosophy, Grammar, Rhetoric, Dialectics, Music, Geometry, Astrology and Theology. The Doric wooden shelving was designed by Juan de Herrera (1530–97).

On each of the four main pillars hang portraits of members of the royal House of Austria – Carlos I, Felipe II, Felipe III and Carlos II. On display are coins and Felipe II's pine Ptolemaic sphere (1582), which placed the earth in the centre of the universe.

THE BASÍLICA

Historically, only the aristocracy were permitted to enter the basílica, while the townspeople were confined to the vestibule at the entrance. The Monks's Choir above is still closed to the public.

The basílica contains 45 altars. Among its highlights are the exquisite statue of *Christ Crucified* (1562) in Carrara marble by Benvenuto Cellini. It is found in the chapel to the left of the entrance, with steps leading up to it. Either side of the altar, above the doors leading to the royal bedrooms in the Palacio de los Austrias, are fine gilded bronze cenotaphs of Carlos I and Felipe II worshipping with their families.

The enormous altarpiece was designed by Juan de Herrera with coloured marble, jasper, gilt-bronze sculptures and paintings. The central tabernacle, backlit by a window, took Italian silversmith Jacoppo da Trezzo (1515–89) seven years to craft. The paintings are by Federico Zuccaro (1542– 1609) and Pellegrino Tibaldi, who also executed the fresco above. The wood for the cross (also used for Felipe II's coffin) came from a Spanish ship, the *Cinco Llagas* (Five Wounds).

PALACE OF THE BOURBONS

In contrast to the simple rooms of the Palacio de los Austrias (Felipe II's royal apartments), the Bourbon apartments are sumptuously furnished. They were created by Carlos IV (reigned 1788– 1808), and are hung with framed tapestries, some by Goya, from the Real Fábrica de Tapices (*see p110*).

A china cabinet displays the dinner service which was part of the trousseau of Victoria Eugenia (Queen Victoria's grand-daughter), when she married Alfonso XIII in 1906.

Dining room in the sumptuous Palacio de los Borbones (Palace of the Bourbons)

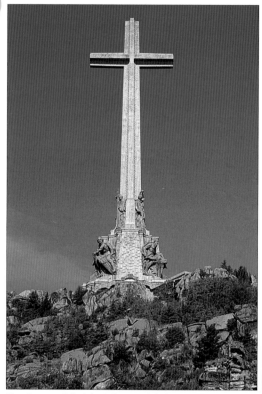

Gigantic cross at Valle de los Caídos, a symbol of Franco's dictatorship

Santa Cruz del Valle de los Caídos ❷

Madrid. North of El Escorial on M600.
Tel 91 890 56 11. 🚌 from El Escorial.
◯ Oct–Mar: 10am–5pm Tue–Sun;
Apr–Sep: 10am–6pm Tue–Sun.
⬤ 1 & 6 Jan, 1 May, 17 Jul, 10 Aug,
24, 25 & 31 Dec. 🎟 (free Wed to EU
residents) 🎫
www.patrimonionacional.es

General Franco had the Holy
Cross of the Valley of the
Fallen built as a memorial to
those who died in the
Spanish Civil War (see p20).
The vast cross is located some
13 km (8 miles) north of El
Escorial (see pp126–9), and
can be seen for miles in every
direction. Some Spaniards
find it too chilling a symbol of
the dictatorship to be enjoy-
able, while for others its sheer
size is rewarding.

The cross is 150 m (490 ft)
high and rises above a basilica
carved 250 m (820 ft) deep

into the rock by prisoners of
war. A number of them died
during the 20-year project.

Next to the basilica's high
altar is the plain white tomb-
stone of Franco and, opposite,
that of José Antonio Primo
de Rivera, founder of the
Falange Española party.
Another 40,000 coffins of
soldiers from both sides in
the Civil War lie here out
of sight, including those of
two unidentified victims.

Manzanares el Real ❸

Madrid. 🚊 6,140. 🚌 🛈 Plaza del
Pueblo 1 (91 853 00 09 / 63 917 96
02). 🛒 Tue & Fri. 🎉 Fiesta de Verano
(early Aug), Cristo de la Nave (14 Sep).

From a distance the skyline of
Manzanares el Real is
dominated by its restored 15th-
century castle. Although the
castle is equipped with some
traditional military features,
such as double machicolations
and turrets, it was used
mainly as a residential palace
by the Dukes of Infantado.
Below the castle is a 16th-
century church, a Renaissance
portico and fine capitals.
Behind the town, bordering
the foothills of the Sierra de
Guadarrama, is **La Pedriza**, a
mass of granite screes and
ravines, popular with climbers,
and part of a nature reserve.

Environs
Colmenar Viejo, 12 km (7.5
miles) to the southeast of
Manzanares, has a superb
Gothic-Mudéjar church.

Sierra Centro de Guadarrama ❹

Madrid. 🚊 Puerto de Navacerrada,
Cercedilla. 🚌 Navacerrada, Cercedilla.
🛈 Navacerrada (91 856 03 08).

The central section of the
Sierra de Guadarrama was
linked to Madrid by train in
the 1920s. The pine-covered
granite slopes are now dotted
with holiday chalets. Villages
such as **Navacerrada** and
Cercedilla have grown into
popular resorts for skiing,
mountain biking, rock climbing, horse riding and walking.

Breathtaking Navacerrada pass in the Sierra de Guadarrama

The **Valle de Fuenfría**, a nature reserve of wild forests, is best reached via Cercedilla. It has a well-preserved stretch of Roman road, as well as picnic spots and marked walks.

Altarpiece in the Monasterio de Santa María de El Paular

Monasterio de Santa María de El Paular ❺

Southwest of Rascafría on M604. *Tel* 91 869 14 25. 🚌 *Rascafría.* 🕐 *Noon, 1pm, 5pm Mon–Sat (no 5pm tour Thu); 1pm, 4pm, 5pm, 6pm Sun.*

Castile's first Carthusian monastery was founded in 1390 on the site of a medieval royal hunting lodge. Although Santa María de El Paular was built in the Gothic style, many Plateresque and Renaissance features were added later.

In 1836, when government minister Mendizábal ordered all church property to be given over to the state, the monastery was abandoned and fell into disrepair. It was not until the 1950s that the state decided to restore it. Today the complex, in a beautiful, tranquil setting, comprises a private hotel *(see p155)*, a working Benedictine monastery and a church.

The church's delicate alabaster altarpiece dates from the 15th century and is thought to be the work of Flemish craftsmen. Its panels are decorated with scenes from the life of Jesus Christ. The sumptuous Baroque *camarín* (chamber), behind the altar, dates from 1718 and was designed by Francisco de Hurtado.

Every Sunday, the monks sing an hour-long Gregorian chant. It is worth asking them to show you the cloister's Mudéjar brick vaulting and double sundial. They are happy to do this if they are not busy.

The monastery constitutes an excellent starting point from which to explore the attractive country towns of **Rascafría** and **Lozoya** in the surrounding Lozoya valley. To the southwest lies the **Lagunas de**

La Granja de San Ildefonso ❻

Plaza de España 17, Segovia. *Tel* 921 47 00 19. 🚌 *from Madrid or Segovia.* 🕐 *Oct– Mar: 10am–1:30pm, 3–5pm Tue–Sat, 10am–2pm Sun & public hols; Apr–Oct: 10am–6pm Tue–Sun.* **Gardens** 🕐 *10am–6pm daily (closing times may vary).* ● *1, 6, & 23 Jan, 1 May, 25 Aug, 24, 25 & 31 Dec.* 🎫 *(free Wed to EU residents).* 🖥 *www.*patrimonionacional.es

This Royal Pleasure Palace stands on the site of a hunting lodge built by Enrique IV in the 15th century.

In 1720, Felipe V embarked on a project to build the palace and numerous artists and architects contributed to the rich furnishings and the splendid gardens. Some rooms were damaged by fire in 1918, but nearly 8 million euros have been spent restoring them.

There are countless salons decorated with *objets d'art* and Classical frescoes. From the ceilings hang huge chandeliers. The church is adorned in high Baroque style, and the Royal Mausoleum contains the tomb of Felipe V and his queen, Isabel de Farnesio.

The spectacular garden fountains portray Felipe V and his queen as Apollo and Diana. They run on Wednesdays, Saturdays and Sundays at 5:30pm.

Serenely beautiful royal gardens at La Granja de San Ildefonso

Segovia ⑦

Tower of San Esteban

Segovia is the most spectacularly sited city in Spain. The old town is set high on a rocky spur and is surrounded by the Río Eresma and Río Clamores. From afar it looks like a ship, the medieval alcázar on its sharp crag forming the prow, the pinnacles of the Gothic cathedral rising up like masts, and the aqueduct trailing behind like a rudder. The view of the old town from the valley below at sunset is magical.

A relatively short journey from Madrid by car, bus or train, Segovia is readily accessible to visitors to the capital and well worth a look. Easy to negotiate on foot, there is plenty to see and do for a day trip or an overnight stay. Weekends, particularly in summer, are the busiest time in Segovia.

The imposing Gothic cathedral of Segovia

Exploring Segovia

Segovia is dotted with many notable churches, including the 11th-century Romanesque **San Juan de los Caballeros**, with a fine sculptured portico; 13th-century **San Esteban** with a five-storey tower; and 11th-century **San Martín** with its arcades, capitals and gilded altarpiece. The **Iglesia de San Millán**, a Romanesque jewel in the newer part of town, has a Mozarabic tower and a 14th-century Gothic crucifix. The **Iglesia de la Vera Cruz**, outside the old town, is a 12-sided crusader's church (1208).

🏛 Cathedral

Plaza Mayor. **Tel** 921 46 22 05.
◯ 9:30am–5:30pm Mon–Sat (6:30pm Apr–Sep); 1:30–5.30pm Sun (6:30pm Apr–Sep). 🈂 👤
Dating from 1525, this massive Gothic structure replaced the old cathedral, which was destroyed in 1520. The old cloister, however, survived and was rebuilt on the new site. Architect Juan Gil de Hontañón devised the austere but elegant design. The pinnacles, flying buttresses, tower and dome form an impressive silhouette.

The interior is light and elegantly vaulted, with stained-glass windows. It has a high altar designed by Sabatini in 1768. Lining the nave and apse are 18 beautiful chapels, most enclosed by graceful ironwork grilles. The most interesting is the Chapel of the Pietà, which took its name from the beautiful sculpture by Juan de Juni. The cloister, whose pointed arches are divided by slender mullions and perforated tracery, is accessed through an outstanding Gothic arch by Juan Guas in the Chapel of Christ's Solace. The cloister leads to the chapterhouse museum, which houses 17th-century Brussels tapestries, paintings, sculptures, silver, furniture, books and coins.

🏛 Museo de Segovia

Casa del Sol, Calle Socorro 11.
Tel 921 46 06 13. ◯ Tue–Sun.
🈂 (free Sat & Sun).
This archaeological museum contains 15,000-year-old Stone Age engravings as well as tools, arms, pottery and metal-work through the centuries. There are Roman coins and inscriptions, wall fragments from Arab houses and a collection of belt buckles.

Also worth seeing are two huge Celtic stone bulls which were excavated in the Calle Mayor. It is thought they may have been divine protectors of people or livestock. In the nearby province of Avila, such icons are linked with burials.

🏛 Casa de los Picos

Just inside the city walls is the Casa de los Picos, a mansion whose 15th-century façade is adorned with diamond-shaped stones. The building houses an art gallery and school.

⛲ Aqueduct

In use until the late 19th century, this aqueduct was built at the end of the 1st century AD by the Romans, who turned ancient Segovia into an important military base. With this feat of engineering, water from the Río Frío flowed into the city, filtered through a series of tanks along the way.

The Roman aqueduct running through the old town

The Alcázar, like a fairy-tale castle rising above the cliff

VISITORS' CHECKLIST

Segovia. 56,000. Plaza del Azoguejo 1 (921 46 67 21). Tue, Thu, Sat. San Juan (24 Jun), San Pedro (29 Jun), San Frutos (25 Oct).

♔ Alcázar

Plaza de la Reina Victoria Eugenia. *Tel* 921 46 07 59. Oct–Mar: 10am–6pm; Apr–Sep: 10am–7pm. public hols. (free 3rd Tue of month for EU residents only). www.alcazardesegovia.com

Although there has been a fortress on this site since the Middle Ages, the present castle is mostly a reconstruction following a fire in 1862. Its rooms are decorated with armour, paintings and furniture for a medieval atmosphere. There is also a weaponry museum.

The virtually impregnable castle had its heyday in the Middle Ages. The rectangular Juan II tower was completed during the reign of Enrique IV in the 15th century and named after his father. It is worth climbing to the top for breathtaking views of Segovia and the Guadarrama mountains. In 1764 Carlos III founded the Royal School of Artillery. Two of its pupils, Daoiz and Velarde, became heroes in the 1808 uprising of *Madrileños* against the French (see p18).

♖ Palacio Episcopal

Plaza De San Esteban. *Tel* 921 46 09 63. to the public.

Built for the Salcedos family, the 16th-century Palacio Episcopal was later acquired by Bishop Murillo.

♙ Monasterio de El Parral

Subida Al Parral 2. *Tel* 921 43 12 98. 10am–12:30pm, 4:15–6:30pm Mon–Sat; 10–11:30am, 4:15–6:30pm Sun.

Just north of the city walls, Segovia's largest monastery has four cloisters and a Plateresque altarpiece. It contains the Plateresque tombs of its benefactor, the Marqués de Villena, and his wife, María.

♙ Iglesia de los Carmelitas

Alameda de la Fuencisla. *Tel* 921 43 13 49. 4–7pm Mon, 10am–1:30pm, 4–7pm Tue–Sun (till 8pm Jun–Sep).

In a secluded Eresma valley, St John of the Cross founded this convent in the 16th century and was Prior from 1588–91. The mystical poet was also co-founder, with Santa Teresa, of a barefooted (*descalzos*) order of Carmelites which ran to the strictest of disciplines.

The tree-lined Plaza Mayor

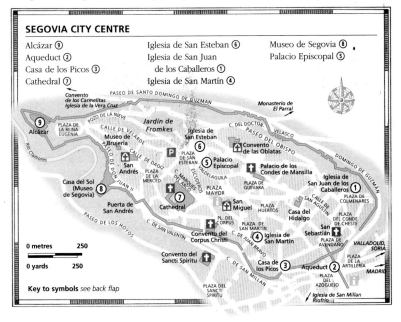

SEGOVIA CITY CENTRE

Alcázar ⑨
Aqueduct ②
Casa de los Picos ③
Cathedral ⑦
Iglesia de San Esteban ⑥
Iglesia de San Juan de los Caballeros ①
Iglesia de San Martín ④
Museo de Segovia ⑧
Palacio Episcopal ⑤

0 metres 250
0 yards 250

Key to symbols *see back flap*

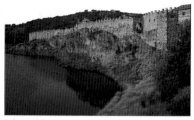

Buitrago del Lozoya, standing next to the river

Buitrago del Lozoya ❽

Madrid. 🏘 *1,800.* 🚌 ℹ️ *Calle Tahona 11 (91 868 16 15).* 🚃 *Sat.* 🎉 *La Asunción y San Roque (15 Aug), Cristo de los Esclavos (15 Sep).*

Picturesquely sited above a meander in the Río Lozoya is the walled town of Buitrago del Lozoya. Founded by the Romans, it was fortified by the Arabs, and became a bustling market town in medieval times. The 14th-century Gothic-Mudéjar castle is in ruins, although the gatehouse, arches and stretches of the original wall survive. Today, the castle is used as a venue for bullfights and a festival of theatre and music in the summer.

The old quarter, within the town's walls, retains its charming atmosphere. The church of **Santa María del Castillo**, dating from the 14th century, has a Mudéjar tower and ceilings moved here from the old hospital. The **town hall**, or *ayuntamiento*, in the newer part of the town preserves a 16th-century processional cross. In the basement is the small **Museo Picasso**. The prints, drawings and ceramics on display were collected by the artist's friend and barber, Eugenio Arias, an inhabitant of the town.

🏛 **Museo Picasso**
Plaza de Picasso 1. *Tel 91 868 00 56.* ⬤ *Mon, Wed pm, Sun pm.*

Sierra Norte ❾

Madrid. 🚏 *Montejo.* ℹ️ *Calle Real 64, Montejo (91 869 70 58).* **www.**sierranorte.com

The black slate hamlets of the Sierra Norte, which was once known as the Sierra Pobre (Poor Sierra), are located in the most rural part of the Comunidad de Madrid (Madrid province). At **Montejo de la Sierra**, the largest village in the area, an information centre organizes riding, rental of traditional houses and visits to the nature reserve of the **Hayedo de Montejo de la Sierra**. This is one of the southernmost beech woods in Europe and a relic of an era when climatic conditions were more suitable for the beech. From Montejo, you can drive on to picturesque hamlets such as **La Hiruela** or **Puebla de la Sierra**, both of which are set in lovely walking country.

The drier southern hills slope down to the **Embalse de Puentes Viejas**, a reservoir where summer chalets cluster around artificial beaches. On the eastern edge of the Sierra Norte lies **Patones**, which supposedly escaped invasion by the Moors and Napoleon due to its isolated location.

Sigüenza ❿

Guadalajara. 🏘 *4,800.* 🚌 ℹ️ *Ermita del Humilladero (949 34 70 07).* 🚃 *Sat.* 🎉 *San Juan (24 Jun), San Roque (15 Aug).* **www.**siguenza.es

Dominating the hillside town of Sigüenza is its impressive castle-parador *(see p155)*. The **cathedral**, in the old town, was begun in the 12th century. It is Romanesque

Semi-recumbent figure of El Doncel on his tomb in Sigüenza cathedral

in style, with later additions, such as the Gothic-Plateresque cloisters. In one of the chapels is the Tomb of *El Doncel* (the young nobleman). It was built for Martín Vázquez de Arce, Isabel de Castile's pageboy *(see p22)*, who was killed in a battle against the Moors in Granada in 1486. The sacristy has a beautiful ceiling carved with flowers and cherubs, by Alonso de Covarrubias.

Intricate diamond stonework on the façade of the Palacio de los Duques del Infantado

Guadalajara ⓫

Guadalajara. 🏠 73,700. 🚉 🚌 ℹ️ *Plaza de los Caídos 6 (949 21 16 26).* 🛒 *Tue, Sat.* 🎉 *Virgen de la Antigua (Sep).* **www**.guadalajara.es

Although Guadalajara's history is largely lost in the modern industrial city, traces of its past splendour survive. It was

founded as the Roman settlement of Arriaca, and then replaced by the Moorish settlement of Wad-al-Hajarah. In 1085 it was taken by Alfonso VI in the Christian Reconquest *(see p15)*, and rose to prominence in the 14th century.

The **Palacio de los Duques del Infantado**, built from the 14th to the 17th century by the powerful Mendoza dynasty, is an outstanding example of Gothic-Mudéjar architecture. The main façade and the two-storey patio are adorned with delicate carvings. Following Civil War bombing, the palace was restored. It now houses the Museo Provincial – the local art museum.

Among the town's churches is the **Iglesia de Santiago**, which has a Gothic-Plateresque chapel designed by Alonso de Covarrubias. In the 15th-century **Iglesia de San Francisco** was the family mausoleum of the Mendoza family, while the cathedral is built on the site of a mosque. The 13th-century **Iglesia de Santa María** has typical Mudéjar horseshoe arches and a bell tower.

🏛 Palacio de los Duques del Infantado
Plaza de los Caídos 13. **Tel** *949 21 33 01.* **Museum** ⭘ *Tue–Sun.* **Palace** ⭘ *Open daily.* 🎫 *(museum free Sat & Sun, palace daily).*

Façade of Colegio de San Ildefonso in Alcalá de Henares

Alcalá de Henares ⓬

Madrid. 🏠 200,000. 🚉 🚌 ℹ️ *Callejón Santa María (91 889 26 94).* 🛒 *Mon & Wed.* 🎉 *Feria de Alcalá (late Aug).* **www**.alcaladehenares-turismo.com

At the heart of a modern industrial town is one of Spain's most renowned university quarters. Founded in 1499 by Cardinal Cisneros, Alcalá's **university** became one of the foremost places of learning in 16th-century Europe, famous for its language teaching. The university was transferred to Madrid in 1836. Although most of the original 40 colleges have since been destroyed, the most historic one, the much-restored Renaissance **Colegio de San Ildefonso**, survives. It has a Plateresque façade (1543) by Rodrigo Gil de Hontañón. Former students include Lope de Vega *(see p28)*. In 1517 the university produced Europe's first polyglot bible, which had parallel texts in Latin, Greek, Hebrew and Chaldean.

Alcalá's other sights are the cathedral, the **Casa-Museo de Cervantes**, birthplace of the author and now an intriguing museum, and the recently restored 19th-century Neo-Moorish **Palacio de Laredo**.

🏛 Casa-Museo de Cervantes
Calle Mayor 48. **Tel** *918 89 96 54.* ⭘ *Tue–Sun.* 🔴 *public hols.* **www**.mcu.es/museos

🏛 Palacio de Laredo
Paseo de la Estación 18. **Tel** *91 880 28 83.* ⭘ *Tue–Sun.* 🎫

MIGUEL DE CERVANTES

Miguel de Cervantes Saavedra, Spain's greatest literary figure *(see p28)*, was born in Alcalá de Henares in 1547. After fighting in the naval Battle of Lepanto (1571), he was held captive by the Turks for more than five years. In 1605, when he was almost 60 years old, the first of two parts of his comic masterpiece *Don Quixote* was published to popular acclaim. Cervantes continued writing novels and plays until his death in Madrid on 23 April 1616, the same date that Shakespeare died.

Lavish, finely woven 18th-century tapestry inside the Palacio de El Pardo

Palacio de El Pardo ⑬

El Pardo, northwest of Madrid on A6. *Tel 91 376 15 00.* 🚌 *from Moncloa.* ⏰ *10:30am–5:45pm Mon–Sat (till 4:45pm Oct–Apr), 9:25am–1:30pm Sun and public hols (from 9:55am Oct–Apr).* ● *during royal visits and public hols.* 🎟 *(free Wed for EU residents).* **www**.patrimonionacional.es

This royal hunting lodge and palace, set in parkland, includes General Franco among its former residents. A tour takes visitors around the palace's original Habsburg wing and identical 18th-century extension by Francesco Sabatini.

The Bourbon interior is decorated with frescoes, gilt mouldings and tapestries, many of which were woven at the Real Fábrica de Tapices *(see p110)*. Today the palace is used to entertain heads of state and royalty. Surrounding the palace is an enormous oak forest, where you can eat at a restaurant or enjoy a picnic.

Museo del Aire ⑭

A5, km 10.5. *Tel 91 509 16 90.* 🚌 *from Estación del Príncipe Pío (Norte) any bus towards Alcorcón or Móstoles.* ⏰ *10am–2pm Tue–Sun.* ● *1 Jan, Easter Thu & Good Fri, 10 & 25 Dec.* ♿ **www**.aire.org

Among the many magnificent flying machines on display at the museum of Spanish aviation, the star exhibit is the Breguet-XIX *Jesús del Gran Poder*, which made the first Spanish transatlantic flight in 1929. Others include the 1911 Vilanova-Acedo, one of the first planes made in Spain, and the Henkel 111 German warplane, the only one ever made. Also on display is *La Cierva* – half-plane, half-helicopter.

Some of the planes are linked with famous people. For example, in 1936 General Franco flew from the Canary Islands to Tetuán to start the Spanish Civil War in the De Havilland *Dragon Rapide*; Juan Carlos I flew a Bell 47G solo; Prince Felipe made his first solo flight in a T-Mentor; and in the Trener Master, Tomás Castaños won the 1964 World Aerobatic Championships.

Prototypes of various Spanish aircraft include the Saeta, Super Saeta and the Casa C–101 Aviojet. The F–104 Starfighter, notorious for its tendency to crash, is one in which Spanish pilots flew a record 10,000 hours without accidents.

On the runway you may see the bulbous Boeing *Guppy*, which flies part of the fuselage (made nearby) of the Airbus to its assembly plant in France.

In addition to aircraft, the museum covers the lives of famous aviators, and features displays of Air Force regalia, flight plans and models. There are also films, videos, photographs and paintings.

Early Lufthansa aircraft at the Museo del Aire

◁ **Cattle grazing on the isolated plains of La Mancha**

Chinchón

Madrid. 🏠 4,800. 🚌 🛈 Plaza
Mayor 6 (91 893 53 23). 🚐 Sat.
🎭 Semana Santa (Easter Week),
San Roque (12–18 Aug).
www.ciudadchinchon.com

Chinchón is arguably Madrid
province's most picturesque
town. The 15th- to 16th-
century, typically Castilian,
porticoed **Plaza Mayor** has a
splendidly theatrical air. It
comes alive for the Easter
passion play (see p34) and
during the August bullfights.
The 16th-century church,
above the square, has an altar
painting by Goya (see p28),
whose brother was a priest
here. Just off the square an
18th-century Augustinian
monastery has been converted
into a parador with a peaceful
patio garden (see p171). There
is a ruined 15th-century castle
on a hill to the west of town.
It is closed to the public but,
from the outside, there are
good views of Chinchón and
the surrounding countryside.

Madrileños often come to the
town at weekends to sample
the superb chorizo and locally
produced *anís (see p163)* in
the town's many taverns.

Chinchón's unique porticoed Plaza Mayor, occasionally used for bullfights

Palacio Real de Aranjuez 🔟

Plaza de Parejas, Aranjuez. **Tel** 91 891
07 40. 🚌 🚐 🅿 Apr–Sep: 10am–
6:15pm Tue–Sun; Oct–Mar: 10am–
5:15pm; gardens daily until 8:30pm,
(6:30pm Oct–Mar) by appointment for
Casa del Labrador. ● 1 & 6 Jan, 1 & 30
May, 5 Sep, 24, 25 & 31 Dec (closed for
restoration until 2009). 💳 (free Wed to
EU residents). 📷 ♿
www.patrimonionacional.es

The Royal Summer Palace and
gardens of Aranjuez grew up
around a medieval hunting
lodge standing beside a natural weir, the meeting point of
the Tagus and Jarama rivers.

Today's palace was built by
Fernando VI and in the 18th
century Carlos III added two
wings. An earlier Habsburg
palace, commissioned by Felipe
II, once stood on this site and
was destroyed by fire. A
guided tour takes you through
numerous Baroque rooms,

including the Chinese Porcelain Room, the Hall of Mirrors
and the Smoking Room,
modelled on the Alhambra in
Granada. It is worth visiting
Aranjuez for the pleasure of
walking in the 3 sq km (1 sq
mile) of shady gardens which
inspired Joaquín Rodrigo's
Concierto de Aranjuez. The
Parterre Garden and Island
Garden survive from the
original 16th-century palace.

The 18th-century Prince's
Garden is decorated with
fountains and trees from the
Americas. The Casa de Marinos
(Sailors' House) is a small
museum housing boats once
used by the royal family.

At the far end of the garden
stands the Casa del Labrador
(Labourer's Cottage), a richly
decorated royal pavilion built
by Carlos IV (see p18).

Pleasant grounds at the Palacio Real de Aranjuez

In summer, a 19th-century
steam train, built to take
strawberries to the market
in Madrid, runs between
here and the capital.

Illescas 🔟

Toledo. 🏠 14,800. 🚌 🛈 Plaza
Mayor 1 (925 51 10 51). 🚐 Thu.
🎭 Fiesta de Milagro (11 Mar), Fiesta
Patronal (31 Aug). **www**.illescas.es

The town of Illescas was the
summer venue for the court
of Felipe II (see p17). While
there is little to see of the
old town, it does have two
interesting churches. The
Parroquial de la Asunción,
built between the 13th and
16th centuries, is easily identified by its Mudéjar tower, one
of the best examples of its
kind in the region.
Nearby is the 16th-
century church of
the **Hospital de
Nuestra Señora de
la Caridad,** which
boasts an important
art collection. The
church owns five
works by El Greco
(see p143), the most
famous being *The
Virgin Dictating to
Saint Ildefonso.* In
its Chapel of Relics
there is a portrait of
Francisco Pacheco
de Toledo by
Pantoja de la Cruz
and, in the sacristy,
there is an original
Ecce Homo by Luis
de Morales.

**🏛 Hospital de
Nuestra Señora de
la Caridad**
Calle Cardenal Cisneros
2. **Tel** 925 54 00 35.
🅿 daily. 📷 ♿

Street-by-Street: Toledo ⑱

Damascene work, typical of Toledo

Picturesquely sited on a hill above the River Tagus is the historic centre of Toledo. Behind the old walls lies much evidence of the city's rich history. The Romans built a fortress on the site of the present-day Alcázar. The Visigoths made Toledo their capital in the 6th century AD, and left behind several churches. In the Middle Ages, Toledo was a melting pot of Christian, Muslim and Jewish cultures, and it was during this period that the city's most outstanding monument – its cathedral – was built. In the 16th century the painter El Greco came to live in Toledo, and today the city is home to many of his works.

The Iglesia de San Román, of Visigothic origin, now contains a museum relating the city's past under the Visigoths.

Puerta de Valmardón

0 metres   100
0 yards   100

To escalator

CARDENAL LORENZANA

CALLE DE SAN ROMÁN

CALLE DE ALFONSO X

★ **Iglesia de Santo Tomé**
This church, with a beautiful Mudéjar tower, houses El Greco's The Burial of the Count of Orgaz.

CALLE DE ALFONSO XII

CALLE DE LA TRINIDAD

Sinagoga de Santa María la Blanca; Monasterio de San Juan de los Reyes

Sinagoga del Tránsito; Casa-Museo de El Greco

Plaza del Ayuntamiento

Archbishop's Palace

Taller del Moro
Once used as a workshop by craftsmen building the cathedral, this Mudéjar palace now houses a museum of Mudéjar ceramics and tiles.

STAR SIGHTS

★ Iglesia de Santo Tomé

★ Cathedral

★ Museo de Santa Cruz

**The Puerta del
ol** has a double
oorish arch and
two towers.

Ermita del Cristo de la Luz

*This small mosque, the
city's only remaining
Muslim building, dates
from around AD 1000.*

Tourist information;
Estación de
Autobuses & RENFE

VISITORS' CHECKLIST

Toledo. 🚶 75,500. ✈ 🚌 *Paseo
de la Rosa*, 925 22 30 99. 🚉
*Avenida de Castilla-La Mancha 3,
925 21 58 50.* ❓ *Plaza del Consis-
torio 1, 925 25 40 30.* 🗓 *Tue.*
🎉 *Corpus Christi (May/Jun), Virgen del Sagrario, (15 Aug).* **Iglesia
de San Román** 🕐 *Tue–Sun.*
Taller del Moro 🕐 *Tue–Sun.*
www.toledoweb.org

The Plaza de Zocodover
is named after the market
which was held here in
Moorish times. It is still the
city's main square, with
many cafés and shops.

PLAZA DE
ZOCODOVER

★ Museo de Santa Cruz

*The city's main fine arts
collection includes several
tapestries from Flanders.
Among them is this
15th-century zodiac
tapestry, with well-
preserved rich colours.*

KEY

— — — Suggested route

★ Cathedral

*Built on the site of a Visigothic
cathedral and a mosque, this
impressive structure is one
of the largest cathedrals in
Christendom (see pp144–5).
The Flamboyant Gothic high
altar reredos (1504) is the
work of several artists.*

Alcázar

*Inside the fortress, a statue
of Carlos V portrays him
triumphant over a Moor.
The Army Museum is due
to open here 2009.*

Toledo cathedral rising above the rooftops of the medieval part of the city

Exploring Toledo

Toledo is easily reached from Madrid by rail, bus or car, and is then best explored on foot. To visit all the main sights you need at least two days, but it is possible to walk around the medieval and Jewish quarters in a long morning. To avoid the heavy crowds, go midweek and stay for a night, when the city is at its most atmospheric.

♠ Alcázar

Cuesta de Carlos V. *Tel* 925 22 16 73. ● until 2009. ⊠ (free Wed). ◪ **Library** *Tel* 925 25 66 80. ◯ 9am– 9pm Mon–Fri, 9am–2pm Sat.

The fortified palace of Carlos I (Holy Roman Emperor Charles V) stands on the site of former Roman, Visigothic and Muslim fortresses. Its severe square profile suffered fire damage before being nearly destroyed in 1936 when the Nationalists survived a 70-day siege by the Republicans. Restoration followed the original plans and the building now houses an army museum. The museum is closed pending the move of the Museo del Ejército *(see p77)* from Madrid to the Alcázar in 2009. The **library**, which contains the Borbón-Lorenzana collection with more than 100,000 books dating from the 16th to the 19th century and 1,000 manuscripts from the 11th to the 19th century, will remain open.

🏛 Museo de Santa Cruz

Calle Cervantes 3. *Tel* 925 22 10 36. ◯ daily. ● Sun pm.

This museum is housed in a 16th-century hospital founded by Cardinal Mendoza. The building has some outstanding Renaissance features, including the main doorway, staircase and cloister. The four wings, in the shape of a Greek cross, are dedicated to the fine arts. The collection is strong in medieval and Renaissance works of art. There are also paintings by El Greco, including one of his last, *The Assumption* (1613), still in its original altarpiece. Displays include two typical Toledan crafts: armour and

***The Assumption* (1613) by El Greco in the Museo de Santa Cruz**

damascened swords, made by inlaying blackened steel with gold wire. Damascene work, including swords, plates and jewellery, is still made in the city. The museum is currently adding an extension, which is due to open in 2009.

🔒 Iglesia de Santo Tomé

Calle Santo Tomé 4. *Tel* 925 25 60 98. ◯ daily. ⊠ (free Wed pm to EU residents).

Visitors come to Santo Tomé mainly to admire El Greco's masterpiece, *The Burial of the Count of Orgaz*. An important patron of the church, the Count paid for much of the 14th-century building that stands today. The painting, commissioned in his memory by a parish priest, depicts the miraculous appearance of St Augustine and St Stephen at his burial, to raise his body to heaven. It has never been moved from the setting for which it was painted, nor restored. Nevertheless, it is remarkable for its contrast of colours. In the foreground, allegedly, are the artist and his son (both looking out) as well as Cervantes. The church is thought to date back to the 12th century, and its tower is one of the best examples of Mudéjar architecture in the city.

Nearby is the **Pastelería Santo Tomé**, a good place to buy locally made marzipan.

🏛 Sinagoga de Santa María la Blanca

Calle de los Reyes Católicos 4. **Tel** 925 22 72 57. ◯ daily. 🏷
(free Wed pm for Spanish citizens).

The oldest and largest of the city's eight original synagogues, this monument dates back to the 13th century. In 1405 it was taken over as a church by the military-religious Order of Calatrava. Restoration has returned it almost to its original beauty – finely carved stone capitals and wall panels stand out against plain white arches and plasterwork. In the chapel is a Plateresque altarpiece. In 1391 a massacre of Jews took place here, a turning point after years of religious tolerance in the city.

Mudéjar arches in the Sinagoga de Santa María la Blanca

🏛 Museo Sefardí

Sinagoga del Tránsito. **Tel** 925 22 36 65. ◯ Tue–Sat am–pm, Sun am. 🏷 (free Sat pm & Sun am). ● 1 Jan, 1 May, 10 Jun, 24, 25 & 31 Dec.

The most elaborate Mudéjar interior in the city is hidden behind the deceptively humble façade of this former synagogue, built in the 14th century by Samuel Ha-Leví, the Jewish treasurer to Pedro the Cruel. The interlaced frieze of the lofty prayer hall harmoniously fuses Islamic, Gothic and Hebrew geometric motifs below a wonderful coffered ceiling.

Adjoining the synagogue is a museum of Sephardi (Spanish Jewish) culture. The manuscripts, costumes and sacred objects on display date from both before and after the Jews' expulsion from Spain at the end of the 15th century.

Ornate ceiling in the Monasterio de San Juan de los Reyes

🔒 Monasterio de San Juan de los Reyes

Calle de los Reyes Católicos 17. **Tel** 925 22 38 02. ◯ daily. 🏷 ● 1 Jan, 25 Dec. ♿

A wonderful mixture of architectural styles, this monastery was commissioned by the Catholic Monarchs in honour of their victory over the Portuguese at the battle of Toro (near Salamanca) in 1476. It was intended to be their burial place, but they were actually laid to rest in Granada. Largely the work of Juan Guas, the church's main Isabelline structure was completed in 1492. Although badly damaged by Napoleon's troops in 1808 (see p18), it has been restored to its original splendour. It retains superb features such as a Gothic cloister (1510) which has a beautiful multicoloured Mudéjar ceiling. Near to the church is a stretch of the Jewish quarter's original wall.

🏛 Casa-Museo de El Greco

Calle Samuel Leví. ● for restoration during 2009. 🏷 (free Sat pm & Sun am). 🌐 www.mcu.es/museos

It is not clear whether El Greco actually lived in or simply near to this house, in the heart of the Jewish quarter, which has been turned into a museum containing an important collection of his works. Canvases on display include *View of Toledo*, a detailed depiction of the city at the time, and the superb series *Christ and the Apostles*. Underneath the museum is a chapel with a fine Mudéjar ceiling and a collection of art by painters of the Toledan School, such as Luis Tristán, a student of El Greco.

🔒 Iglesia de Santiago del Arrabal

Calle Arrabal.

This is one of Toledo's most beautiful Mudéjar monuments. It can easily be identified by its tower, reminiscent of a minaret, which is said to date back to the 12th-century Reconquest (see p15). The church, which was built slightly later, has a beautiful woodwork ceiling. The ornate Mudéjar pulpit and Plateresque altarpiece stand out against the plain interior.

🏛 Puerta Antigua de Bisagra

When Alfonso VI conquered Toledo in 1085, he entered it through this gateway, alongside El Cid. It is the only gateway in the city to have kept its original 10th-century military architecture. The huge towers are topped by a 12th-century Arab gatehouse.

EL GRECO

Born in Crete in 1541, El Greco ("the Greek") came to Toledo in 1577 to paint the altarpiece in the convent of Santo Domingo el Antiguo. Enchanted by the city, he stayed here, painting religious portraits and altarpieces for other churches. Although El Greco was trained in Italy and influenced by masters such as Tintoretto, his works are closely identified with the city where he settled. He died in Toledo in 1614.

Domenikos Theotocopoulos, better known as El Greco

Toledo Cathedral

The splendour of Toledo's massive cathedral reflects its history as the spiritual heart of the Spanish church and the seat of the Primate of all Spain. Still today, the Mozarabic Mass, which dates back to Visigothic times, is said here. The present cathedral was built on the site of a 7th-century church. Work began in 1226 and spanned three centuries, until the completion of the last vaults in 1493. This long period of construction explains the cathedral's mixture of styles: pure French Gothic – complete with flying buttresses – on the exterior and Spanish decorative styles, such as Mudéjar and Plateresque work, in the interior.

Sacristy
El Greco's The Denuding of Christ *above the marble altar, was painted especially for the cathedral. Also here are works by Titian, Van Dyck and Goya.*

The Cloister, on two floors, was built in the 14th century on the site of the old Jewish market.

View of Toledo Cathedral
Dominating the city skyline is the Gothic tower at the west end of the nave. The best view of the cathedral, and the city, is from the parador (see p155).

The belfry in the tower contains a heavy bell known as *La Gorda* ("the Fat One").

The Puerta del Mollete, on the west façade, is the main entrance to the cathedral. From this door, *mollete* (soft bread) was distributed to the poor.

★ Monstrance
The 16th-century Gothic silver and gold monstrance is over 3 m (10 ft) high. It is carried through the streets during the Corpus Christi celebrations (see p34).

STAR FEATURES

★ Monstrance

★ Choir

★ High Altar Reredos

★ Transparente

★ Transparente
This Baroque altarpiece of marble, jasper and bronze, by Narciso Tomé, is illuminated by an ornate sky-light. It stands out from the mainly Gothic interior.

VISITORS' CHECKLIST

Plaza del Ayuntamiento.
Tel 925 22 22 41. ⬜ 8am–6:30pm daily. 🔒 8:45am Mon–Sat, 9:45am Sun (Mozarabic Mass); 8am, 9am, 10am, 10:30am, 5:30pm, 6:30pm daily (also noon & 1pm Sun).
Choir, Treasury, Sacristy and Chapterhouse ⬜ 10:30am–6:30pm Mon–Sat, 2pm–6pm Sun. 🎫 📷 🚫 ♿

Capilla de Santiago

The Capilla de San Ildefonso contains the superb Plateresque tomb of cardinal Alonso Carrillo de Albornoz.

Chapterhouse
Above beautiful 16th-century frescoes by Juan de Borgoña is this spectacular, multi-coloured Mudéjar ceiling.

Puerta de los Leones

★ High Altar Reredos
The polychrome reredos, one of the most beautiful in Spain, depicts scenes from Christ's life.

Puerta Llana (entrance)

The Puerta del Perdón, or Door of Mercy, has a tympa-num decorated with religious characters.

The Capilla Mozárabe has a beautiful Renaissance ironwork grille, carved by Juan Francés in 1524.

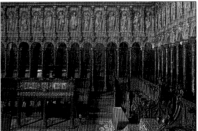

★ Choir
The carvings on the wooden lower stalls depict scenes of the fall of Granada. The alabaster upper ones show figures from the Old Testament.

TRAVELLERS' NEEDS

WHERE TO STAY

When Alfonso XIII *(see p19)* was married in 1906, he was embarrassed that his city, unlike other European capitals, did not have elegant hotels to accommodate his wedding guests. He decided to put things right, and personally instigated the building of the luxurious Ritz and Palace, which are still two of the best hotels in Europe. But, centuries

Hotel doorman

before, Madrid already had a strong tradition of more modest hostelries and guest houses offering shelter to the multitude of visitors from the provinces and from other countries. Today, the city continues to provide an abundance of comfortable lodgings, be they simple pensiones, pleasant three-star hotels in converted town houses, or palatial five-star establishments.

Stately façade of the ME Madrid Hotel *(see p151)* from the Plaza de Santa Ana

WHERE TO LOOK

Central Madrid has plenty of hotels, in every price category, close to the major sights. Some areas, such as Gran Vía and around Puerta del Sol, can be very noisy, both day and night, so sound-proofing is a big consideration. If you are driving, parking in central Madrid is difficult, and a hotel with parking facilities is essential. If it is tranquillity you want, and you do not mind having to take a taxi or the metro to go sightseeing, there are some good hotels in the residential districts of Salamanca (east) or Chamberí (north). A few modern luxury hotels, aimed mainly at business travellers, are located along the Paseo de la Castellana, and on the eastern

side of the M30 ring road, convenient for those needing easy access to the airport.

GRADING AND FACILITIES

Spanish hotels are rated from one to five stars. The top category is Gran Lujo (GL), indicated by five stars. Madrid has 18 hotels in this category – the Ritz, the Westin Palace *(see p69)* and the modern Villa Magna *(see p153)* are among the best. Although the star-

Suite at the Ritz – one of Madrid's most exclusive and expensive hotels *(see p152)*

rating gives a rough indication of standards and prices, it is not an exact science. Three-star hotels, for example, can include anything from charmless grey establishments in need of repair, to real gems with friendly staff and interesting decor. Both four- and five-star hotels should have a good range of extra facilities, and they will be fairly smart, but often less so than a similarly-priced hotel located in a rural part of Spain. Nearly all Madrid hotels in the three- to five-star category have air conditioning and televisions. Very few have gardens or swimming pools.

One- and two-star hotels offer basic facilities, although most now have a telephone and television in the rooms, as well as individual bathrooms. The better ones will have friendly staff, high standards of cleanliness, direct-dial phones and air-conditioning, which is essential in summer.

Hostal-residencias (HR) are hotels without a meal service; otherwise, they are the same as other hotels. Accommodation with basic facilities is also offered in *hostales* (Hs) and *pensiones* (P) at much lower prices than hotels. The two types are essentially the same.

A double room for one person *(habitación doble uso individual)*, which will cost slightly more than a single room, is an option for single travellers needing more space.

Some hotels have their own parking area. Those without often have an arrangement with neighbouring public car parks. There is an additional charge for this service, and it can be quite expensive.

◁ **Outdoor café at Plaza Mayor**

One of Madrid's many inexpensive *hostales* scattered around the centre

PARADORS

Paradors are the deservedly famous state-run hotels in Spain. The best of them are located in converted historic buildings, and many are worth a visit in their own right. Madrid itself has none, but some of the most picturesque paradors are in striking distance of the city, including the first one to open, in 1928, in the Sierra de Gredos. Two unique accommodation options are luxury paradors, one in Toledo *(see p155)* and one in the World Heritage town of Segovia *(see p155)*.

A typical room to be expected from a quality hotel in Madrid

HOW TO BOOK

While Madrid has ample hotel options, you never know whether an important trade fair or conference is going to cause greater demand, so prior booking is advisable. This can be done through a travel agent or directly by fax, phone or email. If you have any special requirements, such as a twin or double bed, interior room or one facing the street, make these known when booking. The receptionist will specify the hour until which your reservation will be held. Some hotels

demand a credit card number or deposit to guarantee a booking. When checking in, you will be asked for ID (a national identity card or passport) and to sign a registration form. Deposit valuables in the safe and tip the porter a few euros.

When leaving, rooms must be vacated before noon, but hotels will look after your luggage if your travel plans call for a later departure.

PAYMENT AND DISCOUNTS

Practically all hotels take major credit cards, but not personal cheques. Rates are increased by seven per cent value-added tax (IVA). Madrid hotels often offer discounts on weekend stays and in August, and it is also possible to buy discount vouchers at travel agents. Companies can usually get a corporate rate – *precio de empresa* – which may mean a reduction of up to a third.

When booking, ask for the room rate, as this is often lower than the listed price. It is even worth asking for a discount.

SPECIAL NEEDS

On the whole Spain is not wheelchair friendly, but newer hotels have ramps, wide elevators (lifts) and certain rooms adapted for disabled people. Enquire with the hotel beforehand, and be specific about your needs; a receptionist might think a ramp up the front steps makes the hotel "wheelchair accessible".

With the new anti-tobacco law, a maximum of 30 per cent of the rooms in any one hotel can be smoking rooms.

SELF CATERING

Some hotels, known as *hotel apartamentos* or *apartbotels*, contain a number of limited self-catering apartments (efficiency units). A few other establishments are entirely self-catering. These are called *apartamentos turísticos*, and usually require a minimum stay of one week.

CHILDREN

Children are welcome in most Madrid hotels, whatever the category. For small children, a cot or an extra bed will be put in the parents' room, often at no additional cost. But, as a rule, hotels provide few facilities for children, and only some of the more expensive offer babysitting – in Spain children tend to go everywhere with their parents.

HOSTELS

The Spanish *hostal* is not a hostel, but a modest hotel. Madrid has two youth hostels, known as *albergues juveniles*: one on Calle de Santa Cruz de Marcenado in central Madrid, the other in the Casa de Campo *(see p112)*. Space is at a premium; to secure a place, book ahead through www.madrid.org/inforjoven, or the **Instituto de Albergues Juveniles** on Gran Vía 10, 3rd floor, telephone: 91 720 11 65.

The opulent Ritz hotel *(see p152)* facing Plaza Canovas del Castillo

Choosing a Hotel

The hotels in this guide have been selected across a wide price range for excellent facilities and location. Many also have a highly recommended restaurant, pretty gardens or bedrooms with balcony views. The chart is divided into chapter areas for easy reference. For details on restaurants, *see pages 164–171*.

PRICE CATEGORIES
For a standard double room per night, with tax, breakfast and service included.

€ under 80 euros
€€ 80–130 euros
€€€ 130–170 euros
€€€€ 170–230 euros
€€€€€ over 230 euros

OLD MADRID

Hostal Santo Domingo
 €

Luna 6, 2nd Floor, 28004 **Tel** *91 531 3290* **Fax** *91 523 2094* **Rooms** *18.* **Map** *2 E5*

Located in the lively Maravillas district, just a few steps away from Callao metro station, is this newly-renovated small hostal. The walls are painted in pastel colours for a soothing interior and all rooms have sound-proof windows and free WiFi – some also have a Jacuzzi. Comfortable with helpful owners. **www.hostalsantodomingo.es**

Hotel Moderno
€€

Arenal 2, 28013 **Tel** *91 531 0900* **Fax** *91 531 3550* **Rooms** *97.* **Map** *7 C2*

This bright and modern hotel could not be more centrally located as it is just off the main square at Sol on a busy street that leads down to the Opera House and the Royal Palace. Rooms are decorated in floral patterns with marble ensuite bathrooms, some with hydromassage bath tubs and private solarium terraces. WiFi available. **www.hotel-moderno.com**

Hotel Opera
 €€

Calle Cuesta de Santo Domingo 2, 28013 **Tel** *91 541 2800* **Fax** *91 541 6923* **Rooms** *79.* **Map** *4 D1*

The Hotel Opera, with its new face lift, is among the capital's top mid-range hotels. Close to the Royal Place and the Opera House, its location is perfect. Opera by name, opera by nature: even the waiters are trained singers and their performances add a romantic, magical touch to the dining experience at this hotel. WiFi available. **www.hotelopera.com**

Hostal Hispano Argentino
 €€

Gran Via 15, 28013 **Tel** *91 532 2448* **Fax** *91 531 7256* **Rooms** *14.* **Map** *2 D5*

Hostal Hispano Argentino is located on the 6th floor of a refurbished Art Deco townhouse on Madrid's Gran Via, the capital's main theatre and cinema drag. Rooms are bright and modern with twin or double beds, and breakfast is served in a small communal lounge solarium. WiFi available. **www.hispano-argentino.com**

Room Mate Alicia
 €€

Calle Prado 2, 28014 **Tel** *91 389 6095* **Fax** *91 369 4795* **Rooms** *34.* **Map** *7 A3*

The ideal location for those wanting to be in the thick of Madrid's vibrant nightlife. This clean cut ultra-modern hotel is affordable to most travellers yet luxurious at the same time. Standard rooms come with a small terrace, and two of the duplex rooms have small private swimming pools and larger terraces. WiFi available. **www.room-matehoteles.com**

Room Mate Mario
 €€

Calle Campomanes 4, 28013 **Tel** *91 548 8548* **Fax** *91 559 1288* **Rooms** *54.* **Map** *4 D2*

An artsy, contemporary hotel, Mario is ideal for those looking for something a bit different at the right price. Decorated by Tomas Alía, one of the most innovative designers to hit Spain's hotel scene in decades, be prepared for the wow factor. WiFi available and breakfast served until late. **www.room-matehoteles.com**

7 Colors
 €€

Calle Huertas 14, 28012 **Tel** *91 429 6935* **Fax** *91 429 6935* **Rooms** *10.* **Map** *7 A3*

Part of the stylish Chic & Basic chain, 7 Colors gives guests a choice of several brightly colour-coordinated rooms that overlook the vibrant Calle Huertas and Plaza Santa Anna. This hotel is the ideal base for partying your way around Madrid. Internet available. **www.7colorsrooms.com**

Suites 33
 €€

Leganitos 33, 28013 **Tel** *91 758 3850* **Fax** *91 542 9911* **Rooms** *33.* **Map** *2 D5*

Built in 2006, this hotel is situated in the heart of Madrid, less than five minutes from Plaza Callao and the busy streets around Puerta del Sol. The elegant, comfortable rooms boast stylish bathrooms, modern furniture and good amenities including a plasma TV, a safety deposit box and WiFi. **www.suites33.com**

Hotel Arosa
 €€€

Calle de la Salud 21, 28013 **Tel** *91 532 1600* **Fax** *91 531 3127* **Rooms** *133.* **Map** *4 F2*

This incredibly central but excellent value for money hotel offers spacious rooms, most of which have been refurbished in the boutique style. Families are welcome, and friendly and attentive staff mean guests keep coming back. Discounted prices can be found on the Internet. **www.bestwestern.es**

Key to Symbols *see back cover flap*

Hotel Meninas

Campomanes 7, 28013 **Tel** *91 541 2805* **Fax** *91 541 2806* **Rooms** *37.*

"Meninas" Hotel, named after the famous painting by Velazquez, is housed in a restored 14th-century t... tucked away down a side street just off the Plaza de Opera. The rooms are decorated in soft beige, cream and brown tones and a buffet breakfast is served in a serene whitewashed vaulted dining room. **www.hotelmeninas.com**

Maria Elena Palace

€€€

Calle Aduana 19, 28013 **Tel** *91 360 4930* **Fax** *91 360 4789* **Rooms** *87.* **Map** *4 F2*

In the vibrant heart of Madrid, close to the Plaza del Sol, this hotel combines the classic with the modern in a relaxing atmosphere. Completely refurbished in 2002, it features an inspiring interior design with "patios" covered by impressive glass and marble domes. **www.mariaelenapalacehotel.com**

Petit Palace Arenal

€€€

Calle Arenal 4, 28013 **Tel** *91 564 4355* **Fax** *91 564 0854* **Rooms** *64.* **Map** *4 E3*

The Petit Palace Arenal is in a vibrant, lively location half way between The Royal Opera House and Sol. Part of a popular chain of hotels, it is renowned for its value for money. Simple monochrome décor and tasteful modern furnishings complement cleverly placed and colourful modern artworks. Pets allowed. **www.hthoteles.com**

Petit Palace Posada del Peine

€€€

Calle Postas 17, 28012 **Tel** *91 523 8151* **Fax** *91 523 2993* **Rooms** *71.* **Map** *4 E3*

Although part of the Petit Palace chain, the Posada del Peine still feels like a modern independent boutique hotel. It is ideally located facing the Plaza Mayor, with elegant and comfortably decorated rooms, and courteous, helpful staff who will direct you to the best sightseeing and restaurants. Pets allowed. **www.hthoteles.com**

Suite Prado

€€€

Calle Manuel Fernandez y Gonzalez 10, 28014 **Tel** *91 420 2318* **Fax** *91 420 0559* **Rooms** *18.* **Map** *7 A3*

Those looking for spacious apartment-style suites at low prices should head for the Suite Prado. The bright and large suites come with a separate white marble bathroom, lounge area and kitchenette, while the rooms are modern and simply furnished and have an independent dining room. Ideal for families with children. **www.suiteprado.com**

Hotel Emperador

 €€€€

Gran Via 53, 28013 **Tel** *91 547 28 00* **Fax** *91 547 2817* **Rooms** *232.* **Map** *2 D5*

The Emperador is famous for its outdoor rooftop pool, open during summer months, with spectacular views of Madrid's skyline towards the Royal Palace, Almudena Cathedral and Retiro Park. This four-star hotel has five-star amenities including a sauna, gym, and business and conference centre. **www.emperadorhotel.com**

Hotel Santo Domingo

 €€€€

Plaza de Santo Domingo 13, 28013 **Tel** *91 547 9800* **Fax** *91 547 5995* **Rooms** *120.* **Map** *4 D1*

This Best Western hotel is located in a small square in the very centre of Madrid, close to Puerta del Sol. Furnished with antique furniture and art, each room is decorated in a different Baroque style. The hotel even houses a small art gallery with rare works by Ravestein, Eduardo Balaca and Vicente Palmaroli. **www.hotelsantodomingo.com**

Hotel de las Letras

 €€€€€

Gran Via 11, 28013 **Tel** *91 523 7980* **Fax** *91 523 7981* **Rooms** *103.* **Map** *3 E1*

This stunning design hotel has been built within a beautifully tiled 18th-century palacette right on Madrid's main shopping and entertainment street. Large and luxurious, many of the rooms have private terraces and a Jacuzzi. The house also operates a well stocked library and a gourmet restaurant. **www.hoteldelasletras.com**

ME Madrid Reina Victoria

€€€€€

Plaza de Santa Ana 14, 28012 **Tel** *91 701 6000* **Fax** *91 522 0307* **Rooms** *192.* **Map** *7 A3*

Occupying the majestic building of the former Gran Hotel is the innovative, ultra-stylish ME Madrid. The rooms boast a martini bar and the latest entertainment technology including a DVD and CD library, a plasma TV, a complimentary iPod and surround-sound speakers. The Penthouse Bar has stunning views of the city. **http://memadrid.travel**

Palacio San Martín

 €€€€€

Plaza de San Martin 5, 28013 **Tel** *91 701 5000* **Fax** *9191 701 5010* **Rooms** *87.* **Map** *4 E2*

This hotel dates back to the 15th century and has been converted from two noblemen's houses into one modern but classic space. The original ornate stone façade, stucco ceilings, wood panelling and a central courtyard have all been preserved. A rooftop terrace restaurant commands panoramic views of Madrid's "Austrias" district. **www.intur.com**

BOURBON MADRID

Cat's Hostel

 €

Cañizares 6, 28012 **Tel** *91 369 2807* **Fax** *91 429 9479* **Rooms** *12.* **Map** *7 A3*

This airy palatial building is home to a very well equipped hostel, situated parallel to Calle Atocha allowing for easy access to Madrid's main bus and train stations as well as the city centre and sights. Guests can have private double rooms with bathrooms or share with up to 12 in dorms. There is also a bar with live concerts. **www.catshostel.com**

Hostal Astoria 🗾📃 €

Carrera de San Jerónimo 30–32, 5°, 28014 **Tel** *91 429 11 88* **Fax** *91 429 2023* **Rooms** *26.* **Map** *7 A3*

Hostal Astoria is on the fifth floor of a recently restored 19th-century building. Only a short walk from Madrid's art gallery triangle, the location is perfect for art lovers. Spacious and spotless rooms are decorated in simple white and yellow with parquet flooring -- all have en-suite bathrooms. Free Internet is provided. **www.hostal-astoria.com**

Hotel Quo Puerta del Sol ♿🗾🧍📃 €€€

Calle Sevilla 4, 28014 **Tel** *91 532 9049* **Fax** *91 531 2834* **Rooms** *62.* **Map** *7 A3*

Designed by one of Madrid's top designers, Tomás Alía, the Quo is not only central and reasonably priced but also very stylish. Red and white pillows contrast with minimalist black and white bedding, and sleek aluminium fittings and cabinets give the rooms a sharp, clean look. Most rooms come with small outdoor patio areas. **www.quopuertadelsolhotel.com**

Husa Paseo del Arte 🗾🍴🧍📺📃P €€€

Atocha 123, 28012 **Tel** *91 298 4800* **Fax** *91 298 4850* **Rooms** *260.* **Map** *7 C4*

Perfectly located, this hotel is close to the city's main museums and just across from Atocha station. Newly renovated, the large rooms have a minimalist decor and free WiFi. Some rooms also have a terrace and good views. The restaurant serves quality Spanish cuisine and excellent breakfasts. **www.hotelhusapaseodelarte.com**

Hotel Vincci Centrum 🗾🍴🧍📃 €€€€

Calle Cedaceros 4, 28014 **Tel** *91 360 4720* **Fax** *91 522 4515* **Rooms** *87.* **Map** *7 B2*

As the name implies this hotel could not have a more central location. All rooms face out on to a reasonably quiet back street and some have quite big outdoor terraces. The funky interior design mixes orange walls with stainless-steel sinks and dark grey and brown carpets, upholstery and bedding. **www.vinccihoteles.com**

Hotel Vincci Soho ♿🗾🍴📃P €€€€

Calle del Prado 18, 28014 **Tel** *91 141 4100* **Fax** *91 141 4101* **Rooms** *170.* **Map** *7 A3*

The Vincci Soho hotel has merged five National Heritage townhouses at the bottom of Paseo del Prado in the historic Barrio de las Letras to form a uniquely stylish hotel that blends the classic with the fashionable. The hotel itself features an *à la carte* restaurant, funky bar-cafeteria and an outdoor terrace with garden. **www.vinccihoteles.com**

Hotel Urban ♿🗾🍴🏊🧍📺📃P €€€€€

Carrera de San Jerónimo 34, 28014 **Tel** *91 787 7770* **Fax** *91 787 7799* **Rooms** *96.* **Map** *7 B2*

The five-star deluxe Urban takes luxury to new heights with its clever design and attentive staff. The hotel is particularly popular with those who appreciate art as it houses an amazing collection of Egyptian, African and Oriental objects. A rooftop infinity pool, solarium and bar enjoy panoramic views of the city. Dogs welcome. **www.derbyhotels.com**

Hotel Villa Real 🗾🍴🧍📃P €€€€€

Plaza de las Cortes 10, 28014 **Tel** *91 420 3767* **Fax** *91 420 2547* **Rooms** *115.* **Map** *7 B2*

The Villa Real is a much more traditional hotel than its neighbouring sister the Urban, but is by no means less luxurious. The hotel features a Roman mosaic and sculpture collection as well as modernist oil paintings. Classically decorated rooms overlook Congress and a small garden at the bottom of Paseo del Prado. **www.derbyhotels.com**

Ritz Madrid ♿🗾🍴🏊🧍📺📃P €€€€€

Plaza de la Lealtad 5, 28014 **Tel** *91 701 67 67* **Fax** *91 701 6776* **Rooms** *167.* **Map** *7 C2*

The Ritz is widely considered to be the city's most classically elegant hotel and has become famed internationally for its suberb cuisine. The hotel stands on a small green plaza on one side of the Paseo del Prado and overlooks the Prado Museum. Rooms are modern but maintain the original Belle Époque style. **www.ritz.es**

Westin Palace ♿🗾🍴🏊🧍📺📃P €€€€€

Plaza de las Cortes 7, 28014 **Tel** *91 360 8000* **Fax** *91 360 8100* **Rooms** *466.* **Map** *7 C1*

Overlooking the Neptune Fountain and its quiet plaza, the Palace combines classic opulence with cutting-edge facilities, such as a state-of-the-art spa and rooftop fitness centre as well as the fantastic Asia Gallery restaurant (see p167). Guests will love relaxing by the bar under the stunning Art Nouveau stained-glass atrium dome. **www.palacemadrid.com**

AROUND LA CASTELLANA

Hostal Macarena 📃 €

Cava de San Miguel 8, 28005 **Tel** *91 365 92 21* **Fax** *91 364 2757* **Rooms** *22.* **Map** *5 A5*

Hostal Macarena is housed in a yellow painted building next to the Plaza Mayor and is slightly more comfortable than its sister hotel Sil Serranos. Good sized rooms are furnished with traditional Spanish dark wood furniture and en-suite bathrooms are kept sparkling clean. **www.silserranos.com**

Hotel Mora 🗾🍴📃 €

Paseo del Prado 32, 28014 **Tel** *91 420 1569* **Fax** *91 420 0564* **Rooms** *62.* **Map** *7 C2*

Located conveniently between the Prado Museum and Recoletos, this chain hotel is also directly opposite Madrid's Atocha railway station. Rooms are simply but comfortably decorated. The hotel has a small restaurant and bar. Staff are particularly helpful and will arrange transport to and from the airport. **www.hotelmora.com**

Espahotel Amador de los Rios
€€€

Calle Amador de los Rios 3, 28046 **Tel** *91 310 7500* **Fax** *91308 0089* **Rooms** *59.*   **Map** *6 D1*

Madrid's most chic aparthotel offers guests a very stylish designer experience. Rooms are a little on the cramped side although the clever design makes maximum use of the limited space. The hotel's terrace boasts a large outdoor swimming pool. **www.espahotel.es**

Galiano
€€€

Calle Alcalá Galiano 6, 28010 **Tel** *91 319 20 00* **Fax** *91 319 99 14* **Rooms** *29.*   **Map** *6 D1*

The Galiano was once a convent and then a nobleman's home and is full of genuine antiques from its regal past. The interior is traditionally decorated with period furniture and there are several spacious communal areas including a large interior garden. The hotel is handy for El Corte Ingles and Madrid's shopping district. **www.hotelgaliano.com**

Hesperia Hermosilla
€€€

Hermosilla 23, 28006 **Tel** *91 246 88 00* **Fax** *91 246 8801* **Rooms** *67.*   **Map** *6 D4*

Located on the corner of Lagasca and Hermosilla Streets, the Hesperia Hermosilla is the best situated and the most reasonably priced hotel in Madrid for upscale shopping. Rooms are elegantly furnished with modern art, and the large ensuite bathrooms have open shower units. **www.hesperia-hermosilla.com**

Husa Serrano Royal
€€€

Marqués de Villamejor 8, 28006 **Tel** *91 576 1156* **Fax** *91 575 3307* **Rooms** *34.*   **Map** *6 E3*

The Husa upgraded all of its rooms and suites in 2006 carefully designing the layout for maximum comfort. The modern interior is very high tech and homely while remaining completely unpretentious. The staff are courteous and friendly and a lavish buffet breakfast is served daily. **www.hotelserranoroyal.com**

Hotel Bauzá
€€€€

Goya 79, 28001 **Tel** *91 435 7545* **Fax** *91 431 0943* **Rooms** *167.*   **Map** *6 D4*

One of the only true design hotels in Madrid with an über-trendy layout and equally triumphant *à la carte* restaurant, which overlooks the busy Calle Goya – a favourite with shoppers. The informal library is the perfect place to relax with a coffee after a busy day in the city. **www.hotelbauza.com**

NH Alcalá
€€€€

Alcalá 66, 28009 **Tel** *91 435 1060* **Fax** *91 435 1105* **Rooms** *146.*   **Map** *4 F2*

A large, chain hotel close to the lovely Retiro gardens, with spacious, well-equipped rooms and amenities that include WiFi and Internet access. This reasonably priced hotel also has a café, bar and private car park. It is within walking distance to the up-market shopping district in Salamanca, and three museums. **www.nh-hotels.com**

NH Zurbano
€€€

Zurbano 79-81, 28003 **Tel** *91 441 4500* **Fax** *91 441 3224* **Rooms** *266.*   **Map** *5 C2*

The NH Zurbano is handy for the airport and Madrid's downtown business district. The hotel is split into two buildings, the first with slightly smaller rooms. The rooms are functional and very quiet, considering the busy location. Special rates for weekends are offered through their website. **www.hotelnhzurbano.com**

Occidental Miguel Angel
€€€€

Miguel Ángel 29–31, 28046 **Tel** *91 442 0022* **Fax** *91 442 53 20* **Rooms** *263.*   **Map** *6 D2*

Not only does the Occidental house one of Madrid's top restaurants, La Broche (see p169), but in 2006 it also inaugurated one of the best spas in Madrid. The Spanish owned hotel is decorated in a classic international style and has interior gardens with a restaurant and café terrace. **www.miguelangelhotel.com**

Gran Melia Fenix

€€€€€

Hermosilla 2, 28001 **Tel** *91 431 6700* **Fax** *91 576 06 61* **Rooms** *215.*   **Map** *6 D4*

Overlooking the flowing fountains of Plaza de Colón, the Gran Melia Fenix is one of Madrid's most emblematic hotels. Club-class rooms and suites on the top floor include a wide private terrace with a hot tub for four. A wide selection of tapas are available throughout the day in the communal areas at no extra cost. **www.granmeliafenix.solmelia.com**

Hotel Orfila
€€€€€

Calle Orfila 6, 28010 **Tel** *91 702 7770* **Fax** *91 702 7772* **Rooms** *32.*   **Map** *5 C4*

This small mansion is hidden in a tranquil residential area next to the British Embassy and just off the Castellana. The hotel retains its original 19th-century façade, cobbled carriage entrance and elegant stone stairwell. Five-star style and treatment is available without the hustle and bustle of a big hotel. Closed 3 weeks in August. **www.hotelorfila.com**

Hotel Villa Magna

€€€€€

Paseo de la Castellana 22, 28046 **Tel** *91 576 7500* **Fax** *91 575 3158* **Rooms** *151.*   **Map** *6 D1*

Easily one of the capital's most lavish hotels, the Villa Magna oozes sophistication. Spacious, sound-proofed rooms have exceptionally comfortable beds. There is a superb Presidential Suite and landscaped garden. The clientele includes business people and shopaholics who want to be close to Madrid's most exclusive boutiques. **www.villamagna.park.hyatt.com**

Hotel Wellington
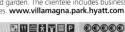
€€€€€

Velázquez 8, 28001 **Tel** *91 575 4400* **Fax** *91 576 4164* **Rooms** *261.*   **Map** *6 F3*

Only 5 minutes walk from the Retiro and the upscale shops of the Calle Goya, the Wellington is one of Madrid's finest hotels. It boasts a large outdoor pool with patio garden, a new beauty Spa and two in-house restaurants serving excellent traditional Basque and Japanese cuisine. **www.hotel-wellington.com**

Intercontinental Castellana

Paseo de la Castellana 49, 28046 **Tel** *91 700 7300* **Fax** *91 319 5853* **Rooms** *307.*   **Map** *6 D1*

This hotel is conveniently situated in the centre of the downtown business district and has spacious rooms and suites that all come with modern amenities. A rooftop spa and fitness area offers beauty treatments and massage. The in-house restaurant offers a superb paella. **www.intercontinental.com**

Palacio del Retiro

Alfonso XII 14, 28014 **Tel** *91 523 7460* **Rooms** *51.*   **Map** *7 D2*

Once a 19th-century palace, this luxurious hotel combines classic grandeur with ultra-hip design. Suites look directly on to Retiro Park and bathrooms include Jacuzzis. Rooms have marble fireplaces and are stylishly decorated. A lounge bar and restaurant provide a sophisticated setting and a small spa offers beauty treatments and massages. **www.ac-hotels.com**

Santo Mauro

Calle Zurbano 36, 28010 **Tel** *91 319 6900* **Rooms** *51.*   **Map** *5 C2*

This hotel, once the Canadian then Philippine embassy, is set on a quiet, tree-lined street near Chamberí. The classic lounges, restaurant and bar have retained their original features, while regal grandeur mixed with cutting edge modernity abounds in the bedrooms, which have been stylishly decorated in soft dark colours. **www.ac-hotels.com**

FURTHER AFIELD

Gran Hotel Velázquez

Velázquez 62 **Tel** *91 575 28 00* **Fax** *91 575 2809* **Rooms** *144.*   **Map** *6 F3*

This attractive medium-sized family hotel is right in the heart of the Salamanca district, close to many of the city's most exclusive boutiques. Over half of the rooms could be classed as suites as they have lounge areas adjoining the bedrooms. If it's sanctuary you're looking for after a hard day's sight-seeing, this is the place for you. **www.hotelvelazquez.com**

Aristos

Avenida de Pío XII 34, 28016 **Tel** *91 345 04 50* **Fax** *91 345 1023* **Rooms** *23.*

The highlight of this hotel, popular with executive business travellers, is El Chaflán (see p171) – a stunning Michelin-starred restaurant. If you are looking for peace and quiet in the leafy suburbs of Madrid this is an ideal spot with reasonable rates and good humoured staff. **www.hotelaristos.com**

NH Abascal

Calle José Abascal 47 **Tel** *91 441 0015* **Fax** *91 442 2211* **Rooms** *183.*

This seven storey hotel was previously occupied by a series of embassies and now seamlessly blends an über-modern interior with a Belle Époque exterior design. Conveniently located in midtown Madrid between the Azca and Nuevos Ministerios, this hotel is particularly popular with business guests. **www.hotelnhabascal.com**

Hosteria de Alcalá de Henares

Colegios 3 **Tel** *918 88 03 30* **Fax** *91 888 0527* **Rooms** *26.*

Housed in an historic building, once a famous seminary, the rooms have a traditional décor with wooden beams and period furniture. There is an exquisite ivy clad interior courtyard is surrounded by wooden weaving balconies, and a grand chandeliered restaurant serving typical Spanish dishes. **www.parador.es**

Hotel Conde Duque

Plaza Conde del Valle Suchil 5, 28015 **Tel** *91 447 7000* **Fax** *91 448 3569* **Rooms** *143.*

The bright and spacious rooms of this family-run, Basque-owned, 40-year-old hotel have been rebuilt and tastefully refurbished in soft blue and green pastels – each is fully soundproofed and has a huge en-suite bathroom. The hotel is set on a relatively calm, tree-lined square on the fringes of Chamberí. **www.hotelcondeduque.es**

Hotel Don Pio

Calle Pío XII 2 **Tel** *91 353 0780* **Rooms** *41.*

Hotel Don Pio is decorated in a classic Spanish style with hand-woven carpets, and oak wood-panelled arches around an interior courtyard which lend it the atmosphere of an enormous private home. Rooms have en suites or connecting rooms for children. **www.hoteldonpio.com**

NH Sanvy

Goya 3, 28001 **Tel** *91 576 0800* **Fax** *91 575 2443* **Rooms** *149.*

Set on the Plaza de Colón, the NH Savy caters for a mixture of Spanish business people and foreign tourists. The hotel has a very modern and functional interior with its own bar, restaurant, function rooms, terrace café and outdoor pool. There is also a special play area for children, nanny service and non-smoking family rooms. **www.nh-hotels.com**

Quinta de los Cedros

Calle Allendesalazar 4 **Tel** *91 515 2200* **Fax** *91 415 2050* **Rooms** *32.*

Modelled on a Tuscan Villa, this intimate hotel feels a million miles away from the busy metropolis although it is only kilometres from Madrid's airport. The hotel interior is charming, relaxing and classically furnished. Rooms are spacious with views out on to the ornamental gardens, and there is free Internet access. **www.quintadeloscedros.com**

Key to Price Guide *see p150* **Key to Symbols** *see back cover flap*

Hotel Adler

Calle Velázquez 33, 28001 **Tel** *91 426 32 20* **Fax** *91 426 3221* **Rooms** *45.* **Map** *6 F3*

This luxury boutique hotel is a restored 17th-century palacette in the upmarket Salamanca district on the busy Velázquez and Goya cross section. The hotel's furnishings are classic but the interior design and modern art collections create a modern look. Friendly staff and a warm atmosphere. **www.adlermadrid.com**

Hesperia Madrid

Plaza de la Castellana 57, 28046 **Tel** *91 210 8800* **Fax** *91 210 8899* **Rooms** *170.* **Map** *6 D1*

The Hesperia is situated on the busy Castellana Avenue, but once inside there's a cosy, softly-lit atmosphere where Japanese minimalism complements ephemeral Italian fittings and furniture. The hotel's Michelin-starred Santceloni restaurant *(see p171)* is divine. Free WiFi Internet service. **www.hesperia-madrid.com**

Puerta America

Avenida de América 41, 28002 **Tel** *91 744 5400* **Fax** *91 744 5401* **Rooms** *342.*

The 12 unique floors at the Puerta America were dreamt up by some of the world's top architects and designers. The hotel has a rooftop pool with views across the city and also a beauty spa and treatment floor. The main restaurant has an extensive menu. Barajas airport and the city centre are only 15 minutes away. **www.hotelpuertamerica.com**

BEYOND MADRID

ARANJUEZ NH Príncipe de la Paz

San Antonio 22, 28300 (Aranjuez) **Tel** *91 809 9222* **Fax** *91 892 5999* **Rooms** *86.*

The NH Príncipe de la Paz is situated in the historic centre of Aranjuez opposite the beautiful Palacio Real. The modern deluxe hotel is housed in a 17th-century building, which has retained its original ornate façade and high airy ceilings. The hotel's interior is distinctly modern and offers every convenience. **www.nh-hotels.com**

MIRAFLORES DE LA SIERRA Palacio Miraflores

Fuente del Pino 6, 28792 (Miraflores de la Sierra) **Tel** *91 844 9050* **Fax** *91 844 9051* **Rooms** *15.*

Only 40 minutes drive from Madrid, this country hotel is located in the Miraflores de la Sierra natural park. Once a palatial house, the building was restored to create this tranquil hotel. Rooms are furnished in antique furniture and look out on to the lawns and gardens. There's also a beauty spa, outdoor pool and restaurant. **www.palaciomiraflores.com**

PEDRAZA El Hotel de la Villa

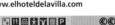

Calle Calzada 5 **Tel** *92 150 86 51* **Fax** *92 150 86 53* **Rooms** *38.*

This grand medieval stone building, complete with thick wooden doors and vaulted beamed ceilings, has been a family-run hotel since the 1950's. The interior is lavishly decorated, and the dining room has a large granite fireplace which is usually roaring in winter. The restaurant also has a good reputation. **www.elhoteldelavilla.com**

SAN LORENZO DE EL ESCORIAL Hotel Botánico

Timoteo Padrós 16 **Tel** *91 890 78 79* **Fax** *91 890 8158* **Rooms** *20.*

The Hotel Botánico has touches of a huge Bavarian villa and is set in lush manicured gardens and orange groves. This is an ideal place to escape from the city and enjoy the tranquil surroundings of San Lorenzo de El Escorial and its marvellous golf course. No luxury is spared in the classic Castilian style suites. **www.valdesimonte.com**

SAN LORENZO DE EL ESCORIAL Hotel Victoria Palace

Calle Juan de Toledo 4 **Tel** *91 896 9890* **Fax** *91 896 9896* **Rooms** *81.*

The hotel Victoria Palace is located in the regal historic town of San Lorenzo de El Escorial. This former palace is decorated in a classic style with oak-beamed ceilings and chandeliers. The hotel is also famous for its gastronomy. The outdoor pool and solarium have views of the town and La Herreria golf course. **www.hotelvictoriapalace.com**

SEGOVIA Parador de Segovia

Carretera de Valladolid, 40003 (Segovia) **Tel** *92 144 3737* **Fax** *92 143 7362* **Rooms** *106.*

What really makes this hotel stand out are the views of Segovia, a World Heritage Site. Bedrooms look out on to the town and are decorated in bright traditional Spanish colours with a hint of its Arab ancestry. The highlight of the hotel is the heated olympic-sized pool set amid lawns, and the award-winning restaurant. **www.parador.es**

TOLEDO Hostal del Cardenal

Paseo de Recaredo 24 **Tel** *925 22 49 00* **Fax** *91 522 2991* **Rooms** *27.*

This rustic country house was once the summer residence of Madrid's pampered Cardinals who restored the building in the 18th century. More recently the Botin family have recreated a classic Toledo mansion complete with Mudéjar-style ceramic tile work, wooden carvings and antique wooden coffered ceilings. **www.hostaldelcardenal.com**

TOLEDO Parador de Toledo

Cerro del Emperador, 45002 (Toledo) **Tel** *925 22 1850* **Fax** *925 22 5166* **Rooms** *70.*

Set on the Cerro del Emperador on the bend of the river Tagus, this Parador comands picture postcard views. The hotel has a large swimming pool and patio garden. Rooms have high ceilings and wooden beams and Mudéjar embroidered rugs and tiling. The restaurant serves typical Castilian fare. **www.parador.es**

RESTAURANTS, CAFES AND BARS

Even if Madrid didn't have its wealth of fabulous museums, palaces and monuments, it would be worth coming here just to experience its abundance of restaurants, cafés and bars. *Madrileños* spend a significant amount of time away from home with family, friends or colleagues, enjoying breakfast, pre-meal *tapas* (*see pp158–9*) or lunch. For the visitor, it is very easy to slip into this unhurried style of eating and drinking.

Tiles at La Chata, a bar in Old Madrid's Calle de la Cava Baja

Regional food from all over Spain is served in picturesque *tabernas* (*see pp30–31*), including some of the oldest existing in Europe, modest *casas de comidas* (local restaurants) and some of the continent's most elegant and creative culinary establishments. Whatever the ambience, whatever the price, tasty food is guaranteed – a restaurant serving mediocre fare is unlikely to survive long in this city of discerning eaters.

Interior view of the finely polished bar at El Espejo (*see p167*)

RESTAURANTS AND BARS

Madrid is populated by legions of executives and white-collar workers who are the mainstay of the city's restaurant trade. They demand good food, fast service and like to linger at the table after the meal. Lunchtime and the *sobremesa* – the casual conversation that follows the meal – are sacred in this city. To serve this market, there are hundreds of places to eat, from simple bistros that offer home cooking and daily menus at low prices, to some of Europe's most stylish establishments.

Some of the most famous restaurants are run by Basques, the acknowledged gastronomic masters of Spain. Every other Spanish region is represented as well, and Madrid also has restaurants serving international food, from Japanese to Russian, but to a lesser degree than other major European cities.

As the majority of their clients are business people, most restaurants close on Sunday. Many close Saturday lunchtime too, and a large number close for the whole of August.

FAST FOOD

In addition to home-grown bars serving *tapas*, Madrid has branches of most of the international franchises, offering American-style hamburgers. Successful Spanish chains include Pans & Co (sandwiches), Telepizza (pizzas, sandwiches and salads) and Vips, a chain of reasonably priced fast food restaurants with a shop attached.

EATING HOURS IN SPAIN

Madrid is notorious for its late meal times, with lunch around 2–3pm and dinner around 10–11pm. For many travellers, eating times take some getting used to.

Madrileños usually have two breakfasts (*desayunos*). The first may be a perfunctory coffee at home. The second, around 10 or 11am, is often eaten in a bar or a café. It might consist of coffee with *churros* – sticks of fried batter for dunking, a thick slice of *tortilla* (potato omelette) or a sandwich (*bocadillo*). Most hotels offer either a continental breakfast of coffee or tea with a roll, or a breakfast buffet.

At lunchtime *Madrileños* adjourn to a bar for a *tapa* – an appetizer served with beer or a *vino* (glass of wine). This is followed by the midday *comida* or *almuerzo* (lunch), often eaten at a restaurant.

A late-afternoon *merienda* (tea) of sandwiches or pastries with coffee, tea or juice tides *Madrileños* over until the time comes for a second round of *tapas* at a bar in the evening, returning home for the *cena* (dinner) or enjoying another meal at a restaurant.

Dining room at Hostería de Pedraza in Pedraza de la Sierra (*see p171*)

An enticing place to rest – a terrace bar on Paseo de Recoletos

READING THE MENU

The Spanish phrase *menú del día* refers to the attractively-priced daily fixed menu. Some gourmet restaurants also offer a *menú de degustación* – a sampler menu which might include several small portions of the house specialities.

On a set day of the week some restaurants may serve an elaborate, traditional dish such as *fabada* (bean stew) or *cocido madrileño*, the classic hearty local dish *(see p159)*.

The Spanish word for menu is *la carta*. It starts with *sopas* (soups), *entremeses* (hors d'oeuvres), *ensaladas* (salad), *huevos y tortillas* (eggs and omelettes) and *verduras y legumbres* (vegetable dishes). The *plato principal* (main course) may be *pescados y mariscos* (fish and shellfish) or *carnes y aves* (meat and poultry). Dessert is *postre*.

PRICES AND TIPPING

All Spanish restaurants must offer a *menú del día*, a comparatively inexpensive daily fixed-price menu comprising two courses and a dessert. Some restaurants do not reveal their daily menu unless it is requested.

Certain dishes, especially seafood, might not be priced on the menu but labelled as *según peso* (according to weight) or *según mercado* (according to the market price that day). It is a good idea to ask for an estimate. Seven per cent value-added tax (IVA) is added to *la cuenta* (the bill)

and tips in cash are customary – around five per cent of the bill. Almost all restaurants take credit cards, though MasterCard and VISA are the most commonly used.

Bodega de Angel Sierra, a local bar in the Plaza de Chueca *(see p90)*

BOOKING

As a rule, booking is essential in Madrid, especially at midday. Phoning a few hours ahead will usually secure a table. At the most popular or fashionable restaurants, however, you should reserve a table one or more days in advance. Arriving early may be no guarantee of a place.

ETIQUETTE AND SMOKING

Apart from the inexpensive and the tourist restaurants, smart casual dress is best in most places, and smart dress should be worn in more exclusive establishments, especially in the evening. Few restaurants have non-smoking sections.

CHILDREN

Children are welcome in most restaurants, even the more exclusive during the day, but they do not receive the royal treatment they get in other parts of Spain, nor are children's menus or high chairs likely to be offered. Children might feel happiest in an informal restaurant, especially if it has an outdoor terrace.

DISABLED PERSONS

Facilities for disabled people are rare in Spanish restaurants and it is always worth phoning in advance (or asking the hotel staff to phone) to enquire about their provision.

WINE CHOICES

Your waiter might offer you an *aperitivo* (aperitif), in which case an excellent choice would be a sherry – a pale, dry *fino* or darker *oloroso* – accompanied perhaps by olives or a *tapa*. Wine is usually served with the main course. Spain has a formidable selection of wines *(see pp162–3)*. Although there is a significant mark-up in restaurants, they can still be reasonably priced, especially *vino de la casa* (house wine).

VEGETARIANS

With few vegetarian establishments in Madrid, you may decide to opt for the egg, salad or vegetable dishes at an ordinary restaurant, but always check the ingredients first.

The entrance to Combarro, with its medieval charm *(see p171)*

The Flavours of Madrid

Madrid offers a dazzling array of eateries, ranging from stylish award-winning restaurants and sleek café-bars to time-worn taverns. People from every corner of Spain have long been drawn to the city and typical Madrileño cuisine reflects this, by fusing cooking styles from all across the country. Visitors can take a culinary tour of the nation's varied regions, sampling Mediterranean rice dishes and Andalucían tapas alongside fish prepared in the Galician style. Surprisingly for a landlocked city, Madrid is noted for its seafood, which arrives daily from the ports. Juicy prawns and tender octopus are among the highlights.

Chorizo

A display of cured hams outside a restaurant in Plaza Mayor

SOUPS AND STEWS

Hearty soups and stews feature prominently on restaurant menus in Madrid. They make the perfect antidote to the city's long and bitterly cold winters, although seasonal *cazuelas* (stews) and *sopa de ajo*, a simple garlic soup, are served at almost any time of the year. A classic Madrileño dish is *cocido*, a slow-cooked casserole of pork, chicken, spicy sausage, black pudding, chunky vegetables and chickpeas. It is usually eaten in three stages: first the broth, then the vegetables, and finally the tender meat. Around Eastertime, look out for the traditional *potaje de garbanzos y espinacas* (chickpea and spinach soup), which is flavoured with salted cod.

ROASTS

Central Spain is famous for its *asadores* (roast houses), where hefty slabs of meat – simply grilled over charcoal (*a la parrilla*) or baked in brick ovens (*al horno de leña*) – are served. Pork (*cerdo*) or lamb (*cordero*) are the most common meats, but you may also find kid (*cabrito*), rabbit (*conejo*) and chicken (*gallina* or *pollo*). In

Pinto beans   **White (butter) beans**   **Red (kidney) beans**

Chickpeas

Black beans   **Armuña lentils**

Selection of pulses commonly used in Madrileño cooking

LOCAL DISHES AND SPECIALITIES

Madrid's sturdy stews and soups, often enriched with lentils and chickpeas, are a menu favourite during Madrid's freezing winters. In late spring and summer, sweet local strawberries and juicy melons feature strongly, offering refreshment in the scorching heat. Numerous *asadores* (roast houses) and *mesones* (taverns) serve roast lamb, pork, kid or game in season. Madrileños are usually happy to eat almost any part of an animal and offal such as tripe, brains, kidneys and pigs trotters are widely served. A classic dish is *callos a la Madrileña* (tripe and spicy sausage, flavoured with paprika). Remember also that Madrileños keep late hours so, unless you want to eat alone, do not go for dinner before 9;30pm and expect lunch to start around 2 o' clock in the afternoon.

Garlic

Sopa de Ajo *This warming garlic soup is thickened with breadcrumbs. An egg and a little paprika are often added.*

Outdoor dining at El Madroño restaurant, Plaza de la Puerta Cerrada

season, game will also be on the menu, particularly partridge (*perdiz*), pigeon (*pichón*) and perhaps even wild boar (*jabalí*).

TAPAS

The *tapeo*, a bar crawl from tapas bar to tapas bar, is an established part of life in Madrid. The city is crammed with tapas bars, from the prettily tiled old taverns to the legion of new bars serving elaborate gourmet snacks. Classic tapas include *croquetas* (croquettes, usually filled with ham or cod), *tortilla de patatas* (a thick potato omelette), *patatas brava*s (fried potato chunks with a spicy sauce), *boquerones en vinagre* (marinated fresh anchovies) and platters of *embutidos* (cured meats) or *quesos* (cheeses). The

Madrileños love pickled and conserved foods, especially shellfish such as *mejillones* (mussels) and *berberechos* (cockles), all perfectly paired with a glass of chilled sherry or *vermut* (vermouth).

The classic Madrileño breakfast: hot churros with a cup of chocolate

DESSERTS AND PASTRIES

Madrileños like to start the day with a breakfast of *porras* or *churros*, sugary fried dough strips, or an *ensaïmada*, a brioche-style pastry originally from Mallorca, served with a cup of hot chocolate. As in most of Spain, each local festival has a special sweet treat. For Easter, *torrijos*, eggy pastries flavoured with lemon and cinnamon, are served. At the *Fiestas de San Isidro* in summer, you can tuck into chocolate-coated *churros* and at Halloween, enjoy *buñuelos*, puffs of choux pastry filled with a thick custard or chocolate sauce.

WHAT TO DRINK

Wine (*vino*) Madrid's own robust reds are a great match for the city's stew and roasts.

Cava This Spanish equivalent of champagne is the favoured celebratory drink in Madrid.

Beer (*cerveza*) *Mahou*, a slightly malty lager, makes a cooling drink in summer.

Anís de Chinchón An aniseed-flavoured liqueur, it comes sweet (*dulce*) or dry (*seco*).

Vermouth (*Vermut*) This classic Madrileño aperitif is good chilled with tapas.

Soft drinks As well as Coca Cola and 7-UP, Bitter Kas, a dark red brew similar in taste to Campari, is very popular.

Tortilla de patatas *This thick omelette, stuffed with slices of potato, is popular served as tapas and for picnic lunches.*

Cocido Madrileño *Various meats, vegetables and chick-peas are cooked together to create this rich, hearty stew.*

Buñuelos de Viento *Puffs of choux pastry are stuffed with a sweet filling, usually a thick chocolate or vanilla cream.*

Choosing Tapas

Tapas, sometimes called *pinchos*, are small snacks that originated in Andalusia in the 19th century to accompany sherry. Stemming from a bartender's practice of covering a glass with a saucer or *tapa* (cover) to keep out flies, the custom progressed to a chunk of cheese or bread being used, and then to a few olives being placed on a platter to accompany a drink. Once free of charge, tapas are usually paid for nowadays, and a selection makes a delicious light meal. Choose from a range of appetizing varieties, from cold meats to elaborately prepared hot dishes of meat, seafood or vegetables.

Mixed green olives

Patatas bravas *is a piquant dish of fried potatoes spiced with a chilli and paprika sauce.*

Albondigas *(meatballs) are a hearty tapa, often served with a spicy tomato sauce.*

Almendras fritas *are fried, salted almonds.*

Banderillas *are canapes skewered on toothpicks. The entire canape should be eaten at once.*

Calamares fritos *are squid rings and tentacles which have been dusted with flour before being deep fried in olive oil. They are usually served garnished with a piece of lemon.*

Jamón serrano *is salt-cured ham dried in mountain* (serrano) *air.*

ON THE TAPAS BAR

Alitas de pollo Chicken wings

Almejas Clams

Berberechos Cockles

Berenjenas horneadas Roasted aubergines (eggplant)

Boquerones Anchovies

Boquerones al natural Fresh anchovies in garlic and olive oil

Buñuelos de bacalao Salt cod fritters

Butifarra Catalonian sausage

Calabacín rebozado Battered courgettes (zucchini)

Calamares a la romana Fried squid rings

Callos Tripe

Chistorra Spicy sausage

Chopitos Cuttlefish fried in batter

Chorizo al vino Chorizo sausage cooked in red wine

Chorizo diablo Chorizo served flamed with brandy

Cogollos fritos Lettuce fried in oil with garlic

Costillas Spare ribs

Criadillas Bulls' testicles

Croquetas Croquettes

Empanada Pastry filled with tomato, onion and meat or fish

Ensaladilla rusa Potatoes, carrots, red peppers, peas, olives, boiled egg, tuna and mayonnaise

Foie gras Liver pâté

Gambas pil pil Spicy, garlicky fried king prawns (shrimp)

Huevos de codorniz Hard-boiled quails' eggs

Judías blancas Butterbeans and whole garlic cloves in white wine vinegar

TAPAS BARS

Even a small village in Spain will have at least one bar where the locals go to enjoy drinks, tapas and conversation. On Sundays and holidays, favourite places are packed with whole families enjoying the fare. In large cities like Madrid it is customary to move from bar to bar, sampling the specialities of each. A *tapa* is a single serving, whereas a *ración* is two or three. Tapas are usually eaten standing or perching on a stool at the bar rather that sitting at a table, for which a surcharge is usually made.

Diners make their choice at a busy tapas bar

Chorizo, *a popular sausage flavoured with paprika and garlic, may be eaten cold or fried and served hot.*

Salpicón de mariscos *is a luxurious cold salad of assorted fresh seafood in a zesty vinaigrette.*

Gambas a la plancha *is a simple but flavourful dish of grilled prawns (shrimp).*

Tortilla española *is the ubiquitous Spanish omelette of onion and potato bound with egg.*

Queso manchego *is a sheep's-milk cheese from La Mancha.*

Pollo al ajillo *consists of small pieces of chicken (often wings) sautéed and then simmered with a garlic-flavoured sauce.*

Lacón a la gallega Boiled and smoked ham slices with paprika

Longaniza roja Spicy red pork sausage from Aragón (Longaniza blanca is paler and less spicy.)

Magro Pork in a paprika and tomato sauce

Manitas de cerdo Pig's trotters

Mejillones Mussels

Merluza a la romana Hake fried in a light batter

Morcilla Black (blood) pudding

Muslitos del mar Crab-meat croquette on a crab claw skewer

Orejas de cerdo Pig's ear

Paella Rice dish made with meat, fish and/or vegetables

Pan de ajo Garlic bread

Patatas a lo pobre Potato chunks sautéd with onions and red and green peppers

Patatas alioli Potato chunks in a garlic mayonnaise

Pernil Ham made from leg of pork, seasoned and air-dried

Pescaditos small fried fish

Pimientos rellenos Stuffed peppers

Pinchito Kebab on a skewer

Pisto Thick ratatouille of diced tomato, onion and courgette

Pulpitos Baby octopus

Rabo de toro Oxtail

Sepia Cuttlefish

Sesos Brains, usually lamb or calf

Surtido de ibéricos Assortment of cured hams

Tortilla riojana Ham, sausage and red pepper omelette

Tostas Bread with various toppings such as tuna or brie

What to Drink in Madrid

Spain is one of the world's largest wine-producing countries and many fine wines are made here, in addition to the famous sherries of southern Spain and the *cavas* (sparkling wines) of Catalonia. Beer is produced throughout Spain, and Madrid's *cervecerías* (beer bars) are especially adept at pulling a refreshing half pint. Some offer *sidra* (apple cider) from northern Spain. The full range of non-alcoholic drinks is available, including mineral water. Spanish coffee is rich and strong and, to round off a meal, many restaurants offer traditional liqueurs such as brandy and *anís*.

Customers enjoying a pre-meal drink at an outdoor terrace bar

Hot chocolate

A plate of *churros* (batter sticks)

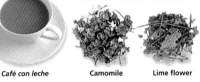

Café con leche

Camomile

Lime flower

HOT DRINKS

Coffee served in Spanish bars is usually espresso. The traditional start to the day is a big cup of *café con leche* (with milk). *Café cortado* has a dash of milk, *café sólo* is black and *café americano* is weaker. Another popular breakfast drink is thick hot chocolate served with *churros* (fried batter sticks). A good cup of tea is hard to find, but herbal teas to try are *manzanilla* (camomile) and *tila* (lime flower).

COLD DRINKS

Madrid's tap water is safe to drink, but Spaniards prefer bottled water *(agua mineral)*, either still *(sin gas)* or sparkling *(con gas)* . Summer favourites include Valencian *horchata*, a sweet milky drink made from ground *chufas* (earth almonds), and *granizado de limón* (iced lemon). *Gaseosa*, or sparkling lemonade, can be drunk either on its own or as *tinto de verano*, mixed with red wine *(see Mixed Drinks)*. Soft drinks and orange juice *(zumo de naranja)* are also widely available.

Sparkling and still mineral water

Horchata, made from *chufas*

WINE

Spain produces some of the best wines in the world. The key standard for the industry is the *Denominación de Origen* (DO) classification, a guarantee of a wine's origin and quality. *Vino de la Tierra* is a classification of wines below that of DO in which over 60 per cent of the grapes come from a specified region. *Vino de Mesa*, the lowest category, covers basic unclassified wines. Spanish *cavas* include best-selling sparkling wines, Freixenet and Codorniú, which are *brut* (dry) or *semi-seco* (slightly sweet). In restaurants, wine is served by the glass, bottle or half-bottle. House wines are sometimes decanted into a carafe.

Penedés white wine

Rioja red wine

Sparkling wine *(cava)*

SPIRITS AND LIQUEURS

Not all of Spain's grapes go into making wine. Much of the harvest
is distilled to make clear spirits, the basis of Spain's many liqueurs.
These include the aniseed flavoured *anís* which can either be
extremely dry (*seco* or *orujo*) or syrupy sweet (*dulce*). Brandy
(*coñac*) de Jeréz, an aged wine spirit, is another popular digestive;
the price is a good indication of quality. Fruits are also used to flavour
liqueurs. One of the most popular variations is *pacharán*, a Navarrese
drink using sloes. Spain, and especially the Canary Islands, has always
produced *ron* (rum) from sugar cane that grows in the south. *Ginebra*
(gin) was introduced by the British when they occupied the island
of Menorca in the 18th century. Whisky is also a favourite, though
imported Scotch is preferred to the domestic brands. A popular drink
with younger people is *cuba-libre*, a rum with cola (*see Mixed Drinks*).

Anís   **Pacharán**

BEER

Spaniards love their *cerveza*
(beer) and Mahou is a popular brand in Madrid.
Bars serve *cerveza
del barril* (draught
beer) in a *caña* (small
glass) or larger *jarra*.
Beer also comes in
bottles of 25 cl,
33 cl or one litre
(*litronas*). Alcohol-
free lager (*cerveza
sin alcohol*) is sold
in many bars.

Bottled beers

SHERRY

Sherry is produced in *bodegas* in
Jeréz de la Frontera, Sanlúcar de
Barrameda and El Puerto de Santa
María. Similar wines are produced in
Montilla near Córdoba, although
they are not officially
called sherry. Pale
fino is dry and light
and makes an excel-
lent aperitif. Amber
amontillado (aged *fino*)
has a strong earthy taste
while *oloroso* is full-
bodied and ruddy.

Two brands of *fino* sherry

**Red wine
and
lemonade**

Sangría

MIXED DRINKS

Sangría is a refreshing
blend of red wine and
gaseosa (lemonade). Other
ingredients include pieces of
freshly chopped fruit, sugar and
liqueurs. Another favourite drink
is *Agua de Valencia*, which is an
invigorating combination of *cava*
(sparkling wine) and orange juice. A
wide range of cocktails is available,
including the ever popular *cuba-libre*.

Cuba-libre   **Tinto de
verano**

HOW TO READ A WINE LABEL

As well as the wine's name and its
producer, the label will tell you the
region it comes from, usually a
Denominación de Origen, and the
vintage year. Wines labelled *cosecha*
are recent vintages and the least
expensive, while *crianza* and *reserva*
wines are aged a minimum of two or
three years, part of that time in oak
casks. *Blanco* (white) can be *seco*
(dry), *semi-seco* (semi-dry) or *dulce*
(sweet). *Rosado* is rosé and *tinto* is
red. The label also gives the content
(usually 75 cl), the alcohol level
(around 12–13 per cent volume) and
sometimes specifies the grape variety.

Brand name   **Company's crest**

**Capacity of
the bottle**

**Estate-bottled
rather than
cooperative**

**The wine's
*Denominación
de Origen***

The vintage   **Symbol for region**

Choosing a Restaurant

The restaurants in this guide have been selected across a wide range of price categories for their good value, exceptional food and interesting location. Some offer tables outside and special menus. The restaurants are listed by area, starting with Old Madrid, then Bourbon Madrid, Around La Castellana, Further Afield and Beyond Madrid.

PRICE CATEGORIES
For a three-course meal for one, including half a bottle of house wine, tax and service:

€ under 20 euros
€€ 20–30 euros
€€€ 30–40 euros
€€€€ over 40 euros

OLD MADRID

Con 2 Fogones
 €

Calle San Bernardino 9, 28015 **Tel** 91 559 6326. **Map** 2 D3

The atmosphere at Con dos Fogones is laid back and sophisticated with a mainly local clientele. Traditional recipes garnered from the owner's mother are cooked by Guatemalan chefs and presented in original style, such as the brie cheese tempura. Smoking permitted.

Inshala
€

Calle Amnistia 10, 28013 **Tel** 91 548 2632. **Map** 4 D2

Located in a side street just off Plaza de la Opera and close to the Palacio Real, this relaxed, multi-ethnic café has a Moorish-style interior. The menu changes every four to six months and includes cuisine from all around the world, be it Italian, Moroccan, Mexican, Argentinian or Japanese. Smoking permitted. Closed Sun & Easter.

Can Punyetes
€€

Calle Señores de Luzón 5, 28013 **Tel** 91 542 0921. **Map** 4 D2

Close to Plaza de la Villa is this traditional Spanish eatery serving Catalonian cuisine. The grilled vegetables and meats are delicious, and the specialities like *escalivada* (oven-baked onion, pepper and aubergine) and *calçots* (chargrilled sweet spring onions) are also worth trying. Smoking permitted. Closed Sun dinner.

El Estragón
€€

Plaza de la Paja 21, 28005 **Tel** 91 365 8982. **Map** 7 A3

Bienvenido Alarcón is head chef at El Estragón Vegetariano (Vegetarian Tarragon). The paella is cooked to perfection (without meat or fish) using white couscous or basmati, organic or brown rice. The novelty factor here shows how paella can be adapted with a multitude of ingredients. Smoking permitted.

El Jardin Secreto
€€

Calle Cònde Duque 2, 28015 **Tel** 91 541 8023. **Map** 2 D4

"The Secret Garden" may not have a garden but it is beautifully situated on a quiet side street, and its popular terrace bar spills on to the street in summer. The menu is light with rose-flavoured soups and goat's cheese and pasta salads. A good selection of pastries and home-baked cakes are on display. Smoking permitted.

Naïa
 €€

Plaza de la Paja 3, 28005 **Tel** 91 366 2783. **Map** 4 D3

This beautifully situated, New York-style eatery was designed by Jorge Varela in a minimalist Zen spirit. An indoor patio garden plays the latest chill-out grooves. Red tuna steak tartare or avocado and gula fish salad make for some of the tastiest cooking in Madrid. Ten euro set menu available Tue–Fri. Smoking permitted. Closed Sun dinner & Mon.

Plato y Placer
 €€

Calle de la Morería 9, 28005 **Tel** 91 365 2075. **Map** 3 C3

The interior of this colourful restaurant is decorated with celebrity memorabilia. The menu is traditional Spanish with a modern twist and includes such dishes as oxtail in filo pastry and "broken eggs" on fried fish. *Cocido Madrileño* (chickpea and meat stew) is available from Wed–Fri lunchtimes. Smoking permitted. Closed Sun dinner & Mon.

Toma
 €€

Calle Conde Duque 14, 28015 **Tel** 91 547 4996. **Map** 2 D4

Toma is a very cool and hidden tiny New York-style eatery. It is run by an American chef who cooks and serves Mediterranean and Japanese cuisine to queues of demanding locals and tourists alike. Only serves lunch on Sundays; the rest of the week opens for dinner only. Smoking permitted.

La Vaca Argentina
 €€

Calle Caños del Peral 2, 28013 **Tel** 91 541 3318. **Map** 4 D2

There are over a dozen La Vaca Argentina outlets all over Madrid specialising in Argentine Pampas-reared beef *assados* cooked to your personal taste. Each restaurant has its own unique style, and specialities include *lomitos* (meat steaks), baguettes stuffed with *solomillo* (pork fillet) and an assortment of homemade sauces. Smoking permitted.

Key to Symbols *see back cover flap*

La Viuda Blanca
Calle Campomanes 6, 28013 **Tel** *91 548 7529.*
Map *4 D1*

This is a cosmopolitan and vibrant eatery that attracts a fashion-conscious crowd. The stunning glass pyramid ceiling creates a bright and relaxed atmosphere, and service is informal but punctual. A very reasonable lunch menu offers a good fixed price option, with dishes such as boletus mushroom risotto. Closed Sun.

Algarabía
Calle de la Unión 8, 28013 **Tel** *91 542 4131.*
Map *4 D2*

This small restaurant serves dishes and wines from the region of La Rioja in the north of Spain. The menu includes potatoes *a la riojana* (with onion, olive oil, garlic and paprika) and various meat dishes, best enjoyed with a glass of red wine. Try the battered asparagus or the lamb with mushrooms. Smoking permitted. Closed Sat lunch & Sun.

Belalúa
San Nicolás 8 **Tel** *91 547 2222.*
Map *3 C2*

A reasonably priced menu celebrates the best of northern Spain's cuisine. A mix of gourmet fish, meat, salads and sweets coupled with an elite crowd spilling out of the nearby opera house make for an entertaining atmosphere. Cheap fixed-price menu at lunch time Mon–Fri. Smoking permitted. Closed Sun & Mon dinner.

Botin
Calle Cuchilleros 17, 28011 **Tel** *91 366 4217.*
Map *4 E3*

Dubbed "the world's oldest restaurant" by the *Guinness Book of Records* (1725), Botin is an antique wonderland built on four floors. Typical Castillian food includes *gazpacho*, suckling pig and a delicious cream tart made with a sweet biscuit base, egg meringue and pastel cream.

Casa Piluca
Plaza Gabriel Miró 7, 28005 **Tel** *91 365 1269.*
Map *3 B3*

Set in old Madrid on the Plaza de las Vistillas, Casa Piluca provides visitors with a taste of typical local and northern cuisine including *cocido madrileño* (chickpea and meat stew). The highlight is the spectacular charcoal grilled fish and meats smothered in garlic and served with a side salad. Offers valet parking. Smoking permitted. Closed Sun & Mon dinner.

Corgui
Calle Rollo 8, 28005 **Tel** *91 547 1005.*
Map *4 D3*

This Mexican-owned restaurant bar, in the heart of Madrid de las Austrias, dishes up a varied Mediterranean and creative cuisine. A nice quiet lunch spot, which becomes more animated by night as the cocktail waitresses get busy. Main courses of note include tempura, *sashimi* and *teriyaki carpaccio*. Smoking permitted. Closed Mon.

Cornucopia
Calle Navas de Tolosa 9, 28013 **Tel** *91 521 3896.*
Map *4 E1*

Cornucopia is a great place for groups as it has three large dining rooms. Try the charcoal grilled tuna steaks marinated in soy, sesame, olive and orange sauces or the vegetable lasagne. The elaborate cakes and desserts can be pre-ordered. There is a 12 euro set menu Mon–Sat lunch. Smoking permitted.

El Pato Mudo
Costanilla de los Angeles 8, 28013 **Tel** *91 559 4840.*
Map *4 E1*

Close to Gran Vía and the Opera, El Pato Mudo specializes in Mediterranean cuisine. The restaurant is known for its rice dishes, and there are eight different choices, including classic black rice (with squid ink), rice with cauliflower and cuttlefish, and the popular duck rice. Smoking permitted.

El Schotis
Calle Cava Baja 11, 28005 **Tel** *91 365 3230.*
Map *4 D4*

El Schotis is just off the Plaza Mayor on the historic Cava Baja, which runs down to the lively La Latina district. The restaurant has been famous for four decades and produces top notch traditional Spanish cuisine. Barbeque-grilled meats dominate the long menu. Smoking permitted. Closed Sun dinner.

La Mordida
Calle Las Fuentes 3, 28005 **Tel** *91 559 1136.*
Map *4 D2*

Tacos and enchiladas are freshly prepared in this colourful restaurant co-owned by the Spanish rock legend Joaquin Sabina. Garish murals of Diego Rivera and Frida Kahlo plaster the walls, and every nook and cranny is stuffed with artworks and trinkets transporting diners to a distant Mexican *pueblo*. Reasonable prices and generous portions. Smoking permitted.

La Parrala
Calle Humilladero 5, 28005 **Tel** *91 366 90 56.*
Map *4 D4*

Burnt ochre red walls and oak panelling characterize this local tapas bar and restaurant. Wine lovers like its simple but varied list, and the menu offers elaborately prepared typical Spanish ingredients such as pumpkin pasties stuffed with *morcilla* (black sausage) coated in pepper and *salmorejo* sauce. Smoking permitted. Closed Sun dinner, Mon, Tue lunch.

Madrid1 Catedral
Carrera San Jerónimo 16 **Tel** *91 523 3556.*
Map *4 F2*

Situated conveniently close to the Reina Sophia and Prado museums, the interior of Madrid1 Catedral is typically Spanish, and is usually bustling with tourists eager to sample the cheap set menus and tapas. Options include paella, garlic rabbit and lentils, an assortment of grilled fish and meats. Ten euro set menu Mon–Fri lunch. Smoking permitted.

Malandrin

 ©©©

*Calle Almendro 9 **Tel** 91 354 0082.* **Map** *4 D3*

Malandrin is located right in the old La Latina district and serves up delicious tapas with a contemporary twist. Also available are a variety of tasty *tostas* (open sandwiches). This *taberna* is popular with locals and tourists alike so arrive early to get a seat. Smoking permitted. Closed Sun dinner & Mon.

Café De Oriente

 ©©©©

*Plaza de Oriente 2, 28013 **Tel** 91 541 3974.* **Map** *3 C2*

Directly opposite the Royal Palace and next to the Opera House, there are few more historically situated places to eat in Madrid. The restaurant is set in the wine cellars next to the remains of the 17th-century convent of San Gil. Try the leg of roasted kid with sweet potato mash. Smoking permitted.

Caripen

 ©©©©

*Plaza de la Marina Española 4, 28071 **Tel** 91 541 1177.* **Map** *4 D1*

Set opposite the Spanish Senate, Caripen was originally a famous flamenco bar popular with Spanish celebrities. Today this Parisian bistro is famed for its duck Magret. Try the *ensalada de berros* (giblets on a base of soft grated cheese, watercress, rocket and dried fruit sitting on a small disk of hard goat's cheese). Smoking permitted. Closed for lunch & Sun.

Casa Lucío

©©©©

*Calle Cava Baja 35, 28005 **Tel** 91 365 3252.* **Map** *4 D4*

Casa Lucío has garnered a reputation for outstanding Spanish cuisine. House specialities include *callos* (tripe), its famous egg dishes and a creamy rice pudding. Its simple appeal attracts many tourists as well as a well-heeled clientele, from artists, actors and politicians to the king of Spain himself. Smoking permitted. Closed Sat lunch & Aug.

El Corral de la Morería

 ©©©©

*Calle Morería 17, 28005 **Tel** 91 365 8446.* **Map** *3 C3*

The oldest performance restaurant in Madrid, El Corral de la Morería has welcomed numerous celebrities and foreign dignitaries. The music is usually Flamenco guitar and includes traditional dancers. The kitchen serves an excellent paella for two, monkfish stew, Basque hake and a partridge recipe from Toledo. Offers valet parking.

La Capilla de la Bolsa

 ©©©©

*Calle Bolsa, 12, 28005 **Tel** 91 521 86 23* **Map** *4 F3*

This atmospheric restaurant once housed the Knights Templar Santa Cruz hermitage. Today, each room is decorated in a different style and the restaurant offers traditional Mediterranean and Spanish cuisine. An assortment of lasagnes, stuffed leg of lamb, sea urchin and prawn croquettes are not to be missed. Reservations advised. Smoking permitted.

Teatro Real

 ©©©©

*Plaza Oriente, 28013 **Tel** 91 516 0670.* **Map** *3 C2*

Located within the Opera House, this is the perfect restaurant for opera lovers, you can even hear the performances from your table. Try the roast suckling pig with toffee cream or the breaded seafood with a mushroom ragout. Desserts include a divine creme caramel with a hazelnut and berry coulis. Closed Aug.

BOURBON MADRID

La Finca de Susana

©©©

*Calle Arlabán 4, 28004 **Tel** 91 369 3557.* **Map** *7 A2*

Excellent value cuisine in stylish surroundings has lunchtime Madrilleños queuing to get in. Set menus cost around 10 euros while an *à la carte* menu provides many more slightly more expensive options. Try the charcoal-grilled vegetables in tempura batter, oven-cooked *bacalao* (cod fish) with spinach or the spicy caramelised duck. Arrive before 1pm.

Indochina

©©©

*Calle Barquillo 10, 28004 **Tel** 91 524 0318.* **Map** *5 B5*

Mixing recipes from Vietnam, Thailand and Malaysia, Indochina has a set menu that consists of five starters and five main dishes, including oxtail stew with bitter hot sauce, Thai noodle pasta with almonds and shrimp, and green papaya salad drizzled with cashew sauce. There is a 13 euro set menu Mon–Fri lunch. Smoking permitted.

Mumbai Massala

 ©©©

*Paseo Recoletos 14, 28001 **Tel** 91 435 7194* **Map** *7 C1*

This typical Indian restaurant has based its menu on Dum Pukt cuisine where recipes are cooked on a low flame so that the rich textures and flavours are preserved. The lamb *rogan josh*, made with tomato, onion and spices, is reputedly the best in Spain. There is a 15 euro set menu Mon–Fri lunch. Smoking permitted.

Olsen

 ©©©

*Calle del Prado 15, 28014 **Tel** 91 429 3659.* **Map** *7 C2*

This pinewood-decorated restaurant opened in February 2005 but has already become renowned for its smorgasbord of Nordic cuisine. The Argentine and Swedish owners have created a tantalising menu with dishes such as Nordic sushi complete with raw Gravlax salmon, prawns, haddock, and herring on sweet potato. Smoking permitted. Closed Mon.

La Paella de la Reina

Avenida Reina 39 **Tel** *91 531 1885.* **Map** *7 A1*

Situated just off Madrid's busy Gran Via avenue, La Paella de la Reina serves up a wide variety of paella combos from the classic seafood paella (mussels, king prawns, clams, squid) to the original "Valenciana" containing rabbit, chicken and mixed vegetables with bits of pork and sausage.

Samarkanda

Estación de Atocha, Glorieta de Carlos V, 28045 **Tel** *91 530 9746.* **Map** *8 D5*

Underneath Atocha station's glass and metal structure, nestled amongst tropical plants, is Samarkanda. The restaurant serves quality Mediterranean food from a six-monthly rotating menu. Offerings include artichokes stuffed with pâté in a hollandaise sauce and codfish fillet in cider. Smoking permitted.

Tocororo

Calle del Prado 3, 28014 **Tel** *91 369 4000.* **Map** *7 C2*

At Tocororo genuine Havana recipes are washed down with expertly shaken cocktails from the vibrant bar. The chef's special dishes include shrimp enchiladas, *ropa vieja* (shredded beef) and *moros y cristianos* (black beans and rice). Week-ends offer live Creole music and dance sessions. Smoking permitted. Closed Mon, 2 weeks in Feb & 2 weeks in Sep.

Asia Gallery

Plaza Las Cortes 7, 28014 **Tel** *91 360 0049.* **Map** *7 C1*

Located within the elegant surroundings of the Westin Palace Hotel, Asia Gallery has triumphed under the skilled direction of Roger Chen. Classic, colonial 1920s design and Cantonese dishes using fresh ingredients attract both local and foreign celebrities. Try the glazed duck, shrimp *mushi*, ginger lobster and the rice pudding mousse. Smoking permitted.

La Ancha

Calle de Zorilla 7, 28014 **Tel** *91 429 8186.* **Map** *7 B2*

Run by a family of caterers since 1930, La Ancha serves good quality, traditional food to the journalists and members of the Spanish Parliament who work nearby. Popular choices include their famous lentil casserole and potato omelette with clams. All the desserts are homemade. Smoking permitted. Closed Sat, Sun & Aug.

AROUND LA CASTELLANA

Bazaar

Calle Libertad 21, 28004 **Tel** *91 523 3905.* **Map** *7 B1*

Right in the heart of the lively, busy Chueca district is an oasis of contemporary creative cooking. The restaurant décor is arthouse New York and the clientele could easily be in Greenwich Village as they lap up Mexican tapas such as cod fish confit or spicy chicken kebabs.

El Espejo

Paseo de Recoletos 31 **Tel** *91 308 2347.* **Map** *6 D5*

This café offers a striking decorative blend of Toulouse Lautrec and Art Deco with plenty of mirrors. The dining room, behind, serves international cuisine. There is also a conservatory-styles space at the front, serving tapas, snacks and coffee all day. There is a reasonably priced menu of the day. Advance reservations are advisable.

Lateral

Calle Velázquez 57, 28046 **Tel** *91 435 0604.* **Map** *6 F3*

Handy for the chic Salamanca shopping district, Lateral is always buzzing, especially before the late night bars and clubs open. The menu offers a good selection of tapas and an assortment of tasty *brochette* recipes. The *sollomillo* (sirloin steak) with caramelised onion is a house favourite. Good selection of wines by the glass. Smoking permitted.

Living in London T Room

Calle de Santa Engracia 4, 28010 **Tel** *91 319 7958.* **Map** *5 A1*

This is a typical English Tea Room complete with steaming Earl Grey, crumpets, scones with cream and a delicious selection of home-made jams and marmalade. A brunch menu includes cappuccino mushroom soup, slices of pizza, hot and cold sandwiches and sweet and savoury pastries. Smoking permitted. Closed Sun morning, including lunch.

Ojalá

Calle San Andrés 1, 28912 **Tel** *91 523 2747.* **Map** *2 F4*

Ojala may seem like a simple local bar with its wooden deck chairs and classroom tables but it is actually a sophisticated restaurant offering gourmet international cuisine, superb cocktails and professional service. The seasonal menu includes Belgian tapas, sushi, Arab dishes and New American cuisine. Ten euro set menu Mon–Fri lunch. Smoking permitted.

Al-mounia

Calle Recoletos 5 **Tel** *91 435 0828.* **Map** *8 D1*

Al-mounia has been serving authentic Arab cuisine in the capital for over 30 years and has been consistently praised for its quality of menu and service. The Moroccan décor transports you to an exotic world where couscous and tagines are steamed with saffron- and ginger-infused vegetables. Offers valet parking. Smoking permitted. Closed Sun & Aug.

Boggo

Calle Velázquez 102, 28046 **Tel** *91 781 1038.*   **Map** *6 F3*

A cool, romantic restaurant, Boggo is the perfect place to impress without breaking the bank. International cuisine is served in an intimate dining room with great upbeat background music and the occasional live jazz concert. Dishes include goat's cheese salad and sole ravioli with yellow pepper cream. Smoking permitted. Opens for dinner only.

Cafe Bisu

Calle José Abascal 8, 28003 **Tel** *91 447 5208.*   **Map** *6 D1*

A mix of dainty Mediterranean cuisine, tapas, *pinchos* and sushi to share are presented with Oriental perfection. The chef recommends mini spring rolls, *terichaki* quail drumsticks, *champinones rellenos* (stuffed mushrooms), *muslos de pollo a la miel* (honey-baked chicken thighs) and *empanadas* (Spanish pastries filled with meat and cheese). Smoking permitted.

Cafe Oliver

Calle Almirante 12, 28004 **Tel** *91 521 73 79.*   **Map** *5 C5*

Cafe Oliver serves Italian, Moroccan, French and Spanish dishes without mixing up the flavours. Main courses offer juicy entrêcote steaks with Sant Marceliny sauce and a selection of wholesome salads. Closed Sun & Mon evenings. Offers valet parking. There is a 12 euro set menu Mon–Fri lunch. Smoking permitted.

Café Saigon

Calle María de Molina 4, 28006 **Tel** *91 563 1566.*   **Map** *6 F1*

Madrid's top Asian eatery has consistently received rave reviews. Head chef, Miguel Ángel García, specialises in innovative Vietnamese cuisine and the menu includes Thai seafood dishes, Chinese spring rolls, aubergine duck curry and Vietnamese ravioli. Try the vanilla ice cream fried in flour and honey and covered in hot chocolate sauce. Smoking permitted.

De Pura Cepa

Calle Fuente del Berro 31, 28009 **Tel** *91 309 2879.*   **Map** *6 F5*

As its name indicates *de pura cepa* means "authentic" in Spanish. This restaurant offers traditional cooking with imaginative touches, and excellent tapas served at the bar at any time of day. Among its dishes it is worth highlighting the squid with crispy onion and the *millefeuille* pastry filled with vegetables, goat's cheese and ham. Smoking permitted.

Divina La Cocina

Calle Colmenares 13, 28004 **Tel** *91 531 3765.*   **Map** *7 B1*

Baroque-style décor creates a decadent atmosphere at this spacious Mediterranean restaurant. Veal stew with a creamy cheese sauce, and sole rolls battered then lightly fried with lemon cream are some of the main courses. Advance booking is recommended. Smoking permitted.

El Buey

Calle General Pardiñas 10, 28071 **Tel** *91 431 4492.*   **Map** *4 F2*

El Buey literally means "the young bull" and it is the charcoal-grilled bullock steak that makes this small restaurant in the Salamanca district so popular. The atmosphere is animated and loud with a good mix of tourists and local upper-crust residents. The tiger prawns cooked in Cava with rice, raisins and pine nuts is worth trying. Closed Sun dinner.

Hard Rock Cafe

Paseo la Castellana 2, 28010 **Tel** *91 436 4340.*   **Map** *5 D4*

You may be wondering why this tacky tourist trap is listed here – the answer is that it has become an icon in Madrid, popular with locals and tourists alike. The atmosphere inside this rock 'n' roll museum is buzzing, and the home-made food is excellent: nachos, hamburgers and a delicious New York-style cheese cake.

Le Dragon

Calle Gil de Santibáñez 2 **Tel** *91 435 6669*   **Map** *6 D5*

A thoroughly Feng-Shui restaurant with a distinctly Soho attitude that serves up typical Chinese fare. The tasting menu allows you to sample the likes of chicken spring rolls with mint sauce. Don't miss the duck ying-yang, crab dim sum or the five perfumes chicken strips. Offers valet parking. Smoking permitted.

Madrilia

Calle Clavel 6, 28004 **Tel** *91 523 9275.*   **Map** *7 A1*

Run by the same team as Cafe Oliver, Madrilia serves simple Italian cuisine in a New York interior right in the heart of Chueca. The carbonara or bolognese pastas are the best options, as well as rocket, Parmesan and sun-dried tomato salad, small pizzas (pizzetta) and gnocchi. Smoking permitted.

Minabo

Calle Caracas 8, 28010 **Tel** *91 308 2277.*   **Map** *5 B3*

Minabo is a Japanese restaurant which mixes typical sushi with Andino and Chinese recipes. The resulting fusion features creative dishes such as the salmon tower in spicy citrus and mango sauce, *sashimi serranito*, *ceviche* or *makis*, all of which provide a satisfying meal. Smoking permitted. Closed Sun.

Moma 56

Calle José Abascal 56, 28003 **Tel** *91 399 4830.*   **Map** *6 D1*

By night Moma is one of the hottest nightspots in Madrid, by day the restaurant serves a selection of over 40 novelty dishes. There is a popular brunch menu which offers the likes of crispy ham scrambled egg with cheddar, meatballs and assorted croquettes. Offers valet parking. Smoking permitted. Closed Sun.

Key to Price Guide *see p.164* **Key to Symbols** *see back cover flap*

Sugar
€€€

Calle Diego de León 11, 28006 **Tel** *91 515 9604.*   **Map** 6 E1

Global cuisine is the best way to describe chef Mario Moñivas' varied menu consisting of recipes from the five continents. The glamorous restaurant is divided into different sections by Oriental chiffon curtains while plasma screens project underwater landscapes. Top of the menu are the grilled entrecôte burgers and the risottos. Smoking permitted. Closed Mon dinner.

Thai Gardens
€€€

Paseo de la Habana 3, 28001 **Tel** *91 577 8884.*

One of the capital's most popular dining experiences attracting many local celebrities, Thai Gardens offers a romantic colonial setting with bamboo and teak furniture, orchids, candles and a private garden at the back. The prize-winning menu offers 70 dishes with fresh ingredients flown in from Bangkok each week. Smoking permitted. Offers valet parking.

El Bodegón
€€€€

Calle Pinar 15, 28037 **Tel** *91 562 8844.*   **Map** 6 D1

The chefs at El Bodegón order fresh fish from the north as well as local produce then adapt traditional Basque recipes into gourmet cooking. The partridge, fresh haricot beans and seafood are particularly good. Reservation is required well in advance. Gentlemen are required to wear a jacket. Valet parking. Smoking permitted. Closed Sat lunch, Sun & Aug.

La Broche
€€€€

Calle Miguel Ángel 29, 28010 **Tel** *91 399 3437.*   **Map** 6 D2

Being one of Ferrán Adriá's disciples, Sergi Arola's creative menu will not disappoint the adventurous gourmet food lover. The menu changes regularly and can include such dishes as marinated sardines stuffed with herring eggs, duck liver with baked vegetables and passion fruit and leek soaked in Amaretto. Reservations are essential. Closed Sat, Sun, Easter & Aug.

Dassa Bassa
€€€€

Calle Villalar 7, 28001 **Tel** *91 576 7397.*   **Map** 7 B1

Young rising culinary star Dario Barrio Dominguez has made this restaurant one of the most fashionable in Madrid. Creative dishes such as oxtail in a wine sauce with chocolate come as a shock to the senses. Offers valet parking. Smoking permitted. Closed Sun, Mon & 3 weeks in Aug.

Iroco
€€€€

Calle Velázquez 18, 28001 **Tel** *91 431 7381.*   **Map** 6 F5

Opened in 1994, Iroco has quickly become a classic due to the excellent international cuisine and wine list. The summer menu, served on the garden patio, includes gazpacho with red pepper ice cream and elaborate desserts such as pineapple and banana rolls with lavender honey. Sunday brunch served from 1–4pm. Smoking permitted.

Jockey
€€€€

Calle Amador de los Ríos 6, 28010 **Tel** *91 319 2435.*   **Map** 6 D4

Jockey was the catering choice of the Princess of Asturias for her wedding. The menu has won dozens of awards and is essentially traditional Spanish recipes cooked with gourmet flair. Recommended are the fresh fish dishes, baked duck and smoked eel mousse. Gentlemen are required to wear a jacket. Valet parking. Smoking permitted. Closed Sun & Aug.

Mosaiq
€€€€

Calle Caracas 21, 28010 **Tel** *91 308 4446.*   **Map** 5 B3

At the extravagantly decorated Mosaic, performing belly dancers add to the Moroccan ambience. The à la carte menu is not overly expensive and there is a tasting menu that consists of the likes of shish kebab, chicken tagine, pitta bread and Arab sweet pastries. Offers valet parking. Smoking permitted.

Nicolás
€€€€

Calle Villalar 4, 28001 **Tel** *91 431 7737.*   **Map** 8 D1

The Art Deco-styled Nicolás offers entrée tapas to whet the appetite, but it's the fish that comes up trumps with dishes such as marinated sardines. Try the excellent *potaje de garbanzos con chipirones* (chickpea and baby squid stew). Smoking permitted. Closed Sun, Mon & Aug.

Santo Mauro
€€€€

Calle Zurbano 36, 28010 **Tel** *91 319 6900.*   **Map** 5 C2

This award-winning restaurant is housed at the back of the luxury Santa Mauro Hotel. Chef Carlos Posada serves up the likes of entrêcote with wild mushrooms and creamy sauce, and a dreamy strawberry *gazpacho* with lobster. There are only eight tables so it is worth booking well in advance. Offers valet parking. Smoking permitted.

Sula
€€€€

Calle Jorge Juan 33, 28001 **Tel** *91 781 6197.*   **Map** 6 F5

This trendy restaurant opened in 2007 and has had rave reviews. Chef Quique Dacosta has created an elegant Mediterranean menu that includes dishes such as peas in scrambled egg with black truffle, and black monkfish with artichokes and a port wine sauce. It also has its own delicatessen. Smoking permitted. Closed Sun & 3 weeks in Aug.

Teatriz
€€€€

Calle Hermosilla 15, 28001 **Tel** *91 577 5379.*   **Map** 6 D4

Formerly a theatre, Teatriz was completely transformed by French designer Philippe Starck in 1989 and now houses a chic restaurant and stylish tapas bar. Live jazz and various artists can often be seen on the old stage. Generous portions of lobster and tuna salad is a menu staple. Closed Aug.

Zalacaín

Calle Álvarez de Baena 4, 28006 **Tel** *91 561 4840.*   **Map** *6 D1*

With three Michelin stars, Zalacaín is arguably Madrid's finest restaurant. Fresh seasonal ingredients appear on the menu like organic entrêcote, steak tartare, *solomillo* (pork fillet) and a range of fish and seafood. A jacket and tie policy operates for gentlemen. Advance booking is essential. Valet parking. Smoking permitted. Closed Sat lunch, Sun, Easter & Aug.

FURTHER AFIELD

Metbar

Calle Serrano 221, 28016 **Tel** *91 344 1321.*

Metbar serves a simple and healthy Spanish and Mediterranean menu with exotic touches such as the *foie milhojas* with Pedro Ximenez-soaked apple crunch. Generous dishes are served up rapidly in this clinical white minimalist space with orange and fuscia coloured fittings. There is a ten euro set menu Mon–Fri. Smoking permitted.

Summa

Avenida Profesor Waksman 5, 28036 **Tel** *91 457 3227.*

Summa specialises in a new wave of Japanese cuisine with a Mediterranean and Latino influence. A sushi bar serves the straight eight- or 16-piece menus alongside wholesome salads. The main dining area offers dishes such as tempura sushi rolls and red tuna steaks. Sushi making classes are also available. Smoking permitted. Closed Sun.

Alduccio

Calle Concha Espina 8 **Tel** *91 564 6897.*

This strictly Italian menu offers a finger-licking foray into the world of home-made pastas. Fetuccini, *carpaccio* and focaccia are the house specialities but if you prefer pizza, calzone, Bolognese or ravioli you will not be disappointed. A large outdoor terrace provides a romantic setting during the summer months. Smoking permitted. Closed Sun & Aug.

Casa Mia

Calle Josefa Valcárcel 10, 28027 **Tel** *91 320 2202.*

On Madrid's northern A2 exit road, this *trattoria* offers real farmhouse recipes straight from the Italian countryside. Dine outside on the lovely terrace in summer, and sit back and enjoy the magicians that entertain diners at weekends! The pumpkin pizza is especially good. Smoking permitted.

Citra

Calle de Castelló 18, 28001 **Tel** *91 575 2866.*

Citra has a cool interior design by the architect Ignacio García de Vinuesa. Clever lighting on a beige, ochre and olive green colour scheme define the lively tapas bar and more formal dining room. House specials are jacket artichoke soup, salmon with vanilla sauce, grilled wood pigeon with sheep cheese and gnocchi and radish sauce. Smoking permitted. Closed Sun.

Dorsia

Avenida de Europa 13–15, 28108 **Tel** *91 490 3025.*

Dorsia is one of Madrid's most popular restaurants, located in the exclusive La Moraleja district. This spacious, modern New York-style diner specializes in gourmet Mediterranean cuisine. Try the tomato and watermelon gazpacho. Smoking permitted. Closed Sun, Mon–Wed dinner.

Mini Lounge

Paseo de la Castellana 123, 28046 **Tel** *91 556 4033.*

This bar, restaurant and night club rolled into one is seriously chic using the same chequered seats as the classic Mini car. Between 8am and 4am, guests can enjoy a selection of well presented and light entrées and salads as well as vegetable prawn stir fry, pasta dishes, meats and fish. Offers valet parking. Smoking permitted. Closed Sun.

Nodo

Calle Velázquez 150, 28046 **Tel** *91 564 4044*

Nodo's cool ultra-modern minimalist interior attracts Madrid's glamorous people. The fusion of Japanese with Mediterranean cuisine works very well with specialities such as garlic tuna *tataki*, red shrimp soaked in black tea with ginger or the grilled beef steaks with red *miso* and Chinese mushrooms. Offers valet parking. Smoking permitted.

Novillo De Plata

Calle Téllez, 20, 28007 **Tel** *91 501 22 81*

This popular Brazilian restaurant offers an unlimited "Rodizio" barbecue. Expect endless portions of beef, pork, *filet mignon*, goat, chicken, duck, ham and pineapple, sausage and fish. Desserts include a papaya cream laced with Cachaça, or *Quindim*, a Brazilian coconut/egg pie. Offers valet parking. Closed Sun dinner.

Sushi Olé

Calle Francisco Silvela 71, 28028 **Tel** *902 022 592.*

Sushi Olé mixes Japanese, Venezuelan and Spanish cuisine to create a fusion that is now being copied by other chefs all over the world. The modern, minimalist interior sits about 30 and service is efficient and speedy. The specialities of the house are *maki*, sushi and *sashimi*. Smoking permitted.

La Alacena de Serrano

Infanta María Teresa 19, 28016 **Tel** *91 220 7009.*

This stylish restaurant is certainly worth the trip from central Madrid. The cuisine is traditional Basque with a modern twist, and popular dishes include succulent lobster rice and *hake kokotxas*. The wine list has been well thought out to compliment the food. Smoking permitted. Closed Sun.

El Chaflán

Avenida Pío XII 34, 28016 **Tel** *91 350 6193.*

Very expensive but definitely worth it, El Chaflán has recently been refurbished in warm modern surroundings. Executive chef Juan Pablo Felipe has won some of the top awards for his distinctive menus. The pork sirloin steak with potatoes and hazelnuts is excellent. Offers valet parking. Smoking permitted. Closed Sat lunch, Sun & last 2 weeks of Aug.

Combarro

Calle de la Reina Mercedes 12 **Tel** *91 554 77 84.*

The days offerings are displayed in the window of one of Madrid's best seafood restaurants. The food harks back to the recipes of the monasteries and old farms of Galicia, as well as the chef's own creations like partridge pastry or wild lamprey with poor-style potatoes. Offers valet parking. Smoking permitted. Closed Sun dinner & Aug.

El Olivo

Calle General Gallegos, 28036 **Tel** *91 359 1535.*

El Olivo serves the best hake in Madrid. The house hare is also delicious and an olive oil and honey ice cream with apple tart is unmissable! A tasting menu offers a sea food selection that includes small flat fritters made from flour and egg with tiger prawns, lobster salad or hard-shelled prawns. Offers valet parking. Closed Sun, Mon & last 2 weeks of Aug.

El Pescador

Calle José Ortega y Gasset 75, 28010 **Tel** *91 402 1290.*

This emblematic seafood restaurant has been on the city's top food list since 1975, when it first opened. The chef's speciality is crab salad prepared in its shell, and rich, tasty hot fish soup can be followed by oven-baked turbot or grilled hake with the obligatory olive oil and parsley. Offers valet parking. Smoking permitted. Closed Sun & Aug.

Kabuki

Calle Presidente Carmona 2, 28020 **Tel** *91 417 6415.*

Kabuki serves the best exotic fish sushi in Madrid – smoked sea bream, macerated monkfish liver, tuna liver or butter fish with truffle pâté keep punters coming back for more. A minimalist Japanese interior is complemented by a hedged-in wooden terrace. Offers valet parking. Smoking permitted. Closed Sat noon, Sun, Easter & Aug.

Mesón Txistú

Plaza Ángel Carbajo 6, 28020 **Tel** *91 570 9651.*

This Basque restaurant has been run by owner Leoncio and his family for over 30 years. The walls are plastered with photos of famous politicians, actors and footballers who have all sampled his food. His Aguinaga eggs are legendary. The menu is pricey but offers a wide selection of meats, fish and a decent wine list. Offers valet parking. Smoking permitted.

Santceloni

Paseo de la Castellana 57, 28046 **Tel** *91 210 8840.*

Set within the five-star Hesperia hotel, Santceloni offers an unforgettable three Michelin-starred gastronomic experience. Lose yourself in the onion hake or roasted pigeon with pumpkin and port. Men are required to wear jackets. Offers valet parking. Smoking permitted. Closed Sat lunch, Sun & Aug.

BEYOND MADRID

ARANJUEZ Casa José

Carretera de Andalucía 17 (Aranjuez) **Tel** *91 891 1488.*

Food buffs travel miles to dine at Casa José. Locally grown ingredients are cooked creatively by the family-run kitchen which has been passed to a second generation of chefs. The chefs are not afraid to experiment serving dishes like hot tomato soup with melting manchego ice cream and croûtons. Smoking permitted. Closed Sun dinner, Mon & Aug.

CHINCHON Parador de Chinchon

Calle de los Huertos 1 (Chinchón) **Tel** *91 894 08 36.*

An old Agustinos monastery, the Parador at Chinchón restaurant serves typical Castillian favourites such as garlic soup, suckling pig, oven roasted lamb or the substantial *cocido madrileño* (a stew combining chickpeas, vegetables, chicken, beef and pork).

SEGOVIA Hostería de Pedraza

Calle Matadero 1 (Pedraza de la Sierra, Segovia) **Tel** *921 50 98 35.*

Located in a former Inquisition house in a typical Castilian village, this restaurant serves traditional Castilian fare such as roast pork and lamb, and hearty stews. The restaurant is beautifully decorated and there is a splendid garden with views over the San Miguel valley. Smoking permitted. Closed Tue.

SHOPPING IN MADRID

From sherry to seafood, the finest-foods in Spain have always made their way across the country to the capital. Madrid still lives off that heritage, despite increasing competition from other parts, especially arch rival Barcelona. Many products are basic Castilian commodities – Manchego cheese, olive oil and leather goods – whose quality lies in the excellent raw materials. Since the swinging 1980s, fashion design has flourished in Madrid. New-look, home-grown fashion outlets now dot Madrid's different shopping areas from the city centre to the upmarket district of Salamanca *(see p97)*. The latest street-wear is available in the Chueca area *(see p92)*. There are colourful food markets all over the city, and in the heart of Old Madrid you'll find superb speciality food and wine stores. Don't miss the El Rastro flea market *(see p61)* on Sundays.

The logo of Spain's best known department store

OPENING HOURS

Spanish shopping hours are not like anywhere else in Europe, thanks to Spanish mealtimes. Most shops are open from 10am to 2pm and from 5pm to 8pm, with only shops in the very centre and department stores staying open during the lunch break. Small shops often close on Saturday afternoons. Sunday opening hours vary; however, all shops tend to open on the first Sunday of each month as well as every Sunday in December and during the sales.

HOW TO PAY

Both cash and credit cards are popular methods of payment in Madrid, whereas cheques are hardly ever accepted. Small shops may sometimes reject credit cards which charge them high commission, so it's always worth double-checking that your card is acceptable. A passport or photo ID will be required when you pay by credit card. Some tourist shops accept payment in US dollars.

VAT EXEMPTION AND TAX

A value-added tax (IVA) is applied to most goods. The standard rate of 16 per cent is charged on clothes and most other products, while the rate for most food-stuffs is seven per cent. A reduced rate of four per cent is applied to basic foods such as cheese and fruit, as well as printed matter and materials for the disabled. At shops with a "Tax-free for Tourists" sign, non-EU residents can claim tax refunds on all purchases over 90 euros, except food, drink, tobacco, motor bikes, cars and medicines.

SALES

Spanish sales are a popular institution, taking place in January and July. Beginning after the Feast of the Epiphany on 6 January, the New Year sales go on well into February. In July the summer fashion sales can turn up some real bargains, especially useful as Madrid's hot season often lasts well into September. Look out for signs advertising , *Rebajas, Ofertas* or *Liquidación.*

Entrance to the Museo del Jamón *(see p178)*

High fashion on Calle de Serrano, Madrid's smartest shopping street

SHOPPING CENTRES

Shopping centres, or *centros comerciales*, have grown rapidly in Madrid. Among the best for upmarket fashion are the **Jardín de Serrano** and **ABC Serrano**, both set in the elegant neighbourhood of Salamanca, where you will also find many specialist luxury shops and the top international designer stores in and around the Calle de Serrano (*see p96)*. If you want to find everything under one roof, go to the huge **La Vaguada** mall on the north side of Madrid.

The department store **El Corte Inglés** is a national institution. Gigantic branches all over the city sell clothes, food, household goods and almost everything else. They offer photo-developing and shoe repair services, too.

Madrid also boasts a number of hypermarkets, mostly located off the M30 ring road.

Display of hand-painted ceramics in Toledo

MARKETS

The legendary **El Rastro** flea market is held on Sundays and public holidays. It is located between the Plaza de Cascorro and streets leading off the Ribera de Curtidores. Do not expect to stumble across a painting by Velázquez, but you will find everything else from valuable antiques to second-hand clothes, jewellery, records, collector items, mountain gear and statues for your garden. This is probably the only market in Madrid where it is possible to knock two-thirds off the starting price. Many shops and stalls in the area are open on weekdays for more relaxed browsing.

Open on Sundays only, the **Mercadillo de Sellos y Monedas** is a small coin, stamp and postcard market held under the arches of the Plaza Mayor. For a browse through old books, visit the

Mercado del Libro, on the south side of the Real Jardín Botánico (see p82). Both new and second-hand books are sold here. On Sundays the stalls are thronged, but most open on weekdays, too.

ANNUAL FAIRS

For many madrileños, the passing of the year is marked by popular annual fairs, many of them outdoors.

The contemporary art fair **ARCO** takes place in February. Whether you want to buy or just browse, it provides a great opportunity to catch up on the latest trends in the art world. In the week prior to Madrid's Fiestas de San Isidro (see p34), which begin on 15 May, you can buy earthen cookware and wine jugs at the **Feria de Cerámica** in the colourful district of Malasaña (see p101). A sure sign that summer is just around the corner is the

arrival of hundreds of book stalls along the leafy avenues of Parque del Retiro (see p77), where publishers and book-shop owners exhibit their wares at the **Feria del Libro** over two weeks, beginning at the end of May.

On the Paseo de Recoletos the **Feria de Artesanos** takes place every December. Craft items from ceramics and jewellery to leather goods, glassware and silks make it ideal for Christmas shopping. Throughout December, the Plaza Mayor is the venue for a traditional Christmas fair, the **Mercado de Artículos Navideños**. Christmas trees are for sale, as well as cork-wood and moss for use in homemade nativity scenes. Stallholders sell figurines, including joke items such as the Catalan *caganers* – bare-bottomed shepherd figures traditionally placed behind the manger.

Sunday morning in the busy El Rastro flea market

DIRECTORY

What to Buy in Madrid

Traditional fan

If flamenco frills and kitsch bulls are not to your taste, you can find a satisfying reminder of your visit in many traditional Spanish goods. Strongly scented saffron, matured ewe's cheese or a fruity extra-virgin olive oil all make prized gifts. Leather goods are particularly sought-after. The beautifully crafted Loewe bags are in a league of their own, but most leather, especially shoes, is extremely good value. Traditional crafts, such as woven baskets, are harder to find, but lovely and inexpensive ceramics are widely available. By looking around, you may even pick up an original piece of clothing.

Chulapo Dolls
These typically Spanish dolls with their endearing pout are dressed in the traditional costume of Madrid's castizos (see p103).

Spanish T-shirt
T-shirts make great gifts, and Custo Barcelona (see p177) offers a wide range of unique designs.

Leather Handbag
The best bags come from Majorca, and are stocked at Piamonte (see p176), although many other shops sell leather, too.

Mantón de Manila
Classical, beautifully embroidered silk shawls, like this one, are easy to find and come in a wide range of colours.

Saffron (Azafrán)
Hand-picked azafrán comes from the autumn crocus. Introduced by the Moors, it is the world's most expensive spice.

Turrón
Luxury nougat and almond paste, pressed into almond-shaped shells, comes in a wooden gift box at Casa Mira (see p178).

Queso Manchego
Used in tapas or served with quince jelly (membrillo) at the end of a meal, Manchego cheese also makes an ideal gift. It is widely regarded as Spain's finest cheese.

Barquillera
Filled with wafer biscuits, this old-fashioned cookie (biscuit) tin has a children's roulette game on the lid. Barquilleras are sold in the pastry departments of El Corte Inglés and Mallorca (see p178).

Modern Fan
A wide range of fans, from the traditional delicate lace variety to colourful, simple modern versions, can be found throughout Madrid.

Modern fan

Traditional Ceramics
The art of hand-painting ceramics with traditional colours and designs continues to thrive in Madrid. The attractive plates and tiles make memorable keepsakes.

Antique ceramic tiles

Decorative ceramic plates

Painted modern candlesticks

Modern Ceramics
Those in search of 20th-century ceramics will not need to look far. As well as traditional designs, Madrid offers a wide range of entirely modern craftwork.

SAUSAGES AND HAMS

Spain has a deep-rooted tradition of pork products, ranging from whole hams to sausages of every shape and size. The annual *matanza*, when pigs were killed and families spent the day preparing food for the months ahead, was an important date on the country calendar. Today, most products are made in a factory. *Jamón serrano* is cured ham, served thinly sliced as a *tapa* or used diced as an ingredient in numerous recipes. The best, and most expensive ham, is *ibérico*, from the small, black-hoofed, free-ranging Iberian pig. Many sausages are seasoned with Spain's favourite spice – paprika; they are called *chorizo*. Those without paprika are called *salchichón*. Other types of sausage are *longaniza* (long, thin sausages), *morcilla* (blood sausage or black pudding, made with rice, onions or potatoes) and *chisto-rras* (small Basque sausages, often flambéed). *Caña de lomo* is cured pork loin.

Jamón serrano

Morcilla

Salchichón

Chorizo

Caña de lomo

Fashion and Accessories

Spaniards are celebrated for their elegance. No woman will leave the house, even if it is simply to go to the market, without dressing impeccably. The most popular styles tend towards classic cuts, with the occasional Baroque flounce. Madrid's cultural boom in the 1980s impacted the fashion world with a look based on sleek, understated design and sophisticated accessories. Footwear and clothing boutiques carry all the well-known international designer labels but, if you want something a little bit different, look out for the Spanish designers.

SHOES

The best shoes are made in Mallorca, with classic footwear by Yanko at the very top of the range. Yanko shoes are so soft and comfortable that they feel like slippers. **Bravo** shoe shops carry many top Mallorcan makes, including Yanko, Lotusse and Barratts.

Another Mallorcan export is the young and comfortable **Camper** shoe. Outlets exist all over Madrid, with customer-friendly displays. The **Geltra** chain stocks the Camper brand in addition to its own good quality range of shoes.

For sophisticated designs – and prices – go to **Farrutx**. For a more avant-garde style, it is worth trying the Catalan shoe outlet **Excrupulus Net**.

If you forgot your trainers, or need to get out of rain-soaked shoes cheaply, try the shops along the Calle de Fuencarral, or go to **Los Guerrilleros** in the heart of Madrid's "kilometre 0" – the area around the Puerta del Sol. Jot down the reference number of the shoe in the showcase and you will get efficient service inside.

Brightly coloured espadrilles are sold in most areas but, for an old-world feel, visit **Casa Hernanz** off the Plaza Mayor.

HANDBAGS AND OTHER LEATHER GOODS

The ultimate in Spanish bags and leather clothing goes by the prestigious name of **Loewe**. Established over a century ago by a German tanner who settled in Spain, Loewe bags are sold all over the world. At the Loewe shop in Calle de Serrano, you can feast your eyes, if nothing else.

Around the corner you will find **Lotusse** selling wallets, bags and coats, as well as its famous shoes. The Mallorcan connection continues nearby at **Boxcalf**, with an enticing range of quality leather clothing and accessories.

Piamonte, in the Chueca district, has become synonymous with attractive bags at affordable prices. They also have belts and an interesting selection of jewellery.

For a touch of Andalusian chic, see the handbags and belts for sale at **El Caballo**.

Manuel Herrero offers value for money in what feels like a bazaar crammed with leather and suede, visitors and persuasive salespeople.

A delightful outlet for classic gloves is the small, but well-stocked **Guante Varadé**.

JEWELLERY

Madrid is full of small shops, stacked with trays of 18-carat gold studs, chains and bracelets, and grand jewellers – whether you walk down the Gran Vía or Calle de Serrano. Most Spanish women adore gold – the heavier the better – and pearls. Popular, man-made "Majorica" pearls, as well as the cultivated variety, can be found all over Madrid. **Casa Yustas**, spread over three floors, stocks Majorica pearls as well as Lladró porcelain.

Del Pino on Calle de Serrano is fun for its variety of costume jewellery across the price range, and the Catalans' innovative **Tous** outlet in Madrid should not be missed.

If you are interested in new creations, visit internationally acclaimed jeweller **Joaquín Berao**. His shop is like a miniature art gallery devoted to thoughtfully understated and tasteful design.

At **Chus Burés**, designer Chus Burés displays his own work and that of other jewellers he has discovered. **Helena Rohner**, whose silver, bronze and enamel jewellery can be found in **Piamonte** (*see Handbags*), is also becoming a popular name. You can visit her workshop, but it is best to call first.

WOMEN'S FASHIONS

The best of Spanish and international fashion is located on Calle de Serrano and Calle de José Ortega y Gasset, as well as in adjacent streets. The best place to find the work of young designers is the Chueca district, in and around Calle del Almirante, with shops such as **Ararat**. If you want original "street" fashion, go to **Glam** in busy Calle de Fuencarral, a street full of fun shops for the young.

In the designer category, **Adolfo Domínguez** – doyen of Madrid's minimalist look – and **Roberto Verino** offer excellent value for money. The more eccentric should try **Agatha Ruíz de la Prada**'s unique creations – also for children – in her shop in Serrano Street. For the best young designs go to **Mezcla**, and for a combination of designer clothes and leather goods, try **Loewe**, but be prepared for high prices.

Another creation in a league of its own is the traditional **Seseña** cape, exclusive to the Madrid fashion house of the same name which also makes more modern versions.

The chain store **Zara** has become an international phenomenon, offering easy-to-wear clothes for women, men and children at very good prices.

Fine lingerie is part of a Spanish tradition, and lingerie shops – called *corseterías* in the more popular parts of town – are everywhere. A cotton nightdress can be an expensive affair but, for a select choice of sleepwear as well as bed linen, visit **¡Oh qué luna!** for original and attractive designs.

Not to be forgotten, Spain is big on babies, and **Prenatal** is well worth a visit for expectant women and for mothers with very young children.

MENSWEAR

Men's fashions can be found in the same areas of Madrid as women's. The traditional tailored look lives on, but Spanish men also like styles from abroad. You will find that many shops which sell off-the-peg clothes have Italian- or English-sounding names, but only sell home-produced merchandise. Prices and quality vary.

For a more interesting purchase, check out the menswear at **Adolfo Domínguez** or **Zara** *(see Women's Fashions)*. **Roberto Verino**, an icon of national fashion for both men and women, is also worth a look. His men's and women's ranges, as well as accessories, are all stocked at his elegant store on Calle Serrano. At the top end, **Loewe**'s store for men has beautiful clothes, adapting fashion trends to its own look. A Loewe silk tie with a Spanish art motif makes a rewarding purchase.

Another name to look out for is Antonio Miró and his

famous shirts, available in **Gallery**, which hosts a range of top international labels.

For casual wear, **Custo Barcelona** is extremely popular and there are clothes for women, too. Its outlets throughout the city offer quality cottonwear with original designs that come in attractive colours. If you are looking for younger and more affordable men's fashion, head to **Caramelo** with several branches in Madrid.

For outdoor clothes, which cater for anything between a walk in the park and a safari, go to **Coronel Tapioca** for comfort at a reasonable price.

DIRECTORY

SHOES

Bravo
Calle de Serrano 42.
Map 6 E4.
Tel 91 435 27 29.

Camper
Gran Vía 54.
Map 4 E1.
Tel 91 547 52 23.
www.camper.es

Casa Hernanz
Calle de Toledo 18.
Map 4 E3.
Tel 91 366 54 50.

Excrupulus Net
Calle del Almirante 7.
Map 5 C5.
Tel 91 521 72 44.

Farrutx
Calle de Serrano 7. **Map** 8
D1. *Tel 91 576 94 93.*

Geltra
Gran Vía 33. **Map** 4 F1.
Tel 91 531 13 53.

Los Guerrilleros
Puerta del Sol 5.
Map 4 F2.
Tel 91 521 27 08

HANDBAGS AND OTHER LEATHER GOODS

Boxcalf
Calle de Jorge Juan 14.
Map 6 E5. *Tel 91 435 34 29.*

El Caballo
Calle de Lagasca 55. **Map** 6 E5. *Tel 91 576 40 37.*

Guante Varadé
Calle de Serrano 54.
Map 6 E3.
Tel 91 575 67 41.

Loewe
Calle de Serrano 26.
Map 6 E4.
Tel 91 577 60 56.
www.loewe.es

Lotusse
El Jardin de Serrano, Calle de Goya 6–8.
Map 6 E4.
Tel 91 577 20 14.

Manuel Herrero
Calle de Preciados 7 & 16.
Map 4 F2.
Tel 91 521 29 90.

Piamonte
Calle Piamonte 16.
Map 5 B5.
Tel 91 360 48 90.

JEWELLERY

Casa Yustas
Plaza Mayor 30.
Map 4 E2.
Tel 91 366 50 84.

Del Pino
Calle Ayala 46. **Map** 6 E3.
Tel 91 435 26 70.

Helena Rohner
Calle del Almendro 4.
Map 4 D3.
Tel 91 366 06 64.

Joaquín Berao
Calle del Conde de Xiquena 13. **Map** 5 C5.
Tel 91 310 16 20.

Chus Burés
Calle Claudio Coello 88.
Map 6 E3.
Tel 91 576 39 01.

Tous
Calle de Ayala 26. **Map** 6
E4. *Tel 91 575 53 86.*
www.tous.es

WOMEN'S FASHIONS

Adolfo Domínguez
Calle de Serrano 18.
Map 6 E5.
Tel 91 577 82 80.

Agatha Ruíz de la Prada
Calle de Serrano 27.
Map 6 E4.
Tel 91 319 05 51.

Ararat
Calle del Almirante 10.
Map 5 C5.
Tel 91 531 81 56.

Glam
Calle de Fuencarral 35.
Map 7 A1.
Tel 91 522 80 54.

Mezcla
Calle de Claudio Coello 81. **Map** 6 E3.
Tel 91 435 42 03.

¡Oh que luna!
Calle de Ayala 32.
Map 6 F4.
Tel 91 431 37 25.

Prenatal
Calle Goya 99. **Map** 7 A1.
Tel 91 431 59 30. www.
prenatal.es

Roberto Verino
Calle de Serrano 33.
Map 6 E4.
Tel 91 426 04 75.

Seseña
Calle de la Cruz 23.
Map 7 A2.
Tel 91 531 68 40.

Zara
ABC Serrano, Calle de Serrano 61.
Map 6 E3.
Tel 91 575 63 34

MENSWEAR

Caramelo
Calle Fuencarral 42.
Map 5 A5.
Tel 91 521 48 29.

Coronel Tapioca
Calle del Carmen 12.
Map 4 F2.
Tel 91 531 59 29.

Custo Barcelona
Calle Mayor 37.
Tel 91 354 00 99.

Gallery
Calle de Jorge Juan 38.
Map 6 E5.
Tel 91 576 79 31.

Loewe
Calle de Serrano 34.
Map 6 E4.
Tel 91 435 30 56.

Antiques, Crafts and Gifts

Spain's rich and varied popular art makes it relatively easy to pick up an original piece of handicraft. It is often possible to obtain the same item, be it a ceramic mortar or a silk shawl, as an antique, a reproduction or even a stylized update. Genuine articles at good prices can still be found, but many rural crafts are fast disappearing. Fortunately, they do not include the age-old arts of producing Manchego cheese, cured ham and wines. Spain's musical tradition is very much alive, and a CD of flamenco-jazz fusion can be a spellbinding gift.

ANTIQUES

Strolling down the Calle de Claudio Coello, in elegant Salamanca, you will pass some outstanding antique shops. The streets around are also full of specialist outlets for rare antiques, ranging from 18th-century lacquered furniture at **María Gracia Cavestany**, to 15th-century Flemish paintings at **Theotokopoulos**, or rustic tools at **Collector**. Some of Madrid's top dealers, such as Pedro Alarcón and Luis Carabe, can be found under one roof at the **Centro de Anticuarios**.

Calle del Prado is lined with antique shops crammed with Castilian-style furniture, books, old tiles, religious artifacts and antique jewellery. Shops on neighbouring Calle de las Huertas deal in old prints.

Hidalgo in El Rastro (see p61) sells collectors' items, such as keys and corkscrews, while reasonably priced bric-à-brac (including some reproductions) can be found at **La Trastienda de Alcalá**, just northeast of the Parque del Retiro (see p77).

Casa Postal, near Plaza de Cibeles, specializes in old postcards and has a great selection of old signs and posters.

MODERN ART, PRINTS AND PHOTOGRAPHS

When it comes to modern art, new trends and new talent, the galleries around Calle de Claudio Coello are well worth visiting. The **Juan Gris** gallery always has works from established as well as up-and-coming artists. **Juana de Aizpuru** has rapidly become one of the most influential galleries in Madrid. Also well known for promoting young artists are **Fúcares** and **Soledad Lorenzo**. You can find sketches by artists such as Picasso, Chillida, Tàpies and Miró at **Estiarte**. Most galleries are closed on Mondays.

CRAFTS

A wide choice of ceramics is offered at **Cántaro**, near the Plaza de España (see p53). Well stocked in regional styles, the shop also carries so-called "extinct" ceramics – pottery which is no longer produced. **Antigua Casa Talavera** opened in the late 19th century and sells hand-painted ceramics including vases, trays and pots produced in different regions of Spain.

The Spanish are proud of their embroidered linen, but hand-embroidered tablecloths or shawls at ridiculously low prices probably come from China. **Casa de Diego** is run by the fourth generation of the same family and sells quality embroidered shawls. One of the best shops for *mantones* (silk shawls) and linen – hand- and machine-made – is **Borca**, just off the Puerta del Sol (see p44).

For a wide selection of hats, including top hats, bowlers and berets, try **La Favorita**. And for fine hand-made guitars, visit **Guitarrería F Manzanero**.

BOOKS AND MUSIC

There is an ample stock of foreign language titles at **Casa del Libro** on Gran Vía. French-owned **FNAC**, nearby, offers a wide choice of books both in English and in other languages. **Booksellers**, a little further afield, has classics but only a limited choice of new books. The second-hand bookstalls of the **Mercado del Libro** behind the Ministerio de Agricultura (see p82) are good for cheap paperbacks and, sometimes, rare volumes.

Art books can be found at **Crisol** branches, while one of the best specialist art bookshops is **Gaudí**, near Chueca.

For all types of music, go to the FNAC or **El Corte Inglés** branches in Calle de Preciados or Paseo de la Castellana. Flamenco buffs must drop in to **El Flamenco Vive**.

GIFTS

Food gifts from Madrid are always appreciated, and olive oil or "green gold" from Catalonia to Andalusia is available at **Patrimonio Comunal Olivarero**, a specialist olive oil shop near Chueca. The **El Corte Inglés** Club du Gourmet in the basement of its Calle de Serrano branch also carries a wide selection of olive oil and other typical Spanish produce, such as sherry vinegar.

At **Casa Mira** you can get *turrón* – Spain's traditional Christmas sweet – all year round. An almond speciality, *turrón* comes in a hard or a soft version. For a less sticky, bite-size treat of soft *turrón* pressed into almond-shaped wafer shells, try *almendras imperiales* (imperial almonds).

For assorted cakes in the centre of Madrid go to **Horno de San Onofre**; for a first-class selection of wines visit **Mariano Madrueño**. Various categories of cured ham are available at **Museo del Jamón** outlets. One of the best cheese shops is **La Boulette** inside the Mercado de la Paz, just off Calle de Serrano. **Mallorca**, Madrid's finest delicatessen, carries the very best of foodstuffs to eat in or take away.

El Arco de los Cuchilleros is one of Madrid's most tasteful gift shops, with jewellery, leather goods and ceramics, while **Así**, conveniently located in the city centre, sells all kinds of dolls as well as reasonably priced household goods.

The Spanish share a national passion for cologne, and there are *perfumerías* (toiletry and cosmetic shops) everywhere.

SOUVENIRS

For a superior tourist shop, go to **La Tienda de Madrid**, which is located in Puerta de Toledo market. You will find souvenirs such as *barquilleras* (traditional biscuit or cookie tins), also sold at **El Corte Inglés** pastry shops and **Mallorca** *(see Gifts)*.

Dolls in typical Madrid costume are available at the **Sanatorio de Muñecas**.

Between the Puerta del Sol and Plaza Mayor, especially on Calle Postas, are outlets for religious artifacts. **Palomeque** specializes in postcards and reproductions of religious art.

Monsy, on the Plaza Mayor, sells a vast range of fans. For a T-shirt that will remind you of your stay, but will not make you feel too touristy, try **El Tintero** in Chueca, which does designs and messages in Spanish.

DIRECTORY

ANTIQUES

Casa Postal
Calle de la Libertad 37.
Map 7 B1.
Tel 91 532 70 37.

Centro de Anticuarios
Calle de Lagasca 36.
Map 6 E5.

Collector
Calle del Conde de Aranda 18. **Map** 8 E1.
Tel 91 575 10 74.

Hidalgo
Galerías Piquer, Shop 23
Ribera de Curtidores 29.
Map 4 E5.
Tel 91 530 56 53.

María Gracia Cavestany
Calle de Jorge Juan 14.
Map 6 E5.
Tel 91 577 76 32.

Theotokopoulos
Calle de Alcalá 97.
Map 8 E1.
Tel 91 575 84 66.

La Trastienda de Alcalá
Calle de Alcalá 64.
Map 8 F1.
Tel 91 576 34 86.

MODERN ART, PRINTS AND PHOTOGRAPHS

Estiarte
Calle de Almagro 44.
Map 5 C3.
Tel 91 308 15 69.

Fúcares
Calle del Conde de Xiquena 12.
Map 5 C5.
Tel 91 319 74 02.

Juan Gris
Calle de Villanueva 22.
Map 6 E5.
Tel 91 575 04 27.
www.galeriajuangris.com

Juana de Aizpuru
Calle de Barquillo 44.
Map 5 B5.
Tel 91 310 55 61.

Soledad Lorenzo
Calle de Orfila 5.
Map 5 C4.
Tel 91 308 28 87.
www.soledadlorenzo.com

CRAFTS

Antigua Casa Talavera
Calle Isabel la Católica 2.
Map 4 D1.
Tel 91 547 34 17.

Borca
Calle del Marqués Viudo de Pontejos 2. **Map** 4 E2.
Tel 91 532 61 53.

Cántaro
Calle de la Flor Baja 8.
Map 2 D5.
Tel 91 547 95 14.

Casa de Diego
Puerta del Sol 12. **Map** 4
F2. *Tel 91 552 66 43.*

Guitarrería F Manzanero
Calle de Santa Ana 12.
Map 4 D4.
Tel 91 366 00 47.

La Favorita
Plaza Mayor 25.
Map 4 E2.
Tel 91 366 58 77.

BOOKS AND MUSIC

Booksellers
Calle Fernández de la
Hoz 40. **Map** 5 C1.
Tel 91 442 79 59.

Casa del Libro
Gran Vía 29. **Map** 4 F1.
Tel 91 521 21 13.
www.casadellibro.com

El Corte Inglés
Calle de Preciados 1–3.
Map 4 F2.
Tel 91 379 80 00.

Crisol
Calle Juan Bravo 38.
Map 6 F2.
Tel 91 423 82 83.
www.crisol.es

El Flamenco Vive
Calle Conde de Lemos 7.
Map 4 D2.
Tel 91 547 39 17.

FNAC
Calle de Preciados 28.
Map 4 E1.
Tel 91 595 61 00.
www.fnac.es

Gaudí
Calle de Argensola 13.
Map 5 C4.
Tel 91 308 18 29.

GIFTS

El Arco de los Cuchilleros
Plaza Mayor 9. **Map** 4 E2.
Tel 91 365 26 80.

Así
Gran Vía 47.
Map 4 E1.
Tel 91 548 28 28.

La Boulette
Mercado de la Paz (Calle de Ayala 28). **Map** 6 E4.
Tel 91 431 77 25.

Casa Mira
Carrera de San Jerónimo 30. **Map** 7 A2.
Tel 91 429 88 95.

El Corte Inglés
Calle de Serrano 47.
Map 6 E3.
Tel 91 432 54 90.

Horno de San Onofre
Calle de San Onofre 3.
Map 7 A1.
Tel 91 532 90 60.

Mallorca
Calle de Serrano 6.
Map 8 D1.
Tel 91 577 18 59.

Mariano Madrueño
Calle del Postigo de San Martín 3.
Map 4 E1.
Tel 91 521 19 55.

Museo del Jamón
Carrera de San Jerónimo 6.
Map 7 A2.
Tel 91 521 03 46.

Patrimonio Comunal Olivarero
Calle de Mejía Lequerica 1.
Map 5 B4.
Tel 91 308 05 05.

SOUVENIRS

Monsy
Plaza Mayor 20.
Map 4 E2.
Tel 91 548 15 14.

Palomeque
Calle del Arenal 17.
Map 4 E2.
Tel 91 548 17 20.

Sanatorio de Muñecas
Calle de Preciados 19.
Map 4 E1.
Tel 91 521 04 47.

La Tienda de Madrid
Mercado Puerta de Toledo, 5th floor. **Map** 3 C5.
Tel 91 364 16 82.

El Tintero
Calle de Gravina 5.
Map 5 B5.
Tel 91 308 14 18.

ENTERTAINMENT IN MADRID

Few European cities take their entertainment as seriously as Madrid. The city is an international mecca for cultural events, putting a great deal of energy into providing its citizens and visitors with the best in traditional and modern entertainment throughout the year. World-famous orchestras, ballets and operas, including Madrid's own *zarzuela*, are daily staples. Dozens of mainstream and alternative theatres offer everything from Spanish Golden Age classics to experimental drama. The country's best flamenco acts bring their southern

Street performer in Parque del Retiro

Spanish art to Madrid's international audiences. Some of Europe's liveliest cafés and bars are found here. The afternoon siesta, once a civilized way to escape the Spanish heat, is now either an excellent remedy for the previous night's revelry, or a way to prepare for the one ahead. Most bars and dance clubs are crowded four nights a week, from Thursday through Sunday, and smaller venues offer jazz, rock, salsa and world music on an almost nightly basis. Be prepared for late nights, however, because most activities begin well after midnight and often continue until after breakfast.

Façade of the Teatro Real *(see p58)*, fronted by a statue of Felipe IV

PRACTICAL INFORMATION

The first stop for visitors to Madrid should be at one of several tourist information offices, where English will be spoken and free information can be obtained. A Madrid Card (www.madridcard.com) can be bought there, giving access to museums, tours, shows and sightseeing buses. For those interested in exploring Madrid with a professional guide, contact **A.P.I.T.** or **COSITUR**. These agencies supply guides with an intimate knowledge of the city.

Most Spaniards speak some English and are usually willing to help confused foreigners. Unfortunately, however, most of the city's entertainment guides are published exclusively in Spanish. *Lookout* is one informative English-language magazine relied upon by Madrid's expatriate community. Another is *In Madrid*, a free

monthly publication found in bookshops, record shops and some bars. You can also pick up a copy at embassies and at the tourist information office at **Barajas Airport** *(see p200)*.

Of the Spanish options, the most complete entertainment guide is the weekly *Guía de Ocio*, which hits newsstands and bookstores on Friday and is usually sold out by Sunday.

Madrid's top three daily newspapers – *El Mundo, El País* and *ABC* – have weekly entertainment supplements. These are more geared towards entertainment features, but their listings are broad and sometimes include last-minute events that you may not find in the *Guía de Ocio*. The *El Mundo, El País* and *ABC* supplements appear on Friday, covering information on music, theatre, cinema and books.

BOOKING TICKETS

The easiest way to purchase tickets to major events, especially theatre, opera and concerts, is by telephone or over the Internet. **Entradas. com** and **Tel-Entrada** are the two main agents. Both accept VISA and MasterCard. Their services are provided free of charge and your tickets will be waiting for you at the venue's ticket booth.

SEASONS AND TICKETS

While there is never a shortage of top events year-round in Madrid, the main concert and theatre seasons run from September to June. During May's Fiestas de San Isidro *(see p34)* and the Festival de Otoño *(see p36)*, from October to November, the authorities

A full house at the Joy Madrid dance club *(see p184)*

Children enjoying the adventure playground in the Plaza de Oriente

book top Spanish and international names in music, theatre and dance. Special events listings can be picked up at tourist offices and at most branches of the Caja Madrid bank.

The record shop **FNAC** sells most big-venue concert tickets, while the **TEYCI** agency sells tickets for bullfighting at Plaza de Toros de Las Ventas, but charges up to 20 per cent commission.

Another agency that sells tickets for a wide variety of events is **El Corte Inglés**, by telephone, or directly from the stores.

FACILITIES FOR THE DISABLED

To find out about wheelchair accessibility, you are advised to telephone the venue itself. *El País* provides a 1–4 rating for some venues in its daily listing: '1' means totally accessible while '4' indicates considerable difficulty.

Getting to and from events is easier. Each bus route runs several low-level vehicles with a wheelchair symbol. **Radioteléfono Taxi** (91 547 82 00) provides special cars – book well in advance and ask for Eurotaxis. Only the new Metro stations have elevators.

CHILDREN'S ACTIVITIES

There is no shortage of activities in Madrid for visitors with children. To give them some space, head for the Casa de Campo *(see p112)*. Simply getting to this park can be fun if you take the high-flying **Teleférico** cable car.

The park is home to the **Zoo-Aquarium**, the modern **Parque de Atracciones** amusement park, a boating lake and several swimming pools. In the centre of Bourbon Madrid is the popular Parque del Retiro *(see p77)* with magic shows, jugglers, clowns and a lake.

The main children's theatre is **Sala San Pol**, but numerous fringe theatres also hold performances for young people.

Flamenco guitarist in the Parque del Retiro

Relaxing at a street café in the Plaza del Dos de Mayo *(see p101)*

Traditional Entertainment

The Spanish take particular pride in their cultural heritage, and attending a performance at one of Madrid's theatres, opera houses, music auditoriums or cabarets is one of the best ways of sharing the experience and traditions of Spain. Madrid plays host to a wide variety of classical art performances, which equal the best on offer in other European cities, but it also provides plenty of opportunities for savouring the traditional art forms of the Spanish people. These include the spontaneity of flamenco, the three-act drama of the *corrida* or bullfight *(see p109)*, and *zarzuela*, Madrid's particular version of the Spanish operetta *(see p75)*.

CLASSICAL MUSIC

The newly renovated **Teatro Real de Madrid** *(see p58)* is probably best known as the home of the city's opera company, but it is also the venue for top national and international classical music concerts.

The two concert halls of the **Auditorio Nacional de Música** also host international classical music performances, along with programmes by the national orchestra, the Orquesta Nacional de España. The Orquesta Nacional is frequently accompanied by Spain's national choir, the Coro Nacional de España.

The **Teatro Monumental** is the main venue for the excellent Orquesta Sinfónica y Coro de RTVE, the orchestra and choir of Spain's state radio and television company. The **Auditorio Conde Duque** also hosts a variety of classical concerts.

OPERA AND ZARZUELA

A visit to the Spanish capital would not be complete without spending a night at the *zarzuela*, Madrid's own variety of comic opera. The best productions are those staged at the **Teatro de la Zarzuela**. Other venues include the **Teatro Albéniz**, due to close for renovation, and the newly reopened **Teatro Príncipe**. Several other theatres also offer *zarzuela* productions during the summer.

The best place to see national opera, as well as touring international productions is the **Teatro Real de Madrid**, next to the Ópera Metro station.

DANCE

There are several venues in Madrid that stage performances of classical and modern dance, in addition to those that put on larger flamenco productions. The **Teatro Albéniz** is the main place to see good international dance companies as well as the top national acts. The three other major venues are the **Teatro Madrid**, the **Nuevo Teatro Alcalá** and the **Teatro de la Zarzuela**.

FLAMENCO

A spontaneous musical art form, flamenco has its roots in the gypsy culture of Andalusia. However, many of the best exponents are now based in the capital.

Flamenco is a late-night art form with shows usually taking place through the evening and into the early hours of the morning. Most venues offer dinner and a show, which may be singing only, or both singing and dancing. Although the familiar rhythmic dancing is often a part of flamenco, the purest form of the art consists of a solo singer accompanied by a guitar.

Casa Patas is still the best place to catch the raw power of genuine flamenco guitar and *cante* singing. Dancing often, but not always, accompanies the singing. Both music and dance can be enjoyed at **Café de Chinitas**. Other venues offering high-quality flamenco performances are **Arco de Cuchilleros**, **Corral de la Morería**, **Candela** and **Torres Bermejas**.

THEATRE

Madrid's most prestigious theatres are the **Teatro de la Comedia** and the **Teatro María Guerrero**. The former is the home of the Compañía Nacional de Teatro Clásico, which stages classic works by Spanish playwrights. The company has relocated to Teatro Pavón on Calle Embajadores while the Teatro de la Comedia undergoes restoration. The Teatro María Guerrero hosts foreign productions as well as modern drama in Spanish. It has recently been renovated. Many other theatres, including **Teatro Alcázar**, **Teatro Muñoz Seca** and **Teatro Reina Victoria**, also stage drama productions.

As well as drama, Teatro Muñoz Seca and Teatro Reina Victoria also offer comedy productions, as do **Teatro Lara** and **Teatro La Latina**, which specializes in *Madrileño* comedy productions. **Centro Cultural Fernán Gómez** (previously called Centro Cultural de la Villa) presents popular theatre. Madrid also has a thriving network of alternative venues, most notably **Cuarta Pared**, **Ensayo 100** and **Teatro Alfil**. **Teatro Häagen Dazs**, **Teatro Lope de Vega** and **Teatro Nuevo Apolo** often stage musicals.

An enormous range of radical and established Spanish and international theatrical talent gathers in the city during the annual Festival de Otoño *(see p36)*.

BULLFIGHTING

Bullfighting continues to be a popular spectacle in Madrid *(see p111)*, as throughout the country, but it is not for the squeamish. The **Plaza de Toros de Las Ventas** bullring is the most important in the world, and holds *corridas* every Sunday from March through to October. During the May Fiestas de San Isidro *(see p34)* there are fights every day. Each fight is made up of six 15-minute *faenas* of three acts, the last of which ends with the killing of the bull or, on very rare occasions, the matador.

FOOTBALL

Winners of the European Cup on' many occasions, **Real Madrid** are the local aristocrats of football. Their Bernabéu stadium, which has a capacity of 105,000, is one of the great theatres of the game. Real Madrid's cross-town rivals are **Atlético de Madrid**. They play at the Vicente Calderón stadium, a smaller and cheaper venue along the Manzanares River. Madrid's third team is **Rayo Vallecano**, who are constantly shifting up and down between the first and second divisions. Tickets are available at the stadiums or through the clubs themselves, but to see the massively popular Real Madrid, you may need to book ahead. Numerous websites offer ticketing services for Real Madrid and other team's games – expect a hefty booking fee. Once in Madrid, try the ticket agents listed on page 181.

DIRECTORY

CLASSICAL MUSIC

Auditorio Conde Duque
Calle del Conde Duque 11.
Map 2 D4.
Tel 91 588 58 34.

Auditorio Nacional de Música
Calle del Príncipe de Vergara 146.
Tel 91 337 01 34.

Teatro Monumental
Calle de Atocha 65.
Map 7 A3.
Tel 91 429 81 19.

Teatro Real de Madrid
Plaza de Oriente. **Map** 3 C2
Tel 91 516 06 00 (info).
Tel 90 224 48 48 (tickets).
www.teatro-real.com

OPERA AND ZARZUELA

Teatro Albéniz
Calle de la Paz 11.
Map 4 F3.
Tel 91 531 83 11.

Teatro Häagen Dazs
Calle de Atocha 18.
Map 4 F3.
Tel 91 420 37 97.

Teatro de la Zarzuela
Calle de Jovellanos 4.
Map 7 B2.
Tel 91 524 54 00.

Teatro Príncipe – Gran Via
Calle de las Tres Cruces 8.
Map 4 F1.
Tel 91 521 83 81.

Teatro Real de Madrid
(see Classical Music)

DANCE

Nuevo Teatro Alcalá
Calle Jorge Juán 62.
Map 6 D5.
Tel 91 426 47 79.

Teatro Albéniz
(see Opera and Zarzuela)

Teatro de la Zarzuela
Calle de Jovellanos 4.
Map 7 B2.
Tel 91 524 54 00.

Teatro Madrid
Avenida de la Ilustración.
Tel 91 730 17 50.

FLAMENCO

Arco de Cuchilleros
Calle de Cuchilleros 7.
Map 4 E3.
Tel 91 364 02 63.

Café de Chinitas
Calle de Torija 7.
Map 4 D1.
Tel 91 547 15 02.

Candela
Calle del Olivar 7.
Map 7 A4.
Tel 91 467 33 82.

Casa Patas
Calle de Cañizares 10.
Map 7 A3.
Tel 91 369 04 96.

Corral de la Morería
Calle de la Morería 17.
Map 3 C3.
Tel 91 365 84 46.

Torres Bermejas
Calle de Mesonero Romanos 11.
Map 4 F1.
Tel 91 532 33 22.

THEATRE

Centro Cultural Fernán Gómez
Plaza de Colón.
Map 6 D5.
Tel 91 480 03 00.

Cuarta Pared
Calle de Ercilla 17.
Tel 91 517 23 17.

Ensayo 100
Calle de Raimundo Lulio 20.
Map 5 A2.
Tel 91 447 94 86.

Teatro Alcázar
Calle de Alcalá 20.
Map 7 A2.
Tel 91 532 06 16.

Teatro Alfil
Calle del Pez 10.
Map 2 F5.
Tel 91 521 58 27.

Teatro Häagen Dazs
Calle de Atocha 18.
Map 4 F3.
Tel 91 420 37 97.

Teatro de la Comedia
Calle del Príncipe 14.
Map 7 A3.
Tel 91 521 49 31.

Teatro Español
Calle del Príncipe 25.
Map 7 A3.
Tel 91 360 14 84.

Teatro La Latina
Plaza de la Cebada 2.
Map 4 D4.
Tel 91 365 28 35.

Teatro Lara
Calle Corredera Baja de San Pablo 15.
Map 2 F5.
Tel 91 521 05 52.

Teatro Lópe de Vega
Gran Via 57. **Map** 4 E1.
Tel 91 547 20 11.

Teatro María Guerrero
Calle de Tamayo y Baus 4.
Map 5 C5.
Tel 91 310 15 00.

Teatro Muñoz Seca
Plaza del Carmen 1.
Map 4 F1.
Tel 91 523 21 28.

Teatro Nuevo Apolo
Plaza de Tirso de Molina 1.
Map 4 F3.
Tel 91 369 06 37.

Teatro Pavón
Calle Embajadores 9.
Map 4 E4.
Tel 91 528 28 19.

Teatro Reina Victoria
Carrera de San Jerónimo 24. **Map** 7 A2.
Tel 91 369 22 88.

BULLFIGHTING

Plaza de Toros de las Ventas
Calle de Alcalá 237.
Tel 91 356 22 00.

FOOTBALL

Atlético de Madrid
Estadio Vicente Calderón, Paseo de la Virgen del Puerto 67.
Tel 902 26 04 03.
www.clubatletico demadrid.com

Rayo Vallecano
Estadio Teresa Rivero, Calle Payaso Fofó.
Tel 91 478 22 53.
www.rayovallecano.es

Real Madrid
Estadio Santiago Bernabéu, Avenida de Concha Espina.
Tel 91 398 43 00.
www.realmadrid.com

Modern Entertainment

Madrid's nightlife starts to rumble at dusk in the city's numerous *tapas* bars and cafés. After a quick bite and yet another *caña* (small glass of beer), you may decide to head off to one of the city's palatial movie houses to see a film, or perhaps you would prefer to hit a lively night spot for a little rock, jazz or salsa to warm up your dancing shoes. The younger *Madrileños*, who may well have to go to school the next day, begin to head for the Metro stations at about 1:30am to catch the last train home, clearing the way for the multitudes of over-20s to take over the dance clubs until daybreak.

CINEMA

Spanish cinema has been undergoing a renaissance in recent years as a new crop of film-makers tries to follow in the footsteps of internationally acclaimed film director Pedro Almodóvar, famous for his *Women on the Verge of a Nervous Breakdown (see p102)*.

For those with a grasp of the language, Spanish cinema is a rewarding experience, especially if enjoyed at one of the vast movie houses along Gran Vía *(see p48)*, such as the **Capitol** or **Palacio de la Música**. At the weekends many cinemas have late-night film programmes which begin only after midnight.

For those with no knowledge of Spanish, Hollywood productions and independent films can be seen in their original-language version at **Golem**, **Ideal**, **Princesa** and **Renoir** among others. These cinemas have sprung up over the years to cater to Madrid's foreign residents and Spaniards who wish to enjoy productions in their purest form with Spanish subtitles. Films shown in their original version are listed in the film section of newspapers and various listings magazines as *VO (versión original)*.

CAFÉS AND BARS

With such a vast array of cafés and bars in Madrid, you'd think supply would outstrip demand. But Madrid's social life revolves around the city's endless watering holes, which are also great places for people-watching and encounters. The **Café del Círculo de Bellas Artes** is a cultural institution overlooking the busy Calle Alcalá, and the view of the Palacio Real *(see pp54–7)* from the **Café de Oriente** is without equal.

Overlooking the lively Plaza de Santa Ana *(see p47)* are the well established **Cervecería Alemana** and **Cervecería Santa Ana** bars. Two quite different bars can be found in the La Latina district. **El Almendro 13** offers sherry on the crowded first floor and popular Spanish cuisine in the basement. **Café del Nuncio** is an old style café with a beautiful outdoor terrace on an old stone staircase over Calle Segovia. And then, of course, there are the *tabernas (see pp30–31)*, the quintessential ingredient of any visit to Madrid. **Viva Madrid** draws in a healthy crowd of young *Madrileños* attracted by the nightly activity around the Plaza de Santa Ana. **España Cañí**, next to Santa Ana, is like an old Andalusian tavern, and is perfect for a quiet drink. **Taberna Alhambra** is larger and airier than España Cañí and a good place from which to people-watch. **Bodega La Ardosa** is another favourite and has been open since 1892. It offers Spanish wines, beers and vermouth and, since the 80s, Guinness and other Irish beers. La Ardosa is not a restaurant but it does have a good selection of tapas. **Casa Labra** was the birthplace of the Spanish socialist party in the late 19th century and, as well as its clandestine history, you can savour its tasty *tapas*. For sheer character born from centuries-old history, visit **Casa Alberto**, **La Bola** and **Taberna Antonio Sanchez**. The elegant surroundings of the **Taberna Casa Domingo** exude a more modern feel, whereas the Belle Epoque décor of **El Parnasillo** can be admired while enjoying a delicious coffee or cocktail.

NIGHTCLUBS

There is a high price to pay for dancing until dawn at one of Madrid's many nightclubs as entrance fees tend to be expensive. Two that are very much in vogue at the moment are **Kapital** and **Joy Madrid**. For something slightly different, however, you might like to try **Berlín Cabaret** where dance is mixed with cabaret acts.

The roomy and somewhat upmarket dance club **Pachá** contrasts with the rest of the music bars in Malasaña, which tend to be reasonably priced but rather claustrophobic. A particular favourite with tourists is the **Villa Rosa** dance club in Old Madrid, or the Madrid de los Austrias. The decorative mosaics of this one-time café are exceptional.

Famous Spanish actor Javier Bardém is the proprietor of the nightclub **El Torero**, where you can dance to Latin and Flamenco style music upstairs, or head downstairs for some funky House music. Salsa enthusiasts can try **Cardamomo** where there are also live flamenco nights. Nightclubs stay open until after 4am.

ROCK, JAZZ AND WORLD MUSIC

For those who would rather seek out good live music, there is no shortage of venues in Madrid. For rock music, **Sala la Riviera** has hosted some internationally famous bands. Located next to the Manzanares river *(see p112)*, this partially-covered venue is particularly popular during the warm summer months. **Moby Dick** and **Siroco** are good places to see some of the vibrant local and national talent. **Café Central** is considered the best place to enjoy jazz in a wonderfully elegant setting. The nearby **Populart** is an excellent venue too. Formerly a pottery shop, it is a relaxed and busy venue. Both the Café Central and Populart are also near to some of the best Latin music clubs in Madrid, where you can see live bands and dance to the sinuous rhythms of salsa into the early hours of the morning. The much larger

Clamores hosts a range of musical performers, from jazz and tango to pop and blues.

Honky Tonk holds some of the city's best rock concerts, so keep an eye out for posters advertising forthcoming events.

GAY CLUBS

The heart of the gay scene is located in the Chueca

district (see p92) of central Madrid. **Why Not** is a small bar that caters mostly to locals and plays music from the 1970s and '80s. There's not much in the way of leather at **New Leather**, but it is still one of the most popular male gay bars in the city. For mixed crowds, **La Lupe** is a favourite hangout that puts on frequent cabaret shows.

DIRECTORY

CINEMA

Capitol
Gran Vía 41. **Map** 4 E1.
Tel 902 33 32 31.

Golem
Calle de Martín de los Heros 14. **Map** 1 A1.
Tel 91 559 38 36.

Ideal
Calle Doctor Cortez 10.
Map 4 F3.
Tel 902 22 09 22.

Palacio de la Música
Gran Vía 35.
Map 4 F1.
Tel 902 22 16 22.

Princesa
Princesa 3. **Map** 1 C5.
Tel 91 541 41 00.

Renoir
C/ Martin de los Heros 12.
Map 1 C5.
Tel 91 541 41 00.

CAFÉS AND BARS

El Almendro 13
Calle Almendro 13.
Map 4 D3.
Tel 91 365 42 52.

Bodega La Ardosa
Calle Colón 13.
Map 5 A5.
Tel 91 521 49 79.

La Bola
C/ Bola 5. **Map** 4 D1.
Tel 91 547 69 30.

Café del Círculo de Bellas Artes
Calle del Marqués de Casa Riera 2.
Map 7 B2.
Tel 91 531 85 03.

Café del Nuncio
Calle Segovia 9.
Map 4 D3.
Tel 91 366 08 53.

Café de Oriente
Plaza de Oriente 2. **Map** 3 C2. *Tel 91 541 39 74.*

Cardamomo
Calle Echegaray 15.
Map 7 A2.
Tel 91 369 07 57.

Casa Alberto
Calle de las Huertas 18.
Map 7 A3.
Tel 91 429 93 56.

Casa Labra
Calle de Tetuán 12.
Map 4 F2.
Tel 91 531 00 81.

Cervecería Alemana
Plaza de Santa Ana 6.
Map 7 A3.
Tel 91 429 70 33.

Cervecería Santa Ana
Plaza de Santa Ana 10.
Map 7 A3.
Tel 91 429 43 56.

España Cañí
Plaza del Angel 14.
Map 7 A3.

El Parnasillo
Calle San Andrés 33.
Map 2 F3.
Tel 91 447 00 79.

Taberna Alhambra
Calle Victoria 9. **Map** 7 A2. *Tel 91 521 07 08.*

Taberna Antonio Sanchez
C/ Mesón de Paredes 13.
Map 4 F5.
Tel 91 539 78 26.

Taberna Casa Domingo
Calle de Alcalá 99. **Map** 8 F1. *Tel 91 576 01 37.*

Viva Madrid
Calle de Manuel Fernández y González 7.
Map 7 A3.
Tel 91 429 36 40.

NIGHTCLUBS

Berlín Cabaret
Costanilla de San Pedro 11. **Map** 4 D3.
Tel 91 366 20 34.

El Torero
Calle de la Cruz 26.
Map 4 F3.
Tel 91 523 11 29.

Joy Madrid
Calle del Arenal 11.
Map 4 E2.
Tel 91 366 37 33.

Kapital
Calle del Atocha 125.
Map 7 B4.
Tel 91 420 29 06.

Pachá
Calle de Barceló 11.
Map 5 A4.
Tel 91 447 01 28.

Villa Rosa
Plaza de Santa Ana 15.
Map 7 A3.
Tel 91 521 36 89.

ROCK, JAZZ AND WORLD MUSIC

Café Central
Plaza del Angel 10.
Map 7 A3.
Tel 91 369 41 43.

Clamores
Calle de Alburquerque 14.
Map 5 A3.
Tel 91 445 79 38.

Honky Tonk
Calle de Covarrubias 24.
Map 5 B3.
Tel 91 445 68 86.

Moby Dick
Avenida del Brasil 5.
Tel 91 555 76 71.

Populart
Calle de las Huertas 22.
Map 7 A3.
Tel 91 429 84 07.

Sala la Riviera
Paseo de la Virgen del Puerto.
Tel 91 365 24 15.

Siroco
Calle de San Dimas 3.
Map 2 E4.
Tel 91 593 30 70.

GAY CLUBS

La Lupe
Calle de Torrecilla del Leal 12.
Map 7 A4
Tel 91 527 50 19.

New Leather
Calle de Pelayo 42.
Map 5 B5.
Tel 91 308 14 62.

Why Not
Calle de San Bartolomé 7.
Map 7 A1.
Tel 91 523 05 81.

OUTDOOR ACTIVITIES

A vast wilderness, ranging from the gentle to the dramatic, lies on the doorstep of Madrid. A scant hour's drive from the city centre will bring you to granite peaks, pine forests, glacial lakes and wild pastureland. Against this backdrop there are endless possibilities for hiking, climbing, horse riding, camping, swimming, skiing or simply finding tranquillity. Stretching across central Spain, the Sierra de Guadarrama and the Sierra de Gredos form a 250-km (155-mile) chain of craggy peaks dipping down to lush

Cycling in Madrid

pastureland, where you can track a mountain stream in spring, ski in winter or picnic in the wilderness in summer. Within Madrid, golf and tennis facilities are on hand, and waterworlds have begun to appear everywhere in response to the hot summers. Beyond Madrid, the area surrounding Toledo is famous for its hunting and, further afield, Cuenca's river gorges and ravines are an ideal setting for adventure sports. Details on all outdoor activities are available at **Comunidad de Madrid Tourist Information** offices.

Enjoying a game of golf in the attractive countryside of El Escorial

GOLF AND TENNIS

Madrid's finest sports grounds are to be found at the semi-private **Club de Campo**. The entrance fee for non-members is high, but the excellent facilities and lovely setting make it well worth the cost for

A pleasant break from sightseeing at one of Madrid's tennis courts

weary tourists who need a day away from the museums. Tennis, squash and golf are all on offer here. The club also provides designated play areas for children. Tennis courts can be reserved over the telephone, but for golf you must turn up at the club in person. When deciding which day to plan your activities, it is worth bearing in mind that admission prices rise at the weekends.

El Olivar de la Hinojosa is a new golf course just off the road to Barajas airport *(see p200)*. It accepts reservations over the telephone. At both the Club de Campo and El Olivar you can rent golf equipment.

If you want a game of tennis in the centre of town, you can reserve a court at the **Canal de Isabel II** sports centre. This modern, attractively designed

complex, which is conveniently located in north-central Madrid, boasts excellent facilities as well as a pleasant bar and restaurant. The **Puerta de Hierro** sports complex, alongside the Río Manzanares *(see p112)*, also has tennis courts and a swimming pool.

WALKING AND CYCLING

For keen walkers, there are numerous day hikes within easy access of the city – even if you don't have a car. Just an hour away by train, Cercedilla is an excellent starting point for trails into the Valle de la Fuenfría. One such trail is the old Roman road *(calzada romana)*. Dating from around the 1st century AD, the road once ran over the mountain to Segovia. A tram which links Cercedilla with the area's ski resorts climbs to the Puerto de Navacerrada for more substantial trails higher up.

Further east, the regional park which encompasses Manzanares el Real *(see p130)* leads into a valley of fast-flowing streams and pools, climbing sharply to the source of the Río Manzanares. The valley tends to attract large numbers of picnickers – one good reason for an early start.

Because only limited roadside bicycle trails are available, many cyclists opt for mountain biking instead. **Karacol Sport** near Atocha Station *(see p83)* rents bicycles which can then be taken by train to Cercedilla. For other destinations, check

An ideal site for birdwatching and walking outside the city

with RENFE first *(see p204)*. In addition to organizing walks, **Asociación Sport Natura** and other specialist outlets provide bikes and transport at weekends to areas such as the Sierra Pobre, east of the Guadarrama.

Remember to take sensible precautions when walking or cycling in the intense Spanish summer heat. It is essential to wear a hat and a high-factor suncream and to take an adequate supply of water with you. Walkers venturing into high-mountain areas should always check the weather forecast first, as conditions here can change very rapidly.

HORSE RIDING

The sierras and *cañadas* (old sheep trails) surrounding Madrid are ideal for horse riding. Spaghetti westerns were once filmed in this wild region of the country. At the **Club de Campo**, on the edge of the city, horses can be hired for rides through Madrid's expansive Casa de Campo *(see p112)*. You can also hire a steed by the hour or even for the day at **El Potril**.

Centro Equestre Alameda del Pardo is situated in the village of El Pardo about 5 km northwest of Madrid and offers routes through the extensive forest surrounding the famous Palacio de El Pardo *(see p138)*.

High up on the route from Cercedilla to the Puerto de Navacerrada, set back from the tram line, **Picadero los Ciruelos** also offers a wide choice of day horse riding routes or even longer outings. In the rugged Sierra Pobre near Buitrago del Lozoya, **Rutas Ecuestres Sierra Norte** organizes routes from Braojos de la Sierra, which is accessible by direct bus once a day from Madrid.

For an overnight stay or longer stays, the Sierra de Gredos offers superb horse riding set against imposing peaks. You can hire horses at **Turismo Ecuestre Almanzor**, down the road from the Parador Nacional de Gredos. Further along, **Gredos Rutas a Caballo (GRAC)** also organizes day- or week-long outings. During holiday periods, especially Easter week, you should book your accommodation well in advance. Also make sure the riding centre is open on the day you plan to go, and specify your riding level.

Rugged terrain of the sierras – perfect for horse riding

Skiing at the popular resort of the Puerto de Navacerrada

SKIING

In a year of good snowfall, skiing through pine trees under an azure sky can be a glorious experience. The most popular resort near Madrid is the **Puerto de Navacerrada**. It has 15 slopes and a daunting chairlift up to the "Bola del Mundo" at 2,200 m (7,200 ft). Further away, **Valdesquí** offers better snow conditions and 24 slopes, while **La Pinilla** in the Segovia region is probably the least crowded. All the equipment you need, including skis, snowboards and sleds, can be rented at the resorts.

On weekends during the skiing season, the route to the Puerto de Navacerrada tends to be congested with traffic. Avoid driving if you can and take the tram from Cercedilla. A reliable source of information is **ATUDEM** (Asociación Turística de Estaciones de Esquí y Montaña), a group that specializes in alpine skiing and will provide details on any of the resorts.

MOUNTAINEERING AND CLIMBING

Some perfect drops for novice climbers can be found at La Pedriza de Manzanares, as well as at La Cabrera at the eastern end of the Guadarrama mountains. Patones, in the Sierra Pobre, offers ideal rock faces. For the experienced mountaineer, the huge granite needles and walls in the Sierra de Gredos present a greater challenge. Information on courses and guides is available at the **Federación Madrileña de Montañismo**. **Club Ibérico de Expediciones** organises four-wheel drive (4WD) trips out of Madrid for weekends. They take care of the accommodation and the food and also offer tuition in driving the 4WD off-road vehicles. A company called **Gente Viajera** organizes weekend courses near Cuenca in which those with a seriously robust constitution can be taught the exciting art of rappelling (abseiling) down river gorges.

Climbing at Escalada en Patones

SHOOTING

Like the rest of Spain, the rugged terrain surrounding Madrid is ideal for hunting. But, unless you are fortunate enough to hunt on one of the many private estates, you will not find much game in the remaining free shooting zones. The best option is to go to Toledo or Ciudad Real, both of which are rich in game, from birds to wild boar and deer. To avoid hassles for permits, contact **Cacerías Ibéricas** in advance. They will do the paperwork, organize the outing and provide equipment. **Viajes Marsans** will do everything except provide your equipment.

WATER SPORTS

Madrid's sizzlingly hot summers make watering holes a dire necessity. There is a splendid swimming pool at the **Club de Campo Villa de Madrid** although, in spite of its great size, it can be uncomfortably full on a hot day. The sports complex at **Puerta de Hierro** has a huge, neck-deep basin just for cooling off, as well as a proper lane pool for swimmers. By far the best pool in Madrid is the **Centro de Natación M-86**, but it is only open to the public from June to the end of August. The **Canal de Isabel II** sports complex, which is also conveniently situated in town, has a much appreciated outdoor pool, as well as a

One of the reservoirs on the outskirts of Madrid – ideal for canoeing

Causing a splash outside Madrid

children's pool. There are also a number of large reservoirs outside Madrid, which are perfect for sailing, windsurfing and canoeing. Contact

Asociación Sport Natura, which provides equipment and transport at weekends to its centre at Embalse del Atazar near El Berrueco.

THEME PARKS

Nearly 500 animals run wild at **Safari Madrid** outside Aldea del Fresno, making this a great outing for children. There is also a daily show of birds of prey. A nearby added attraction is the park and beach along the Alberche river.

Aquópolis, a 40-minute drive from the city, is Madrid's most complete waterworld, with slides and innumerable

other water features. Bring a picnic, and enjoy a day out for the family.

For an alternative form of nature park visit **Faunia**, a biological park that recreates the world's ecosystems and natural surroundings to suit the different species of animals.

The thrilling **Parque de Atracciones** *(see p114)* has the latest stomach-churning rides from roller coasters to vertical drops, as well as all the old favourites. There is also a zone for small children. A **Warner Bros. Park** in Madrid has roller-coaster rides and recreations of film sets and a Hollywood Boulevard.

DIRECTORY

Comunidad de Madrid Tourist Information
Calle del Duque de Medinaceli 2, Madrid.
Map 7 B3.
Tel 91 429 49 51.
www.madrid.org/turismo

GOLF AND TENNIS

Canal de Isabel II
Avenida de Filipinas 54, Madrid.
Tel 91 533 17 91.

Club de Campo Villa de Madrid
Carretera de Castilla, km 2, Madrid.
Tel 91 550 20 18 (tennis).
Tel 91 550 20 27 (water sports).
Tel 91 550 20 10 (riding school).

El Olivar de la Hinojosa
Campo de las Naciones, Via de Dublin, Madrid.
Tel 91 721 18 89.

Puerta de Hierro
Carretera de El Pardo, km 1, Madrid.
Tel 91 376 86 80.

WALKING AND CYCLING

Asociación Sport Natura
Avenida Donostiarra 4 posterior, Madrid.
Tel 91 403 61 61.

Karacol Sport
Calle de Tortosa 8, Madrid.
Map 7 C5.
Tel 91 539 96 33.

HORSE RIDING

Centro Ecuestre Alameda del Pardo
Carretera Fuencarral, km 2.3, El Pardo.
Tel 91 372 09 58.

Club de Campo
See Golf and Tennis.

El Potril
Avenida de las Caudalosas, Brunete.
Tel 91 816 42 91.

Gredos Rutas a Caballo (GRAC)
Calle Triguras 4, Hoyos del Espino (Avila).
Tel 920 34 90 85.

Picadero los Ciruelos
Camino los Ciruelos 30, Carretera Camorritos, Cercedilla.
Tel 91 852 07 67.

Rutas Ecuestres Sierra Norte
Calle Generalísimo 13, Braojos de la Sierra.
Tel 91 868 09 44.

Turismo Ecuestre Almanzor
Barajas de Gredos, Navarredonda de Gredos (Avila).
Tel 920 34 80 47.

SKIING

ATUDEM
Calle del Padre Damián 43, 2nd Floor 26, Madrid.
Tel 91 359 75 26.

La Pinilla
Tel 921 55 06 51.

Puerto de Navacerrada
Tel 90 288 23 28.

Valdesquí
Tel 91 852 39 41.

MOUNTAINEERING AND CLIMBING

Federación Madrileña de Montañismo
Avenida Salas de los Infantes 1, Madrid.
Tel 91 527 38 01.

Club Ibérico de Expediciones
Avenida Complutense 16 Camarma de Esteruelas.
Tel 606 72 94 21.

Gente Viajera
Calle de Santa Alicia 19, Madrid.
Tel 91 478 01 11.

SHOOTING

Cacerías Ibéricas
Calle de San Pedro el Verde 49.3, Toledo.
Tel 925 21 25 52.

Viajes Marsans
Gran Via 84, Madrid.
Map 4 E1.
Tel 90 230 60 90.

WATER SPORTS

Canal de Isabel II
See Golf and Tennis.

Club de Campo
See Golf and Tennis.

Centro de Natación M-86
Calle de José Martínez de Velasco 3, Madrid.
Tel 91 433 71 12.

Puerta de Hierro
See Golf and Tennis.

Sport Natura
See Walking and Cycling.

THEME PARKS

Aquópolis
Avenida de la Dehesa, Villanueva de la Cañada.
Tel 91 815 69 11.

Faunia
Motorway A3, Exit 6, Valdebernardo.
Tel 91 301 62 10.

Parque de Atracciones
Casa de Campo, Madrid.
Tel 90 234 50 01.

Safari Madrid
Motorway A5, Salida 32, Aldea del Fresno.
Tel 91 862 23 14.

Warner Bros. Park
Carretera A4, Exit 22, San Martin de la Vega.
Open Mar–Oct.
Tel 91 821 12 34.

SURVIVAL GUIDE

PRACTICAL INFORMATION

Spain has finally begun to market itself beyond the attractions of its coastline, and now has a solid tourist infrastructure. In Madrid there are national tourist offices, while the smaller towns have regional offices. All offer help with finding accommodation, restaurants and activities in their area. One of Madrid's best offices is at Plaza Mayor. August is Spain's

Old street sign

vacation (holiday) period, during which many businesses close. Roads are very busy at the beginning and end of the month. Find out in advance whether your visit coincides with Madrid's many fiestas because, although these are attractions, they often entail widespread closures. It is a good idea to plan leisurely lunches, as most of Spain stops from 2pm to 5pm.

LANGUAGE

Spain's official language is *castellano* (Castilian). It is spoken by everyone and is certainly the language you will experience most frequently in Madrid. There are three main regional languages – *català* (Catalonia), *euskera* (Basque country) and *gallego* (Galicia). Places that deal with tourists usually employ at least one English-speaker.

MANNERS

Madrileños are a warm, open, spirited people who are justly proud of their city. Drawn to the capital from all parts of the country, they have brought with them a strong and varied cultural tradition. As a result, this lively city teems with culture and the arts.

It is common for the Spanish to greet and say goodbye to strangers at bus stops and in elevators (lifts), shops and other public places. They often talk to people they do not know. It is customary for people to shake hands when introduced. Women usually kiss on both cheeks when they meet; friends and family members embrace or kiss. In bars or restaurants, it is unusual to sit at someone else's table.

VISAS AND PASSPORTS

Visas are not required by citizens of most EU countries but it is wise to check entry requirements before you go. A list is available from Spanish embassies, which specifies 35 other countries, including Canada, Australia and the US, whose nationals do not need a visa for visits of less than 90 days. For an extension, apply to the *Gobierno Civil* (a local government office) with proof of employment or of sufficient funds to cover a long stay. Visitors from

all other countries need a visa. British visitors can no longer travel on a Visitor's Passport and must have a full passport.

TAX-FREE GOODS AND CUSTOMS INFORMATION

Non-EU residents can reclaim IVA (VAT) on single items worth over 90 euros and bought in shops displaying a "Tax-free for Tourists" sign. Food, drink, tobacco, cars, motorcycles and medicines are exempt. You pay the full price and ask the sales assistant for a *formulario* (tax exemption form). When you leave Spain, ask customs to stamp your *formulario* (this must be within six months of purchase). You will receive the refund by mail or as a credit on your credit card account.

Branches of Spain's Banco Exterior at Madrid's Barajas Airport give refunds on *formularios* that have been stamped by customs.

Sign indicating tax-free goods

TOURIST INFORMATION

Madrid and all major historic towns in the vicinity have *oficinas de turismo* (tourist information offices), which provide maps, transport details and hotel and restaurant lists. On arrival, it is worth visiting the tourist office at **Barajas Airport** (Terminal One) where there is also a hotel reservation desk and a RENFE *(see p200)* desk offering information on rail travel; there is also a new tourist information office in Terminal Four. New tourist

---

MADRID TIME

Madrid is one hour ahead of Greenwich Mean Time (GMT) and 6 hours ahead of Eastern Standard Time (EST). Spain uses the 24-hour clock, so 1pm = 13:00 hours.

City and Country	Hours ahead or behind Spain	City and Country	Hours ahead or behind Spain
Athens (Greece)	+ 1	Moscow (Russia)	+ 2
Auckland (New Zealand)	+ 11	New York (US)	– 6
Bangkok (Thailand)	+ 6	Paris (France)	0
Berlin (Germany)	0	Perth (Australia)	+ 7
Cape Town (South Africa)	+ 1	Rome (Italy)	0
Chicago (US)	– 7	Sydney (Australia)	+ 9
Dublin (Ireland)	– 1	Tokyo (Japan)	+ 8
Hong Kong (China)	+ 7	Toronto (Canada)	– 6
London (UK)	– 1	Vancouver (Canada)	– 9
Los Angeles (US)	– 9	Washington DC (US)	– 6

◁ **The start of Madrid's sweeping Gran Vía with its relentless flow of traffic**

kiosks can be found in Plaza de Cibeles, Plaza del Callao, Plaza de Colón and Plaza de Felipe II. Tourist Information Offices are usually open Monday to Saturday from 8am until 8pm, and from 9am until 2pm on Sundays and public holidays.

OPENING HOURS

Most museums and monuments close on Sunday afternoons and all day Monday. Major art museums do not close over lunch. Churches have more restricted opening hours; some open only for services.

FACILITIES FOR THE DISABLED

COCEMFE sign for disabled access

Spain's national association for the disabled, **Confederación Coordinadora Estatal de Minusválidos Físicos de España (COCEMFE)**, operates Servi-COCEMFE – a tour company which publishes guides to disabled facilities in Spain and can help plan a vacation (holiday) to your requirements.

Tourist information offices and the social services supply information on local conditions and facilities. Metro maps and other information in Braille are available from the Spanish national organization for the blind, **Organización Nacional de Ciegos (ONCE)**. If you prefer to let someone else do the work, the Spanish travel agent **Viajes 2000** specializes in vacations for the disabled. In the United States, the **Society for the Advancement of Travel for the Handicapped (SATH)** publishes the useful *ACCESS to Travel* magazine which deals with destinations, attractions, accommodation, transportation and other information for disabled people.

STUDENT INFORMATION

Holders of the International Student Identity Card (ISIC) are entitled to benefits, such as discounts on travel and reduced admission to museums and galleries. Information is available from all international student organizations and, in

Students in Madrid

Madrid, from the government-run youth information centre, **Centro de Información Juvenil (CIJ)**. One company that specializes in student travel is **Turismo y Viajes Educativos (TIVE)**.

ELECTRICAL ADAPTOR

Spain's electricity supply is 220 volts, but the 125-volt system still operates in some old buildings. Plugs for both have two round pins.

A three-tier, standard travel converter will enable you to use appliances from abroad on both supplies. Hair dryers, however, should be used only with 220-volt sockets.

DIRECTORY

EMBASSIES

Australia
Plaza del Descubridor Diego de Ordás 3, 2nd floor.
Tel 91 353 66 00.
www.immi.gov.au

Canada
Calle de Núñez de Balboa 35. **Map** 6 F4.
Tel 91 423 32 50.
www.canada-es.org

New Zealand
Calle Pinar 7, 3rd Floor.
Map 6 E1.
Tel 91 523 02 26.

South Africa
Calle de Claudio Coello 91, 6°. **Map** 6 E2.
Tel 91 436 37 80.
www.sudafrica.com

Republic of Ireland
Paseo de la Castellana 46, 4th floor. **Map** 6 E2.
Tel 91 436 40 93.

United Kingdom
Calle de Fernando El Santo 16. **Map** 5 C4.
Tel 91 700 82 00.
www.ukinspain.com

United States
Calle de Serrano 75. **Map** 6 E2. *Tel 91 587 22 00.*
www.embusa.es

TOURIST OFFICES IN MADRID

Municipal Tourist Office
Plaza Mayor 27. **Map** 4 E3.
Tel 91 588 16 36.
www.esmadrid.com

Comunidad de Madrid
C/ del Duque de Medinaceli 2. **Map** 7 B3.
Tel 90 210 00 07.

Barajas Airport
Terminal 1 (International).
Tel 91 305 86 56.

Estación de Chamartín
Tel 91 315 99 76.

Estación de Atocha
Map 8 D5.
Tel 91 528 46 30.

SPANISH TOURIST OFFICES ABROAD

Canada
34th Floor, 2 Bloor Street West, Toronto, M4W 3E2
Tel (416) 961 3131.

United Kingdom
79 New Cavendish St (2nd floor), London W1W 6XB.
Tel (020) 7486 8077.
www.tourspain.co.uk

United States
666 Fifth Avenue,
New York, NY 10103.
Tel (212) 265 8822.
www.okspain.org

ORGANIZATIONS FOR DISABLED TRAVELLERS

Viajes 2000
Paseo de la Castellana 228.
Tel 91 323 10 29.

COCEMFE
Calle de Luis Cabrera 63.
Tel 91 744 36 00.

ONCE
Centro Bibliográfico Cultural - Braille,
Calle de La Coruña 18.
Tel 91 589 42 00.

SATH
347 Fifth Avenue,
Suite 610
New York, NY 10016.
Tel (212) 447 7284.

STUDENT ORGANIZATIONS

CIJ
Gran Vía 10. **Map** 7 B1.
Tel 91 720 11 82.
www.madrid.org/
inforjoven

TIVE
Calle de Fernando el Católico 88. **Map** 1 B1.
Tel 91 543 74 12.
www.madrid.org/
inforjoven

Personal Security and Health

In Madrid, as in other cities with a high concentration of tourists, you should take steps to guard against theft. Carry credit cards, money and a photocopy of your passport in a money belt, and never leave anything visible in your car when you park it. If you lose your documents, contact your embassy (see p193) and the police. If you are unwell, there will always be a local pharmacy (farmacia) open. In Spain, pharmacists are qualified to advise and sometimes even to prescribe.

Spanish pharmacy sign

IN AN EMERGENCY

The new telephone number for all emergency services is 112. Depending on the nature of the problem you have, ask for *policía* (police), *ambulancia* (ambulance) or *bomberos* (fire brigade).

In cases of medical emergency, hospitals will accept admissions to the *urgencias* (casualty department).

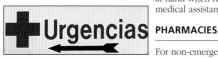

Sign identifying a *Cruz Roja* (Red Cross) emergency treatment centre

MEDICAL TREATMENT

All EU nationals are entitled to Spanish social security cover. To claim, you must obtain the European Health Insurance Card from the UK Department of Health or from a post office before you travel. You give this card to anyone who treats you and it comes with a booklet, *Health Advice for Travellers*, which explains exactly what health care you are entitled to and where and how to claim. You may find you have to pay and reclaim the money later.

Not all treatments are covered by the European Health Insurance Card and some are costly, so arrange for medical cover before travelling.

If you want private health care, ask at your hotel, embassy or tourist office for the name of a doctor. If necessary, ask for an English-speaker.

Visitors from the US should check with their insurance companies before leaving home to be sure they are covered if medical care is

needed. Some medical facilities require payment for treatment in full at the time of service. Get an itemized bill to submit to your insurance company. In some cases, insurance companies require you to provide an official translation before they reimburse you. Travellers may wish to take out extra private travel insurance for emergency hospital care, doctors' fees and repatriation. Have your policy at hand when requesting medical assistance.

PHARMACIES

For non-emergencies, a pharmacist *(farmacéutico)* can advise and, at times, prescribe without a doctor's consultation. Some medicines available only on prescription at home may be sold over the counter in Spain. The *farmacia* sign is an illuminated green cross. The addresses of those open at night or at weekends are displayed in the windows of all the local pharmacies or may be found in local newspapers.

Guardia Civil   **Policía Municipal**

PERSONAL SECURITY

Although violent crime is rare in Madrid, it is wise to take sensible precautions when out and about.

To guard against theft, wear your bag or camera strapped across your body and always keep your possessions in sight, especially at the airport.

At night, avoid walking alone in poorly lit areas and, if possible, take a taxi back to your lodgings late at night.

SPANISH POLICE

There are essentially three types of police in Spain. The first is the *Guardia Civil* (paramilitary Civil Guard) who mainly police rural areas, country roads, highways and state buildings and take part in anti-terrorist operations. Their uniform is olive green in colour, but their black patent leather tricorns, for which they are renowned, are now donned only on ceremonial occasions.

The *Policía Nacional* wear a blue uniform and they deal mainly with national security, terrorism and major crime in towns with a population of more than 30,000. They also police immigration, work permits and residence documents. There is a special female department in Puerta del Sol which has been set up to deal with crimes against women. There is also a service for tourists who have been victims of crime. This is based at the police station on Calle Leganitos 19 and can be reached on 91 548 85 37.

The third branch is the *Policía Municipal*. They are involved with traffic regulation, the imposition of fines and the policing of local communities.

DIRECTORY

EMERGENCY SERVICES

Police (Policía)
Tel 091

Ambulance (Ambulancia)

Fire Brigade (Bomberos)
*Tel 112 for ambulance, fire &
police.*

Red Cross (Cruz Roja)
Tel 91 522 22 22.
www.cruzroja.es

Patrol car of the Policía Nacional, Spain's main urban police force

Cruz Roja (Red Cross) ambulance

Spanish fire engine

LEGAL ASSISTANCE

Some insurance policies cover legal costs – after an accident, for instance. If you are not covered, telephone your embassy. They should be able to provide you with a list of bilingual lawyers.

If you are arrested, you have the right to telephone your embassy. The *Colegio de Abogados* (Lawyers' Association) can also inform you where best to obtain legal advice or representation.

If you require an interpreter, it is best to consult either your embassy *(see p193)* or the *Páginas Amarillas* (Yellow Pages) telephone directory under *Traductores* (Translators) or *Intérpretes* (Interpreters). Both *Traductores Oficiales* and *Traductores Jurados* are qualified to translate legal and official documents.

PUBLIC CONVENIENCES

Public pay-toilets have sprung up on some streets in Madrid but, on the whole, public conveniences are rare. Most people walk into a bar or café, a department store or a hotel and ask for *los servicios*, although it would be preferable to be a customer. On highways (motorways), there are toilets at service stations. Women often have to ask for the key *(la llave)*. Always carry toilet tissue with you as it is often not provided.

PERSONAL PROPERTY

Vacation (holiday) insurance is there to protect you financially in the event of the loss or theft of your property,

but it is always advisable to take preventative measures – by making use of hotel safes, for example, and playing down the obvious tourist image.

It should not be necessary to carry large sums of money with you, as Spain has more ATMs (cashpoints) than any other country in Europe, and they take EuroCard and all major credit cards. If you have more than one card, do not carry them together. Travellers' cheques are another option, but you will need your passport with you to cash them.

If you discover a loss or theft, report it to the local *comisaría* (police station). To claim insurance you must do this immediately, as many companies give you only 24 hours. You must make a *denuncia* (formal written statement) to the police and obtain a copy to give to your insurers. The process can take some time.

If you lose your passport, your embassy can supply a replacement but cannot provide financial assistance.

Sometimes lost property is found and handed in. If this is the case, it will probably end up at Madrid's main post office in the Plaza de Cibeles or at your embassy, so it is worth checking these two places.

OUTDOOR HAZARDS

Spain is prey in summer to forest fires fanned by winds and fuelled by bone-dry vegetation. Avoid fire hazards by extinguishing cigarettes in car ashtrays and taking empty bottles away with you.

The sign *coto de caza* in woodland areas identifies a hunting reserve where you must follow the country code. *Toro bravo* means fighting bull – do not approach. A *camino particular* sign indicates a private driveway.

If climbing or hiking, go properly equipped and tell someone when you expect to return. You can also keep in touch by cellular (mobile) phones, which work in most parts of the country.

Banking and Local Currency

You may enter Spain with any amount of money, but if you intend to export more than 6,000 euros, you should declare it. Traveller's cheques may be exchanged at banks, *cajas de cambio* (foreign currency exchanges), some hotels and some shops. Banks generally offer the best exchange rates. The cheapest exchange may be offered on your credit or debit card, which you can use in cash dispensers (automated teller machines, ATMs) displaying the appropriate sign.

24-hour cash dispenser (ATM)

BANKING HOURS

Although Spanish banks are beginning to extend their opening hours throughout the country, expect extended hours only at the large central branches in the city centre.

As a general rule, banks are open from 8am to 2pm on weekdays. Some are also open until 1pm on Saturdays, except in the summer when most are closed on Saturdays.

CHANGING MONEY

Most banks have a foreign exchange desk with the sign *Cambio* or *Extranjero*. Remember to always take your passport with you as ID to effect any transaction.

You can draw up to 300 euros on major credit cards at a bank. If you bank with either **Barclays Bank** or **Citibank** it is possible to cash a cheque in the usual way at one of their branches in Spain.

Foreign currency exchange offices (bureaux de change), with the sign *Caja de Cambio* or "Change", may state that they charge no commission but their exchange rates are invariably worse than those found at banks. One benefit is that they are often open outside normal banking hours. There are several offices located on Gran Vía around the Plaza del Calleo as well as in many of the popular tourist areas.

Cajas de Ahorro (savings banks) also exchange money. They open from 8:30am to 2pm on weekdays and some are also open on Thursday afternoons from 4:30pm to 7:45pm.

CHEQUES AND CARDS

Traveller's cheques can be purchased at **American Express** (AmEx), **Travelex** or your bank. All are accepted in Spain. If you exchange American Express cheques at an AmEx office, commission is not charged.

Banks require 24 hours' notice to cash cheques larger than 3,000 euros. If you draw more than 600 euros on traveller's cheques, you may be asked to show the purchase certificate.

The most widely accepted card in Spain is the **VISA** card, although **MasterCard (Access)/Eurocard** and American Express are also useful currency. **Diners Club** is widely accepted in Madrid, but less so in establishments outside the city. The major banks will allow cash withdrawals on credit cards. All cash dispensers accept most foreign cards, although the level of commission charged on your withdrawal will depend on your own bank.

When you pay with a card, cashiers will usually pass it through a card reading machine. In shops you will always be asked for additional photo ID. As leaving your passport in the hotel safe is preferable, make sure you have an alternative original document on hand (photocopies will rarely do) such as a driver's license.

As is common throughout Europe, credit cards are not always accepted in some smaller bars and restaurants. Checking first will avoid unnecessary embarrassment.

Logo for BBVA, the Banco Bilbao Vizcaya Argentaria

CASH DISPENSERS

If your card is linked to your home bank account, you can use it with your PIN to withdraw money from cash dispensers. Nearly all take VISA or MasterCard (Access). Cards with Cirrus or Maestro logos can also be widely used in cash machines.

When you enter your PIN, instructions are displayed in English, French, German and Spanish. Many dispensers are inside buildings so customers must swipe their card through a door-entry system.

DIRECTORY

FOREIGN BANKS

Barclays Bank
Plaza de Colón 1, 28046 Madrid.
Tel 91 336 10 00.

Citibank
C/ Velázquez 31, 28001 Madrid.
Tel 91 426 07 82.

LOST CARDS AND TRAVELLER'S CHEQUES

American Express
Pl de Las Cortes 2, 28014 Madrid.
Tel 902 37 56 37.

Diners Club
Tel 901 10 10 11.

MasterCard
Tel 900 97 12 31 (toll free).

Travelex/T Cook MC
Tel 900 94 89 71 (toll free).

VISA
Tel 900 99 11 24 (toll free).

THE EURO

Introduction of the single European currency, the euro, has taken place in 15 of the 27 member states of the EU. Austria, Belgium, Finland, France, Germany, Greece, Ireland, Italy, Luxembourg, The Netherlands, Portugal, Spain, Slovenia, Malta and Cyprus chose to join the new currency; the UK, Denmark and Sweden stayed out, with an option to review the decision. The euro was introduced on 1 January 1999, but only for banking purposes. Notes and coins came into circulation on 1 January 2002. After a transition period allowing the use of both national currencies and the euro, Spain's own currency, the peseta, was completely phased out by March 2002. Euros can be used across participating member states.

Bank Notes

Euro bank notes have seven denominations. The 5-euro note (grey in colour) is the smallest, followed by the 10-euro note (pink), 20-euro note (blue), 50-euro note (orange), 100-euro note (green), 200-euro note (yellow) and 500-euro note (purple). All notes show the 12 stars of the European Union.

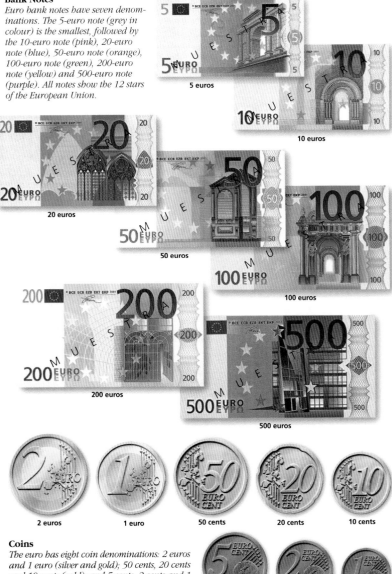

5 euros

10 euros

20 euros

50 euros

100 euros

200 euros

500 euros

2 euros

1 euro

50 cents

20 cents

10 cents

Coins

The euro has eight coin denominations: 2 euros and 1 euro (silver and gold); 50 cents, 20 cents and 10 cents (gold); and 5 cents, 2 cents and 1 cent (bronze). The reverse (number) side of euros are the same in all Euro-zone countries, but the front is different in each state.

5 cents

2 cents

1 cent

Communications

The Spanish telecommunications company, Telefónica, was digitized in 1995 and 1998 saw the end of the state monopoly. Most public telephones operate with a card or coins. International calls are expensive. The postal service *(correos)* is identified by a crown insignia in red or white on a yellow background. Registered mail and telegrams can be sent from *correos* offices; they also sell stamps, as do state-run *estancos* (tobacconists). Madrid also has an increasing number of internet cafés.

Logo of the Spanish telecom system

TELEPHONING IN SPAIN

As well as public telephone boxes *(cabinas)*, there are nearly always payphones in bars. Both types take coins. There will be a high minimum connection charge, especially for international calls. Phonecards can be bought at newsstands and *estancos*. Some phones are equipped with multilingual electronic instruction displays.

There are also public telephone offices called *locutorios* where you can make a call and pay for it afterwards. The cheapest are those run by Telefónica; private *locutorios*, often found in shops, cost more. Calls from a *cabina* or a *locutorio* can cost as much as 35 per cent more than calls made from a private phone in someone's home. Calls from hotels can also be expensive.

There are four charge bands for international calls: EU countries; non-EU European countries and Northwest Africa; North and South America; and the rest of the world.

Collect calls within the EU may be dialled directly, but most others must be made through the operator.

The first digit in each area code is 9. For example, Madrid's code is 91. To call

USING A COIN AND CARD TELEPHONE

1 Lift the receiver, and wait for the dialling tone and for the display to show *Inserte monedas o tarjeta*.

2 Insert either coins *(monedas)* or a card *(tarjeta)*.

3 Key in the number firmly, but not too fast – Spanish phones prefer you to pause between digits.

4 As you press the digits, the number you are dialling will appear on the display. You will also be able to see how much money or how many units are left and when to insert more coins.

5 When your call is finished, replace the receiver. The phonecard will then re-emerge automatically or any excess coins will be returned.

Spanish phonecard

USEFUL SPANISH DIALLING CODES

- To call another province, first dial the area code (beginning with 9, e.g. Barcelona 93). Area codes are listed in the A-K phone book or obtained from directory enquiries.
- Use area codes for calls within a province.
- To make an international call, dial 00, wait for the tone, then dial the country code, the area code and the number. Country codes are: UK 44; Eire 353; US and Canada 1; New Zealand 64; Australia 61; South Africa 27.
- If calling Spain from another country, dial that country's international access code, the code for Spain (34) and the full area code.

- For operator/directory service, dial 11818.
- For international directories, dial 11825.
- To make a collect (reversed-charge) call within the EU, dial 1005 followed by the country code; to the US or Canada, dial 1005 followed by 11 or 15 respectively. Numbers for other countries can be found in the front of the A-K telephone directory under *Indicativos Internacionales*.
- To report technical faults, dial 1002.
- The speaking clock: 093, restaurant and hotel info: 11888, wake-up calls: 096.

Madrid from abroad, first dial your country's international access code, then Spain's country code (34), and then Madrid's area code (91).

City telephone numbers generally have seven digits, while those in smaller towns have six digits only.

MAIL (POSTAL SERVICE)

The postal service (correos) in Spain can be rather slow. Urgent or important items can be sent by urgente (express) or certificado (registered) mail, although to be sure of fast delivery it is wise to use a private courier.

Mail can be registered and telegrams sent from all correos offices. Stamps for letters and postcards can be bought from an estanco (tobacconist). Postal rates fall into four price bands: the EU; the rest of Europe; the USA; and the rest of the world. Parcels have to be weighed and stamped at a post office and must be securely tied with string or a charge may be made to have them sealed by a clerk.

The main correos offices open 8am–9pm from Monday to Friday and 9am–2pm on Saturday. Branches in the suburbs of cities and in smaller towns and villages open from 9am–2pm Monday to Friday and from 9am–1pm on Saturday.

Spanish mailbox

Standard issue stamps

ADDRESSES AND LETTERS

In Spanish addresses the house number follows the name of the street. The floor of an apartment block is indicated by the number which appears after the hyphen. Therefore, 4-2° means an apartment on the second floor

of number four. All postcodes have five digits, with the first two standing for the province.

If you mail your letters at a central post office they are usually likely to arrive more quickly than if you were to mail them in a local mailbox (buzón). Cities have yellow pillar boxes; towns and villages normally have small, wall-mounted mailboxes.

Poste restante letters should be addressed care of the Lista de Correos and the town. You will be able to collect them from main post offices.

To send and receive money by mail ask for a giro postal.

When dealing with businesses in Spain, it is always quicker and more convenient to phone or fax. The mail tends to be used only as a last resort. Fax facilities are available in some locutorios, in hotels and in many private shops. Look for a telefax sign.

TELEVISION AND RADIO

Televisión Española is Spain's state television company, which broadcasts two channels by the names of TVE1 and TVE2.

Several of the autonomous regions have their own television stations. Madrid's is called Telemadrid and is a useful source of news.

There are four national independent television stations in Spain: Antena 3, Tele-5 (Telecinco), Cuatro and La Sexta. There are also several satellite channels which you will only be able to receive if you pay a subscription for a station decoder.

Most foreign films shown on Spanish television (and in cinemas) are dubbed. Subtitled films will appear in listings as V.O. (versión original).

The satellite channels CNN, Eurosport and Cinemanía can be received throughout Spain.

The state radio station, Radio Nacional de España, has four channels. Radio 2 and 3 play music, while Radio 1 and 5 broadcast news programmes.

NEWSPAPERS AND MAGAZINES

Most of the kiosks around Puerta del Sol, Gran Vía, Calle de Alcalá and Paseo de la Castellana stock foreign newspapers and periodicals. English newspapers available on the day of publication are the International Herald Tribune, the Financial Times and The Guardian Europe. Many other English-language and European titles are sold, usually a day after their publication.

The European newspaper and popular weekly current affairs magazines, such as Time, Newsweek and The Economist, are readily available throughout Madrid.

The most widely read of the Spanish newspapers, in descending number of sales, are Marca, El País, El Mundo and ABC. Marca is a sports newspaper while the others cover international news.

The main weekly listings magazines for arts and events are the Guía del Ocio, which appears on Fridays; Metrópoli, free in El Mundo on Fridays; On Madrid, free with El País, on Fridays (see p180); and the magazine Salir on Fridays.

Local newspapers in Spanish can be a useful source of detailed information about events in the city and throughout the region.

Publications in English edited in Madrid are Guidepost, with business and general information; In Madrid, free each month and available in pubs, bookshops and record shops; and Lookout, with articles about Spanish life.

Spanish daily papers

TRAVEL INFORMATION

Spanish road and rail links were improved for the Expo in Seville and the Olympics in Barcelona in 1992, and Madrid, with its central location, is probably one of the easiest places in Spain to get to. The city is also a good starting point for trips to other destinations, whether Spanish, European or international.

Sign for the airport

While Barajas Airport, one of Europe's busiest, caters for domestic and European travel, it is also one of the main gateways to South America. By road, there are seven main points of entry to Madrid, and its train stations offer regular services to many European cities, as well as high-speed links with destinations all over Spain.

FLYING TO MADRID

Barajas airport is served by dozens of international airlines and charter companies. **Iberia**, the national carrier, has daily flights linking all Western European capitals except Dublin, and once- or twice-weekly flights to the capitals of Eastern Europe. **Air Europa** and **Spanair** also fly between London and Madrid. **British Airways** and **EasyJet** are the only UK airlines to offer direct scheduled flights. **Virgin** offers a service via Brussels.

US airlines **Continental** and **Delta Air Lines** link Madrid to New York, while **American Airlines** links Madrid to Miami. Iberia now flies direct to New York, Montréal and Toronto.

GETTING TO AND FROM THE AIRPORT

It takes about 20 minutes by taxi or bus to reach the city centre from Barajas Airport. The airport buses go to Avenida de América station. Taxis should cost no more than 30 euros. It takes a mere 12 minutes on the Metro to reach the central station of Nuevos Ministerios, where numerous airlines have check-in facilities.

Buses to the airport go from Avenida de América station: Terminal 1, 2 and 3 (bus 200); Terminal 4 (bus 204). They run every 12 minutes between 6am and 11:30pm and the journey costs around 1 euro.

AIR FARES

Air fares to Madrid vary throughout the year. They are generally at their highest in the summer months due to high demand. Special deals for weekend breaks in the city are often offered during winter and may include a number of nights at a hotel with vouchers to visit the sights. Iberia and British Airways invariably have some cheap return-flight deals on offer throughout the year. Air Europa, Spanair and EasyJet also offer competitive deals worth looking out for.

DOMESTIC FLIGHTS

Iberia operates a frequent shuttle service *(puente aéreo)* between Madrid and Barcelona. It flies every

Pont Aeri
Puente Aéreo

Sign for the shuttle service linking Madrid and Barcelona

quarter of an hour and passengers can buy tickets just 15 minutes prior to departure.

Air Europa and Spanair also have scheduled services between Madrid and Barcelona. **Air Nostrum**, Spanair and Air Europa operate flights between Madrid and the regional capitals and, even though they are not quite as frequent as the *puente aéreo*, their prices tend to be slightly lower. As a rule, the earlier you can book a flight, the greater will be your discount. To benefit from the cheapest tickets, you must book at least one week in advance.

ARRIVING BY TRAIN

The Spanish national rail network, **RENFE** (*Red Nacional de Ferrocarriles Españoles*), has two long-distance train stations in Madrid – **Atocha** *(see p83)* south of the centre and **Chamartín** in the north. Atocha receives trains from Portugal and the south and west of Spain, as well as the high-speed AVE trains from Seville, Córdoba, Zaragoza, Toledo, Barcelona, Lleida, Segovia, Valladolid and Málaga. Those coming from France or northern and eastern Spain go to Chamartín station. Since the two stations are linked by a tunnel under the city, some trains stop at both stations and often the intermediate stations, Nuevos Ministerios and Recoletos.

The new AVE service between Madrid and Barcelona via Guadalajara and Zaragoza

National carrier, Iberia, connecting Spain with the rest of Europe

Atocha station, one of Madrid's first glass and wrought-iron structures

is scheduled to extend to the French border by 2010. This will open the door to a high-speed rail line linking Madrid and Barcelona with similar lines in France and the rest of the European Union network.

There are also TALGO expresses, which use both the AVE and European tracks, and slower, long-distance *(largo recorrido)* trains. TALGO high-speed services mean that it is now possible to travel between the main cities extremely quickly.

Overnight sleeper trains arrive from Lisbon, Paris and parts of Spain. Cars can be loaded in advance to travel with the train. Bicycles can be carried only in the sleeping compartments of these trains and must be dismantled and packaged up, or unpackaged on regional trains, but only during non-peak periods.

ARRIVING BY CAR

Many people drive to Spain via the French highways (motorways). From the UK there are also car ferries from Plymouth to Santander and from Portsmouth to Bilbao.

From whichever direction you approach Madrid, make sure you are able to identify your highway (motorway) turn-off by its street name. Madrid has two major ring roads, the outer M40 and the inner M30. If you need to cross the city, it is advisable

Typical road signs in Madrid

to take one of the two and get as close as possible to your destination before turning off. All highways (motorways) lead to the M30 but most do not continue into the city.

For information on Spanish driving law, see p203.

ARRIVING BY BUS

Travelling by bus (coach) is usually a relatively cheap form of travel and, in Spain, it can quite often be a quicker way to get around than trains, especially from destinations such as the costas (coast). Buses offer travellers a modern airline-style service on fast highways. **Eurolines** buses operate regular services throughout Europe.

There are three main long-distance bus stations in Madrid. **The Estación Sur de Autobuses**, situated just southeast of the city centre, serves the whole of Spain. The second is **Estación Auto-Res**, which operates services to Valencia, eastern Spain, Lisbon and northwest Spain. And the third, **Estación De Avenida de América**, is located east of the city centre. Buses from this station serve towns in northern Spain.

The transport interchange at Calle de Méndez Alvaro also provides convenient access to the city buses, the Metro and to regional trains.

DIRECTORY

AIRPORT

Barajas Airport Information
Tel 91 305 83 43.
www.aena.es

IBERIA

Flights
Tel 902 40 05 00 *(Spain)*.
Tel (0845) 601 2854 *(UK)*.
Tel (800) 772 4642 *(US)*.
www.iberia.com

OTHER AIRLINES

Air Europa
Tel 902 40 15 01.
www.air-europa.com

Air Nostrum
Tel 902 40 05 00.

American Airlines
Tel 902 11 55 70 *(Spain)*.
Tel (817) 267 1151 *(US)*.
www.aa.com

British Airways
Tel 902 11 13 33 *(Spain)*.
Tel (0870) 850 9850 *(UK)*.
www.britishairways.com

Continental
Tel 900 96 12 66 *(Spain)*.
Tel (800) 231 0856 *(US)*.
www.continental.com

Delta Air Lines
Tel 91 749 66 30 *(Spain)*.
Tel (800) 241 4141 *(US)*.
www.delta.com

EasyJet
Tel 902 29 99 92 *(Spain)*.
www.easyjet.com

Spanair
Tel 902 13 14 15 *(Spain)*.
www.spanair.com

Virgin
Tel 902 88 84 59 *(Spain)*.
Tel (01293) 616 161 *(UK)*.
www.virgin-express.com

TRAINS

Atocha
Plaza del Emperador
Carlos V. **Map** 7 C5.
Tel 902 24 02 02.

Chamartín
Calle de Agustín de Foxá.
Tel 902 24 02 02.

Príncipe Pío
Estación del Norte.
Map 3 A1.
Tel 902 24 02 02.
www.renfe.es

BUS STATIONS AND COMPANIES

Estación Sur de Autobuses
Calle de Méndez Alvaro,
corner Calle de la Retama.
Tel 91 468 42 00.

Eurolines
Tel 91 506 33 60 *(Madrid)*.
Tel (020) 7730 8235 *(UK)*.
www.eurolines.es

Auto-Res
Calle Fernández Shaw 1.
Tel 902 02 09 99.
www.auto-res.net

Continental-Auto
Avenida de América 9.
Tel 902 42 22 42.
Tel 902 33 04 00 *(tickets)*.

Getting Around Madrid

Most of the tourist sights are clustered together in the centre of Madrid within walking distance of each other. There are also other interesting attractions further afield, and you will have to decide how to get there. Plan your day in advance, bearing in mind that some museums and shops close between 2pm and 5pm, and try to cover one area at a time. The Metro is by far the best way to travel around Madrid because the trains are quick and clean. However, if you have more time and prefer to see where you are going, the city bus service is excellent, and there is no shortage of taxis in Madrid if you don't mind spending a bit extra.

Sightseeing in one of the city's bright red buses outside the Puerta de Toledo

GETTING AROUND BY BUS

Buses are an excellent way to see the city. If you plan to make a number of bus trips, it is best to buy a *Metrobus* – a ten-trip ticket good for buses and the Metro. It costs around 6.5 euros, so is better value than tickets bought individually. The new *Tourist Travel Pass* costs from 3.5 euros and is cost-effective for travel within Madrid and further afield. *Metrobuses* are available at *estancos* (tobacconists), news kiosks, the **EMT** booths in Plaza de Colón, Plaza de Cibeles, Plaza del Callao, Plaza de Manuel Becerra and Puerta del Sol and all metro stations. Details of bus, Metro services

and regional trains are available at these booths and at tourist offices. Bus stop signs display the bus numbers and basic routes. Either pay the driver or put your *Metrobus* ticket in the machine. Request a stop by pressing a button next to the exit doors.
People in wheelchairs can board buses displaying the words *piso bajo* (low floor).
Some useful bus routes: 2 crosses central Madrid east to west; 5 starts at Puerta del Sol, going northwest to Chamartín railway station via Plaza de Cibeles; 27 travels from north to south the length of the Paseo de la Castellana from Plaza de Castilla to Glorieta de Embajadores via Paseo del Prado and Calle de Atocha; C makes a circuit around Madrid via Calle de Atocha.
Day buses run from 6am until 11:30pm. Twenty night buses, or *buhos* (owls), run every half an hour between midnight and 3am and then each hour until 6am. All leave from the Plaza de Cibeles.

THE METRO

The metro is the quickest, cheapest and easiest way to travel around Madrid, avoiding the madness of the city's traffic at street level. Many of the main Metro stations have shops and bars, and Retiro station even boasts an art gallery.
The Metro is open from 6am to 1:30am and consists of over 200 stations which are linked by 12 colour-coded lines plus the Ópera-Príncipe Pío link. A *Metrobus* ticket for ten trips on the Metro (except the Metrosur and TFM lines) or bus can be bought at any of the stations. For a map of the Metro, see the inside back cover of this book.
New Metro extensions now provide fast and convenient links with the IFEMA Parque Ferial exhibition centre as well as Barajas Airport.

Sign for a Metro station

TAXIS

Madrid has some 15,000 taxis, identifiable by the red diagonal stripe on the door. If they are available, the green light on the roof will be illuminated and a card in the window will say *"libre"*.
Within Madrid's city limits, including the airport, taxis are obliged to turn on their meters once hired. The initial charge is about 1.5 euros, but there are various additional charges, including fees for the airport, each piece of luggage, a dog (except guide dogs), IFEMA Parque Ferial and leaving from a train station between 11pm and 6am Saturdays, Sundays and public holidays.
You can order a cab by telephone through **Radio Taxi** or **Radioteléfono Taxi**. For a car specially adapted for the disabled, call Radioteléfono Taxi and ask for Eurotaxis.

City taxis with their logo and official numbers

Organized coach trips with Juliá Travel, one way to see the sights

BUS TOURS

A sightseeing service is operated by **Madrid Vision**, whose double-decker buses are equipped with multilingual headphone commentaries. There are 14 points along the route where you can get on or off, and it is possible to use the buses all day. The bus tours run all year round.

Juliá Travel also offers a variety of bus trips around the city, which can include visits to a *corrida* or bullfight (*see p109*) or an evening flamenco performance (*see p182*).

DRIVING

In Spain you must carry a valid driver's licence with you when driving, as well as your insurance documents. If you are not an EU citizen, it is essential to have an international driver's licence. In the United States, these are available through the AAA.

Driving around Madrid is quite an experience for the uninitiated as *Madrileños* tend to drive aggressively. Signs are often misleading or missing altogether, service stations are few and parking is usually difficult. Read the map before setting off, but watch out for one-way systems, tunnels and overpasses (flyovers). In rush hour, traffic hardly moves and the M30 inner ring road often comes to a standstill. If you get lost while driving, hail a taxi, shout the address and follow the driver.

In urban areas the speed limit is 50 km/h (31 mph), while it is 100 km/h (62 mph) on main roads and 120 km/h (75 mph) on highways (motorways).

CAR RENTAL (HIRE)

To rent a car in Spain you should have an international driver's licence (if you are an EU citizen your ordinary licence is usually sufficient) and be over 21 years of age. You can pay using cash, credit card or traveller's cheques.

On the ground floor of Barajas Airport's International Terminal 1 are various car rental firms, including **Avis, Europcar, Hertz** and **National Atesa**. Cars can also be rented at Atocha and Chamartín railway stations. You are strongly advised to take out full insurance, and air-conditioning is recommended.

In the city, your hotel or a travel agent will be able to arrange car rental for you.

Some of the leading car rental agencies operating in Spain

PARKING

Parking in Madrid is difficult, so you may want to select a hotel with parking facilities. There are also underground parking garages (car parks) which charge by the hour. A green sign saying *"libre"* means that space is still available; a red sign saying *"completo"* means the car park is full.

Parking illegally can result in being towed away, with a fine of 180 euros to recover your vehicle. In the city centre green and blue lines on the road denote different parking zones. Green zones are for residents, although non-residents can park for one hour. Blue zones offer non residents two hours parking. Tickets must be purchased from appropriately coloured machines. When parking, lock your doors and do not leave anything of value in your car. If you must leave items in the car, stow them in the boot (trunk).

No parking at any time of the day

DIRECTORY

BUS AND METRO INFORMATION

EMT Bus Information
Tel 91 406 88 10.

Metro Information
Tel 902 44 44 03.
www.metromadrid.es

TAXIS

Radio Taxi
Tel 91 447 51 80.

Radioteléfono Taxi
Tel 91 547 82 00.

BUS TOURS

Juliá Travel
Gran Vía 68. **Map** 4 F1.
Tel 91 559 96 05.
www.juliatravel.com

CAR RENTAL

Avis
Tel 902 18 08 54.
Tel 902 20 01 62 (Barajas Airport).
Tel (800) 331 1084 (US).
www.avis.com

Europcar
Tel 902 10 50 30.
Tel 902 10 50 55 (Barajas Airport).
www.europcar.com

Hertz
Tel 901 10 10 01.
Tel 91 372 93 00 (Barajas Airport).
Tel (800) 654 3001 (US).
www.hertz.com

National Atesa
Tel 902 10 01 01.
Tel 91 393 72 32 (Barajas Airport).
www.atesa.com

Pepecar
Parking Plaza de España.
Tel 807 41 42 43.
www.pepecar.com

BICYCLES

Karacol Sport SA
Calle de Tortosa 8. **Map** 7 C5.
Tel 91 539 96 33.

CYCLING

Riding a bicycle around Madrid in weekday traffic is dangerous. Only on Sundays and public holidays can cycling in Madrid be fun. **Karacol Sport SA** near Atocha train station rents bikes.

Travelling Outside Madrid

Logo of the Spanish national railways

The main sites around Madrid can be visited in a day but, if you plan to visit several, you might like to consider staying outside Madrid, at a hotel or at one of an increasing number of rural hostelries. The most convenient way to travel is by car, but trains are also very easy to use with services to all the main historic towns and cities. Even Córdoba, Seville, Barcelona and Valencia are accessible using the AVE and Alaris high-speed trains which afford superb views of the countryside. Tour companies offer coach trips to Toledo, El Escorial and Segovia. A trip usually includes the main sites and a meal. If you intend to use a scheduled bus service, use the most direct, as some buses stop at every village.

AVE trains at Atocha station

TRAIN SERVICES

Madrid is served by six types of train: *cercanías* (commuter), *regional* (local) *largo recorrido* (long-distance), TALGO (long-distance express), Alaris (to Valencia) and AVE (high-speed link to Ciudad Real, Puerto-llano, Córdoba, Seville, Guadalajara, Zaragoza, Calatayud, Lleida, Málaga, Barcelona, Toledo, Segovia and Valladolid).

There are frequent services to Alcalá de Henares and Guadalajara on the *cercanías* C-2 from Chamartín, Nuevos Ministerios, Recoletos and Atocha. *Cercanías* leave from Atocha to Aranjuez every half an hour. During weekends from mid-April to mid-July and mid-September to mid-October, a Strawberry Train *(Tren de las Fresas)*, pulled by a steam engine, serves Aranjuez from Atocha. Strawberries are included and booking is required. To Puerto Navacerrada and the

ski resorts, take *cercanías* C-8b from Atocha to Cercedilla and then change to *cercanías* C-9. Use C-8a for San Lorenzo de El Escorial, and C-8b or the *regional* from Atocha station for Segovia. Sigüenza is served by *regional* trains from Chamartín, with three or four trains a day. Toledo is served by *regional* trains from Atocha. Trains run every two hours.

TICKETS AND FARES

Information and tickets can be obtained by phoning **RENFE**, from **RENFE** offices and stations, or from travel agents. Rail fares depend on the speed and quality of the train, therefore TALGO, Alaris and AVE trains are more expensive.

Bicycles can be taken only on *regional* trains on weekends and public holidays and

at specified non-peak times in the week. *Largo recorrido* and TALGO trains will take them if dismantled and kept in the sleeping compartments.

Fares rise on weekends and public holidays. Children, aged four to 11, get a 40 per cent discount, while students, aged 12 to 25, get a 20 per cent discount. Return tickets are valid for 15 days and carry the same discounts. For long journeys, RENFE may offer special rates on certain days. **Iberrail** also offers economical rail-plus-hotel deals. For a one-way journey, ask for *ida* and for a return, ask for *ida y vuelta*

TAKING YOUR OWN CAR

A Green Card and a bail bond from a motor insurance company are needed to extend your comprehensive cover to Spain. In the UK, the RAC, AA and Europ Assistance offer rescue and recovery policies with European coverage.

By law you must always carry with you your vehicle's registration document, a valid insurance certificate and your driving licence. Always be able to show a passport or a national ID card, and display a country of registration sticker on the rear of the vehicle.

The headlights of right-hand-drive vehicles must be adjusted. This can be done with stickers sold at ferry ports or on ferries. You risk on-the-spot fines if you do not carry a red warning triangle, spare light bulbs and a first-aid kit.

Driving along a mountain road through Spain's spectacular countryside

A filling station run by a leading chain with branches throughout Spain

In winter you should carry chains if you intend to drive in mountain areas. In summer, take drinking water if you are travelling in a remote area.

Spain's fastest roads are its *autopistas*, usually highways (motorways) and sometimes with tolls *(peajes)*. The *carretera nacional* is the network of main roads prefixed by "N".

Madrid is served by seven main *autovías*, numbered A1 to A6, which fan out in different directions, and the A42, which goes to Toledo. In addition, there are two ring roads with links between the highways. The inner ring road is the M30 and the outer one, with direct access to and from the airport, is the M40, which links four toll highways – the R2, R3, R4 and R5.

For road and traffic information in Spanish call the toll-free number for **Información de Tráfico de Carreteras**.

BUYING FUEL

In Spain *gasolina* (gas/petrol) and *gasóleo* (diesel) are sold by the litre. *Gasolina sin plomo* (unleaded gas/petrol) is available everywhere.

SPEED LIMITS AND FINES

Speed limits in Spain for cars without trailers are: 120 km/h (75 mph) on *autopistas* (toll highways/motorways); 100 km/h (62 mph) on *autovías* (non-toll highways/motorways); 90 km/h (56 mph) on *carreteras nacionales* (main roads) and *carreteras comarcales* (secondary roads); 50 km/h (30 mph) in built-up areas. There are instant fines of 6 euros for every kilometre over the limit. Tests and fines for drinking and driving are increasingly common, and some prison sentences have been given for speeding or for dangerous driving.

TOUR BUSES AND LOCAL BUSES

By far the easiest and most relaxing way to visit the sights is by tour bus. Madrid's main tour bus company, **Juliá Travel** *(see p203)*, will take direct bookings. **Pullmantur** tours have to be booked at a travel agency. **Madrid Vision** also offers several sightseeing tours.

Major towns and many villages are served by local buses. Buses for the following destinations depart from **Estación Sur de Autobuses**, south of the city centre (metro station Méndez Álvaro). Aranjuez and Sigüenza are served by **Autocares Samar**, San Martín de Valdeiglesias by **Autocares Cevesa**, Segovia by **La Sepulvedana** and Toledo by **Continental-Auto**.

Alcalá de Henares is served by **Continental-Auto** (Avenida de América), Chinchón by **La Veloz** (Plaza de Conde Casal), Manzanares el Real by **Hijos de J Colmenarejo** (Plaza de Castilla), Puerto de Navacerrada by **Larrea SA** (Metro Moncloa), San Lorenzo de El Escorial by **Autocares Herranz** (Metro Moncloa).

Buses can often be quicker than trains. **Alsa** operates a competitively priced service from the costas, for example.

Spanish touring bus, a quick and convenient way to see the sights

DIRECTORY

TRAIN SERVICES

Iberrail
Tel 91 571 66 92.
www.iberrail.es

RENFE
Tel 902 24 02 02.
www.renfe.es

TRAFFIC INFORMATION

Información de Tráfico de Carreteras
Tel 900 12 35 05.
www.dgt.es

CAR RESCUE SERVICE

RACE
Calle General Perón 40.
Tel 902 40 45 45.
www.race.es

TOUR BUSES AND LOCAL BUSES

Autocares Cevesa
Tel 91 539 31 32.

Autocares Herranz
Tel 91 896 90 28.

Autocares Samar
Tel 91 468 42 36.

Continental-Auto
Avenida América station.
Tel 902 42 22 42.
www.continental-auto.es

Alsa
Estación Sur de Autobuses.
Tel 902 42 22 42.
www.enatcar.es

Hijos de J Colmenarejo
Tel 91 314 64 08.

Larrea SA
Tel 91 851 55 92.

Madrid Vision
Tel 91 779 18 88.
www.madridvision.es

Pullmantur
Tel 91 556 11 14.

La Sepulvedana
Tel 902 22 22 82.
www.lasepulvedana.es

La Veloz
Tel 91 409 76 02.

MADRID STREET FINDER

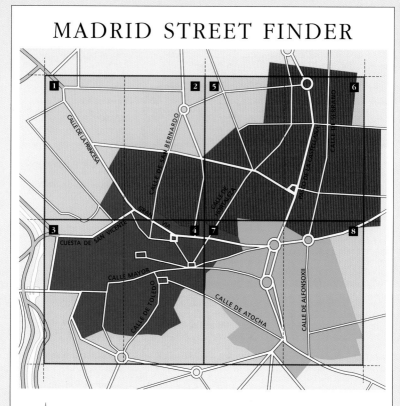

KEY TO STREET FINDER

Major sight	Taxi	Post office
Place of interest	Parking	Railway line
Other building	Tourist attraction	Pedestrianized street
Train station	Hospital with emergency room	
Metro station	Police station	**SCALE OF MAP PAGES**
Main bus stop	Church	0 metres — 200
Bus station	Convent or monastery	0 yards — 200

A

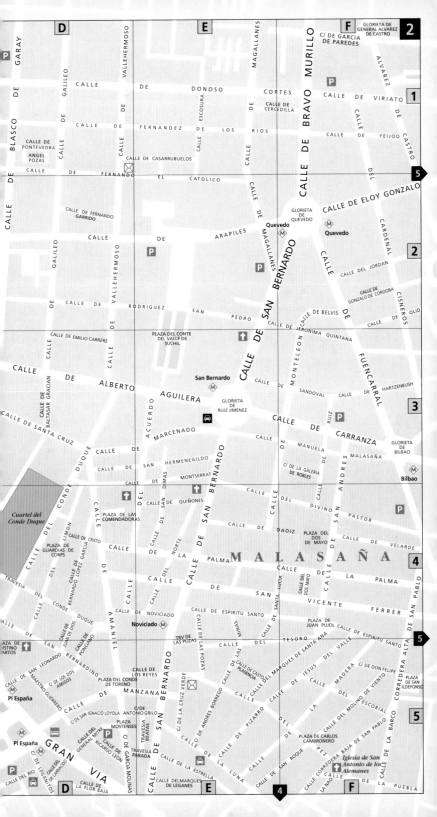

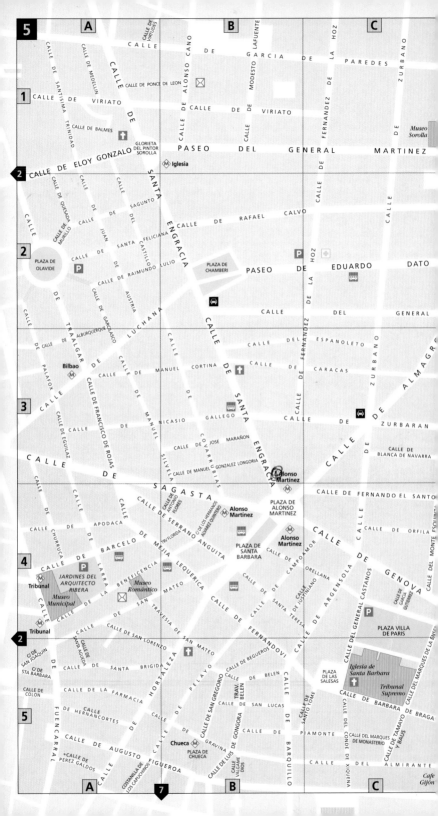

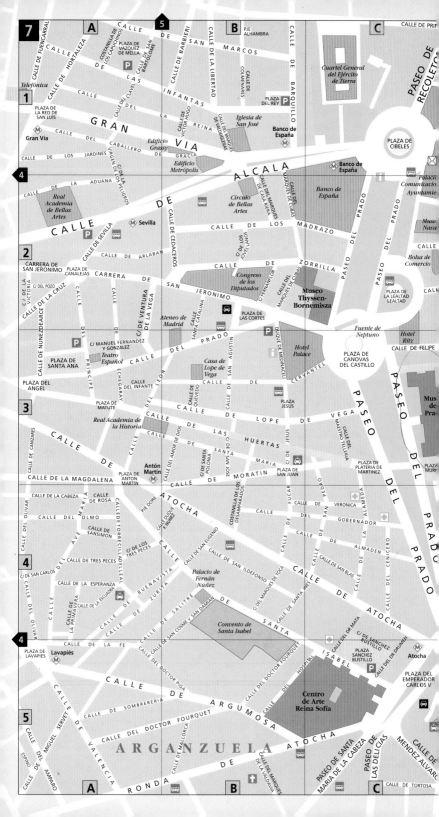

D **E** **6** **F** **8**

CALLE DE RECOLETOS
CALLE DEL CONDE DE ARANDA
CALLE DEL
CALLE DE SERRANO
CALLE DE
COLUMELA
CALLE DE SALUSTIANO OLOZAGA
CALLE DE VILLALAR
CALLE DE CLAUDIO COELLO
CALLE DE LAGASCA
C/ DE VELAZQUEZ
CALLE DE O'DONNELL
PEDRO MUÑOZ SECA
ALLE MARQUES DEL DUERO
Palacio de Linares
Puerta de Alcalá
PLAZA DE LA
Retiro Ⓜ
Retiro Ⓜ
PLAZA DE COSTA RICA **1**
C A L L E
D E **A L C A L A**
CALLE DE RUIZ DE ALARCON
INDEPENDENCIA
PUERTA DE HERNANI
PLAZA DE GALICIA
AVENIDA DE MEJICO
PLAZA DEL MAESTRO VILLA
PASEO DE BOLIVIA
CALLE DE VALENZUELA
CALLE DE ALFONSO XII
GTA TITERES
PLAZA DE NICARAGUA
PASEO DE COLOMBIA
REPUBLICA DOMINICANA
PODE LA
CALLE DE MONTALBAN
Museo Nacional de Artes Decorativas
DE ALFONSO
CALLE DE
ROSALOI DEL ESTANQUE
PASEO SALON DEL ESTANQUE
Estanque
GTA DE LA SARDANA **2**
E CALLE DE
JUAN DE MENA
XII
PASEO DE LA ARGENTINA
DE
ANTONIO MAURA
MORETO
CALLE DE ALFONSO
PUERTA DE ESPAÑA
Salon de Reinos
CALLE DE MENDEZ NUÑEZ
PASEO DE VENEZUELA
Real Academia Española
CASON DEL BUEN RETIRO
Casón del Buen Retiro
PASEO PARTERRE
PASEO DEL PARAGUAY
PLAZA DE
HONDURAS
Palacio de Velazques
RUIZ
CALLE DE LA ACADEMIA
PUERTA DE FELIPE IV
PASEO DE LA REPUBLICA DE CUBA
Iglesia de San Jerónimo el Real
CALLE DEL CASADO DEL ALISAL
PASEO DEL MARQUES DE PONTEJOS **3**
ALARCON
CALLE ALBERTO BOSCH
CALLE DE ALFONSO XII
Palacio de Cristal
CALLE DE ESPALTER
P A R Q U E
PUERTA DE MURILLO
D E L
LA CHOPERA
PASEO DE ROJAS CLEMENTE
PASEO DE CELESTINO MUTIS
R E T I R O
GLORIETA DEL ANGEL CAIDO **4**
PASEO DE JOSE QUER
PASEO DE CELESTINO MUTIS
REAL JARDIN BOTANICO
CALLE DE ALFONSO
PASEO DEL DUQUE DE FERNAN NUNEZ
GOMEZ
CALLE DE CLAUDIO MOYANO
PUERTA DEL ANGEL CAIDO
VIVEROS MUNICIPALES
Ministerio de Agricultura
CALLE DEL DOCTOR VELASCO
CALLE DEL POETA ESTEBAN VILLEGAS
PASEO DE LA INFANTA ISABEL
Atocha Ⓜ
Museo Nacional de Antropología
Observatorio Astronomico
CALLE DE LUIS CAMOENS
CALLE DE JUAN VALERA
CALLE DE ANDRES TORREJON **5**
AVENIDA DE LA CIUDAD DE BARCELONA
CALLE DE ALFONSO XII
CALLE DE JUAN BAUTISTA S. SACRETTI
CALLE DE JOSE ANSELMO CLAVE
JULIAN
CALLE DE AGUSTIN QUEROL
Estación de Atocha
Atocha Ⓜ Renfe
Atocha Renfe Ⓜ
PASEO DE LA REINA
CRISTINA
GAYARRE
CALLE DE FUENTERRABIA
Real Fábrica de Tapices

D **P** **P** **E** **F**

General Index

Acknowledgments

Dorling Kindersley would like to thank the following people whose contributions and assistance have made the preparation of this book possible.

Contributor

Adam Hopkins is an indefatigable travel writer and author of *Spanish Journeys: A Portrait of Spain.*

Mark Little, an American who grew up in Spain, is a freelance writer based in southern Spain. For many years he was the editor of *Lookout* magazine.

Edward Owen has been, for many years, a foreign correspondent based in Madrid, contributing to *The Times* and *The Express* in London and *Time Magazine* among other publications.

James Russo, a freelance journalist, is also a staff writer for Spain's state news agency, EFE. He has lived in Spain since the 1980s.

Kathy White is a freelance journalist who has contributed to *The Christian Science Monitor* and *Newsweek*. She also worked for the French Service of the BBC and was foreign desk assistant at Channel 4 News.

Design and Editorial Assistance

Special thanks to Hilary Bird for preparing the index, Juan Fernández for providing feedback on the content of the guide, Joy Fitzsimmons for visualizing the artworks, Elly King for the final design check, ERA Maptech for creating the maps, Graphical Innovations for outputting the text film, Barbara Minton for support from DK Publishing, Inc., Roberto Rama, Victoria Cano (Word on Spain) and Cristina Barrallo for fact checking, Mary Sutherland for providing feedback on the Survival Guide, Anna Freiberger, Juliet Kenny, Marianne Petrou, Tom Prentice, Mani Ramaswamy, Ellen Root, Zoë Ross, Meredith Smith and Lynda Warrington for design and editorial assistance and Stewart Wild for proofreading. Project assistance given by Fay Franklin, Annette Jacobs, Vivien Crump, Gillian Allen, Douglas Amrine, Joanne Blackmore, Monica Allende and Pamela Shiels.

Additional Photography

Ian Aitkin, Isabel Real Martinez, Ian O'Leary, Conrad van Dyk

Photography Permissions

© Patrimonio Nacional, Madrid: Monasterio de las Descalzas Reales; El Escorial; La Granja de San Ildefonso; Palacio Real; Palacio Real Aranjuez; Palacio de Fernán Núñez propriedad de Renfe Sede de la Fundación de los Ferrocarriles Españoles.

Dorling Kindersley would like to thank all the cathedrals, churches, museums, restaurants, hotels, shops, galleries, and other sights too numerous to thank individually.

Picture credits

t=top; tl=top left; tlc=top left centre; tc=top centre; trc=top right centre; tr=top right; cla=centre left above; ca=centre above; cra=centre right above; cl=centre left; c=centre; cr=centre right; clb=centre left below; cb=centre below; crb=centre right below; bl=bottom left; b=bottom; bc=bottom centre; bcl=bottom centre left; br=bottom right; d=detail

Works of art have been reproduced with the permission of the following copyright holders:

Gernika Picasso © Succession Picasso/ DACS 1999 85br; *Lugar de Encument* Chillida © DACS 1999 97c; *Mosaic* Miró © ADAGP, PARIS and DACS, London 1999 105t, front cover c.

The publisher would like to thank the following individuals, companies and picture libraries for their kind permission to reproduce their photographs:

Ace Photo: Bill Wassman 180b; AISA, Barcelona: 7inset, 16cb, 19b, 23bl, 23bc, *Retrato de Camilo Jose Cela* Alvaro Delgado © DACS 1999 28t, 29t, 56c, 76b, 78t, 80t, 81b, *La Tertulia del Café de Pombo* Jose Gutiérrez Solana © DACS 1999 85t, 102b; Alamy Images: Dan Atkin 158cl; Robert Fried 159tl; David Kilpatrick; La Belle Aurore/ Steve Davey 118tr; Phil Robinson/PjrFoto 10cla; Alex Segre 161tr; Ken Walsh 24; Max Alexander: 116; Museo Arqueológico Nacional, Madrid: 94, 95; The Art Archive: Museo del Prado, Madrid/ Dagli Orti (A) - St Cecilia Patron Saint of Music, Nicholas Poussin (1594–1665) 81cr.

Bridgeman Picture Library: *The Adoration of the Shepherds* El Greco 78ca, *The Annunciation* Fra Angelico 79cb, *The Clothed Maja* Goya 79t, *The Naked Maja* Goya 79ca, *The Three Graces* Rubens 78cb, *The Martyrdom of St Philip* Jose Ribera 79c, *St Dominic of Silos Enthroned as Abbot* Bermejo 80c. Carrerey Carrera: 10tc; Corbis:

Patrick Ward 77tc; Joe Cornish: 132c; Corral De La Moreria: 114tc; Cover: Quim Llenas 29b; Matias Nieto 37c; El Deseo: 102tr; Agencia Efe, Madrid: 35b, 36b.

European Commission: 197; Mary Evans Picture Library: 16b, 121inset, 147inset, 191inset.

Fundación Lázaro Galdiano: 27t, 98/99; Hulton Getty: 135b; Godo Fotos: 129b; Roland Halbe: 10bl, 114bl, 118cl; Robert Harding Picture Library: James Strachan 53tr, 113t; P. Robinson 40

Images Colour Library: A.G.E. Fotostock 25tr, 109cra; Horizon 109c; Index, Barcelona: 15b, 16c, 18b, 20b, 22ca, 22cbl, 23tl, 23tc, 23br, 28c, 28b, 29c; Nick Inman: 195c, 201t.

Anthony King: 76t. Lonely Planet Images: Guy Moberly 119bl; Richard Nebesky 114cr; Damien Simonis 117br.

Arxiu Mas, Barcelona: 12b; Museo Del Prado, Madrid: 78b; Museo Thyssen Bornemisza, Madrid: 25cr, 70tr; *Harlequin with Mirror,* Picasso © Succession Picasso/ DACS 1999 70cl; 70bl; *Portrait of Baron Thyssen-Bornemisza* © Lucian Freud 70bc; 71tl, 71cra, 71crb; *Autumn Landscape in Oldenburg,* Karl Schmidt-Rottluff © DACS 1999 71bl; 72 (3), 73 (2).

Naturpress, Madrid: 186b; J.L. González Grande 187b; A. Ibannez & Fco González 188c; Diana Kvaternik 25bc; W Kvaternik-R. Olivas 2/3, 36c, 186c, 188t, 189t; Luis Olivas 34b; Petro Retamar 188b; Carlos Vegas 35c; Jaime Villanueva 1, 21c, 25ca, 34c, 111t, 186t; Museo Naval, Madrid: 65br.

Oronoz, Madrid: 15t, 16t, 17t, 17c, 17b, 19c, 21t, 22tl, 22tr, 22cr, 26t, 26c, 26b, 47b, 56t, 56b, 57t, 57c, 57b, 67b, 75ca, 75b, 80b, 81t, 116br; Moro Cabeza Crispolo 119tr; *Portrait II* Miró © ADAGP, PARIS and DACS,

London 1999 84t, *Woman in Blue* Picasso © Succession Picasso/DACS 1999 84ca, 100b, 101b, 109cla, 122, 123. Prisma, Barcelona: 11t, 11br, 14, 18t, 18c, 20t, 20c, 23tr, 23clb, 60b.

Centro De Arte Reina Sofia, Madrid: *Retrato de Josette* Juan Gris © ADAGP, PARIS and DACS, London 1999 27b; *Landscape in Cadaqués* Dalí © Salvador Dalí – Foudation Gala – Salvador Dalí/DACS 1999 84c, 84b; *Toki-Egin (Homenaje a San-Juan de la Cruz),* 1952 Eduardo Chillida © DACS 2002 85bl; *Guitarra ante el Mar* Juan Gris © ADAGP, PARIS and DACS, London 1999 86t; *El Profeta* Pablo Gargallo © ADAGP, PARIS and DACS, London 1999 86c; *Minotauromaquia* Picasso © Succession Picasso/DACS 1999 86b; *Muchacha en la Ventana* Dalí © Salvador Dalí – Foundation Gala – Salvador Dalí/ DACS 1999 87t; *Toda la Ciudad Habla de Ello* Eduardo Arroyo © DACS 1999 87b; RENFE: 204tl.

6 TOROS 6 magazine: 109cr. M Angeles Sanchez: 35t, 103b; Juan Carlos Martínez Zafra 52b; Archivo Del Senado: Oronoz 53b; Science Photo Library: Geospace 8; Stockphotos: Marcelo Brodsky 34t; Tony Stone: 172b. Peter Wilson: 38; World Pictures: 165c.

Jacket: Front - AISA - Archivo Iconográfico S.A., Barcelona: main image; DK Images: Kim Sayer clb. Back - DK Images: Ian Aitkin tl; Max Alexander cla; Kim Sayer clb; Peter Wilson bl. Spine - AISA- Archivo Iconográfico S.A., Barcelona: t; DK Images: Kim Sayer b.

Front End Paper: All special photography except Max Alexander tr.

All other images © Dorling Kindersley. For further information see www.DKimages. com

---

SPECIAL EDITIONS OF DK TRAVEL GUIDES

DK Travel Guides can be purchased in bulk quantities at discounted prices for use in promotions or as premiums. We are also able to offer special editions and personalized jackets, corporate imprints, and excerpts from all of our books, tailored specifically to meet your own needs.

To find out more, please contact:
(in the United States) **SpecialSales@dk.com**
(in the UK) **Sarah.Burgess@dk.com**
(in Canada) DK Special Sales at **general@tourmaline.ca**
(in Australia) **business.development@pearson.com.au**

Phrase Book

In an Emergency

Help!	¡Socorro!	soh-**koh**-roh
Stop!	¡Pare!	**pah**-reh
Call a doctor!	¡Llame a un ! médico	yah-meh ah **oon** meh-**dee**-koh
Call an ambulance!	¡Llame a una ambulancia!	yah-meh ah **oonah** ahm-boo-**lahn**-thee-ah
Call the police!	¡Llame a la policía!	yah-meh ah lah poh-lee-**thee**-ah
Call the fire brigade!	¡Llame a los bomberos!	yah-meh ah lohs bohm-**beh**-rohs
Where is the nearest telephone?	¿Dónde está el teléfono más próximo?	**dohn**-deh ehs-**tah** ehl teh-**leh**-foh-noh mahs prohx-ee-moh
Where is the nearest hospital?	¿Dónde está el hospital más próximo?	**dohn**-deh ehs-**tah** ehl ohs-pee-**tahl** mahs prohx-ee-moh

Communication Essentials

Yes	Sí	see
No	No	noh
Please	Por favor	pohr fah-**vohr**
Thank you	Gracias	**grah**-thee-ahs
Excuse me	Perdone	pehr-**doh**-neh
Hello	Hola	**oh**-lah
Goodbye	Adiós	ah-dee-**ohs**
Good night	Buenas noches	**bweh**-nahs noh-chehs
Morning	La mañana	lah mah-**nyah**-nah
Afternoon	La tarde	lah **tahr**-deh
Evening	La tarde	lah **tahr**-deh
Yesterday	Ayer	ah-**yehr**
Today	Hoy	oy
Tomorrow	Mañana	mah-**nya**-nah
Here	Aquí	ah-**kee**
There	Allí	ah-**yee**
What?	¿Qué?	keh
When?	¿Cuándo?	**kwahn**-doh
Why?	¿Por qué?	pohr-**keh**
Where?	¿Dónde?	**dohn**-deh

Useful Phrases

How are you?	¿Cómo está usted?	**koh**-moh ehs-**tah** oos-**tehd**
Very well, thank you.	Muy bien, gracias.	mwee bee-**ehn grah**-thee-ahs
Pleased to meet you.	Encantado de conocerle.	ehn-kahn-**tah**-doh deh koh-noh-**thehr**-leh
See you soon.	Hasta pronto.	ahs-tah **prohn**-toh
That's fine.	Está bien.	ehs-**tah** bee-**ehn**
Where is/are ...?	¿Dónde está/están ...?	**dohn**-deh ehs-**tah**/ehs-**than**
How far is it to ...?	¿Cuántos metros/ kilómetros hay de aquí a ...?	kwahn-tohs **meh**-trohs/kee-**loh**-meh-trohs eye deh ah-**kee** ah
Which way to ...?	¿Por dónde se va a ...?	pohr **dohn**-deh seh **bah** ah
Do you speak English?	¿Habla inglés?	**ah**-blah een-**glehs**
I don't understand	No comprendo	noh kohm-**prehn**-doh
Could you speak more slowly please?	¿Puede hablar más despacio por favor?	pweh-deh ah-**blahr** mahs dehs-pah-thee-oh pohr fah-**vohr**
I'm sorry.	Lo siento.	loh see-**ehn**-toh

Useful Words

big	grande	**grahn**-deh
small	pequeño	peh-**keh**-nyoh
hot	caliente	kah-lee-**ehn**-the
cold	frío	**free**-oh
good	bueno	**bweh**-noh
bad	malo	mah-loh
enough	bastante	bahs-**tahn**-the
well	bien	bee-**ehn**
open	abierto	ah-bee-**ehr**-toh
closed	cerrado	thehr-**rah**-doh
left	izquierda	eeth-key-**ehr**-dah
right	derecha	deh-**reh**-chah
straight on	todo recto	toh-doh **rehk**-toh
near	cerca	**thehr**-kah
far	lejos	**leh**-hohs
up	arriba	ah-**ree**-bah
down	abajo	ah-**bah**-hoh
early	temprano	tehm-**prah**-noh

late	tarde	**tahr**-deh
entrance	entrada	ehn-**trah**-dah
exit	salida	sah-**lee**-dah
toilet	lavabos, servicios	lah-**vah**-bohs sehr-**bee**-thee-ohs
more	más	mahs
less	menos	**meh**-nohs

Shopping

How much does this cost?	¿Cuánto cuesta esto?	**kwahn**-toh **kwehs**-tah **ehs**-toh
I would like ...	Me gustaría ...	meh goos-ta-**ree**-ah
Do you have?	¿Tienen?	tee-**yeh**-nehn
I'm just looking.	Sólo estoy mirando, gracias.	**soh**-loh ehs-**toy** mee-**rahn**-doh **grah**-thee-ahs
Do you take credit cards?	¿Aceptan tarjetas de crédito?	ah-**thehp**-than tahr-**heh**-tahs deh **kreh**-dee-toh
What time do you open?	¿A qué hora abren?	ah **keh** oh-rah **ah**-brehn
What time do you close?	¿A qué hora cierran?	ah keh oh-rah thee-**ehr**-rahn
This one.	Éste	**ehs**-the
That one.	Ése	**eh**-she
expensive	caro	**kahr**-oh
cheap	barato	bah-**rah**-toh
size, clothes	talla	**tah**-yah
size, shoes	número	**noo**-mehr-oh
white	blanco	**blahn**-koh
black	negro	**neh**-groh
red	rojo	**roh**-hoh
yellow	amarillo	ah-mah-**ree**-yoh
green	verde	**behr**-deh
blue	azul	ah-**thool**
antiques shop	la tienda de antigüedades	lah tee-**ehn**-dah deh ahn-tee-gweh-**dah**-dehs
bakery	la panadería	lah pah-nah-deh-**ree**-ah
bank	el banco	ehl **bahn**-koh
book shop	la librería	lah lee-breh-**ree**-ah
butcher's	la carnicería	lah kahr-nee-theh-**ree**-ah
cake shop	la pastelería	lah pahs-teh-leh-**ree**-ah
chemist's	la farmacia	lah fahr-**mah**-thee-ah
fishmonger's	la pescadería	lah pehs-kah-deh-**ree**-ah
greengrocer's	la frutería	lah froo-teh-**ree**-ah
grocer's	la tienda de comestibles	lah tee-**yehn**-dah deh koh-mehs-**tee**-blehs
hairdresser's	la peluquería	lah peh-loo-keh-**ree**-ah
market	el mercado	ehl mehr-**kah**-doh
newsagent's	el kiosko de prensa	ehl kee-**ohs**-koh deh **prehn**-sah
post office	la oficina de correos	lah oh-fee-**thee**-nah deh kohr-**reh**-ohs
shoe shop	la zapatería	lah thah-pah-teh-**ree**-ah
supermarket	el supermercado	ehl soo-pehr-mehr-**kah**-doh
tobacconist	el estanco	ehl ehs-**tahn**-koh
travel agency	la agencia de viajes	lah ah-**hehn**-thee-ah deh bee-**ah**-hehs

Sightseeing

art gallery	el museo de arte	ehl moo-**seh**-oh deh **ahr**-the
cathedral	la catedral	lah kah-teh-**drahl**
church	la iglesia	lah ee-**gleh**-see-ah
	la basílica	lah bah-**see**-lee-kah
garden	el jardín	ehl hahr-**deen**
library	la biblioteca	lah bee-blee-oh-**teh**-kah
museum	el museo	ehl moo-**seh**-oh
tourist information office	la oficina de turismo	lah oh-fee-**thee** nah deh too-**rees**-moh
town hall	el ayuntamiento	ehl ah-yoon-tah-mee-**ehn**-toh
closed for holiday	cerrado por vacaciones	thehr-**rah**-doh pohr bah-kah-thee-**oh**-nehs
bus station	la estación de autobuses	lah ehs-tah-thee-**ohn** deh owtoh-**boo**-sehs
railway station	la estación de trenes	lah ehs-tah-thee-**ohn** deh **treh**-nehs

Staying in a Hotel

Do you have a vacant room?	¿Tiene una habitación libre?	tee-**eh**-neh oo-nah ah-bee-tah-thee-**ohn lee**-breh
double room	habitación doble	ah-bee-tah-thee-**ohn doh**-bleh
with double bed	con cama de matrimonio	kohn **kah**-mah deh mah-tree-**moh**-nee-oh
twin room	habitación con dos camas	ah-bee-tah-thee-**ohn** kohn dohs **kah**-mahs
single room	habitación individual	ah-bee-tah-thee-**ohn** een-dee-vee-doo-**ahl**
room with a bath	habitación con baño	ah-bee-tah-thee-**ohn** kohn bah-nyoh
shower	ducha	**doo**-chah
porter	el botones	ehl boh-**toh**-nehs
key	la llave	lah **yah**-veh
I have a reservation.	Tengo una habitación reservada.	tehn-goh **oo**-na ah-bee-tah-thee-**ohn** reh-sehr-**bah**-dah

Eating Out

Have you got a table for …?	¿Tiene mesa para …?	tee-**eh**-neh meh-sah pah-**rah**
I want to reserve a table.	Quiero reservar una mesa.	kee-eh-roh reh-sehr-**bahr** oo-nah **meh**-sah
The bill please.	La cuenta por favor.	lah **kwehn**-tah pohr fah-**vohr**
I am a vegetarian	Soy vegetariano/a	soy beh-heh-tah-ree-**ah**-no/na
waitress/ waiter	camarera/ camarero	kah-mah-**reh**-rah kah-mah-**reh**-roh
menu	la carta	lah **kahr**-tah
fixed-price menu	menú del día	meh-**noo** dehl **dee**-ah
wine list	la carta de vinos	lah **kahr**-tah deh **bee**-nohs
glass	un vaso	oon **bah**-soh
bottle	una botella	oo-nah boh-**teh**-yah
knife	un cuchillo	oon koo-**chee**-yoh
fork	un tenedor	oon teh-neh-**dohr**
spoon	una cuchara	oo-nah koo-**chah**-rah
breakfast	el desayuno	ehl deh-sah-**yoo**-noh
lunch	la comida/ el almuerzo	lah koh-**mee**-dah/ ehl ahl-**mwehr**-thoh
dinner	la cena	lah **theh**-nah
main course	el primer plato	ehl pree-**mehr plah**-toh
starters	los entremeses	lohs ehn-treh-**meh**-sehs
dish of the day	el plato del día	ehl **plah**-toh dehl **dee**-ah
coffee	el café	ehl kah-**feh**
rare (meat)	poco hecho	poh-**koh eh**-choh
medium	medio hecho	**meh**-dee-oh **eh**-choh
well done	muy hecho	mwee **eh**-choh

Menu Decoder

al horno	ahl **ohr**-noh	baked
asado	ah-**sah**-doh	roast
el aceite	ah-**thee-eh**-teh	oil
las aceitunas	ah-theh-**toon**-ahs	olives
el agua mineral	**ah**-gwa mee-neh-**rahl**	mineral water
sin gas/con gas	seen gas/kohn gas	still/sparkling
el ajo	**ah**-hoh	garlic
el arroz	ahr-**rohth**	rice
el azúcar	ah-**thoo**-kahr	sugar
la carne	**kahr**-neh	meat
la cebolla	theh-**boh**-yah	onion
el cerdo	**therh**-doh	pork
la cerveza	thehr-**beh**-thah	beer
el chocolate	choh-koh-**lah**-teh	chocolate
el chorizo	choh-**ree**-thoh	spicy sausage
el cordero	kohr-**deh**-roh	lamb
el fiambre	fee-**ahm**-breh	cold meat
frito	**free**-toh	fried
la fruta	**froo**-tah	fruit
los frutos secos	**froo**-tohs seh-kohs	nuts
las gambas	**gahm**-bahs	prawns
el helado	eh-**lah**-doh	ice cream
el huevo	oo-**eh**-voh	egg
el jamón serrano	hah-**mohn** sehr-**rah**-noh	cured ham
el jerez	heh-**reìz**	sherry

la langosta	lahn-**gohs**-tah	lobster
la leche	**leh**-cheh	milk
el limón	lee-**mohn**	lemon
la limonada	lee-moh-**nah**-dah	lemonade
la mantequilla	mahn-teh-**kee**-yah	butter
la manzana	mahn-**thah**-nah	apple
los mariscos	mah-**rees**-kohs	seafood
la menestra	meh-**nehs**-trah	vegetable stew
la naranja	nah-**rahn**-hah	orange
el pan	pahn	bread
el pastel	pahs-**tehl**	cake
las patatas	pah-**tah**-tahs	potatoes
el pescado	pehs-**kah**-doh	fish
la pimienta	pee-mee-**yehn**-tah	pepper
el plátano	**plah**-tah-noh	banana
el pollo	**poh**-yoh	chicken
el postre	**pohs**-treh	dessert
el queso	**keh**-soh	cheese
la sal	sahl	salt
las salchichas	sahl-**chee**-chahs	sausages
la salsa	**sahl**-sah	sauce
seco	**seh**-koh	dry
el solomillo	soh-loh-**mee**-yoh	sirloin
la sopa	**soh**-pah	soup
la tarta	**tahr**-tah	pie/cake
el té	teh	tea
la ternera	tehr-**neh**-rah	beef
las tostadas	tohs-**tah**-dahs	toast
el vinagre	bee-**nah**-greh	vinegar
el vino blanco	**bee**-noh **blahn**-koh	white wine
el vino rosado	**bee**-noh roh-**sah**-doh	rosé wine
el vino tinto	**bee**-noh **teen**-toh	red wine

Numbers

0	cero	**theh**-roh
1	uno	**oo**-noh
2	dos	dohs
3	tres	trehs
4	cuatro	**kwa**-troh
5	cinco	**theen**-koh
6	seis	says
7	siete	see-**eh**-teh
8	ocho	**oh**-choh
9	nueve	**nweh**-veh
10	diez	dee-**ehth**
11	once	**ohn**-theh
12	doce	**doh**-theh
13	trece	**treh**-theh
14	catorce	kah-**tohr**-theh
15	quince	**keen**-theh
16	dieciséis	dee-eh-thee-**seh-ees**
17	diecisiete	dee-eh-thee-see-**eh**-teh
18	dieciocho	dee-eh-thee-**oh**-choh
19	diecinueve	dee-eh-thee-**nweh**-veh
20	veinte	**beh**-een-teh
21	veintiuno	beh-een-tee-**oo**-noh
22	veintidós	beh-een-tee-**dohs**
30	treinta	**treh**-een-tah
31	treinta y uno	treh-een-tah ee **oo**-noh
40	cuarenta	kwah-**rehn**-tah
50	cincuenta	theen-**kwehn**-tah
60	sesenta	seh-**sehn**-tah
70	setenta	seh-**tehn**-tah
80	ochenta	oh-**chehn**-tah
90	noventa	noh-**vehn**-tah
100	cien	**thee**-ehn
101	ciento uno	thee-**ehn**-toh **oo**-noh
102	ciento dos	thee-**ehn**-toh **dohs**
200	doscientos	dohs-thee-**ehn**-tohs
500	quinientos	khee-nee-**ehn**-tohs
700	setecientos	seh-teh-thee-**ehn**-tohs
900	novecientos	noh-veh-thee-**ehn** tohs
1,000	mil	meel
1,001	mil uno	meel oo-noh

Time

one minute	un minuto	oon mee-**noo**-toh
one hour	una hora	**oo**-na oh-rah
half an hour	media hora	meh-dee-a **oh**-rah
Monday	lunes	**loo**-nehs
Tuesday	martes	**mahr**-tehs
Wednesday	miércoles	mee-**ehr**-koh-lehs
Thursday	jueves	hoo-**weh**-vehs
Friday	viernes	bee-**ehr**-nehs
Saturday	sábado	**sah**-bah-doh
Sunday	domingo	doh-**meen**-goh